Teacher Proof

C000002222

'Tom Bennett is the voice of the modern teacher.'
Stephen Drew, Senior Vice-Principal, Passmores Academy,
UK, featured on Channel 4's *Educating Essex*

Do the findings from educational science ever really improve the day-to-day practice of classroom teachers?

What can teachers do to find the proof within the pudding, and how can this help them on a wet Wednesday afternoon?

Drawing from a wide range of recent and popular education theories and strategies, Tom Bennett highlights how much of what we think we know in schools hasn't been 'proven' in any meaningful sense at all. He inspires teachers to decide for themselves what good and bad education really is, empowering them as professionals and raising their confidence in the classroom and the staffroom alike. Readers are encouraged to question and reflect on issues such as:

- the most common ideas in modern education and where these ideas were born;
- the crisis in research right now;
- how research is commissioned and used by the people who make policy in the UK and beyond;
- the provenance of education research: who instigates it, who writes it, and how to spot when a claim is based on evidence and when it isn't;
- the different ways that data can be analysed;
- what happens to the research conclusions once they escape the laboratory.

Controversial, erudite and yet unremittingly entertaining, Tom includes practical suggestions for the classroom throughout. This book will be an ally to every teacher who's been handed an instruction on a platter and been told, 'the research proves it'.

Tom Bennett has been a full time teacher since 2003, and the resident Behaviour Guru for the *Times Educational Supplement* since 2009. This is his fourth book.

Teacher Proof

Why research in education doesn't always mean what it claims, and what you can do about it

Tom Bennett

Routledge
Taylor & Francis Group

LONDON AND NEW YORK

First published 2013
by Routledge
2 Park Square, Milton Park, Abingdon, Oxon OX14 4RN

Simultaneously published in the USA and Canada
by Routledge
711 Third Avenue, New York, NY 10017

Routledge is an imprint of the Taylor & Francis Group, an informa business

British Library Cataloguing in Publication Data
A catalogue record for this book is available
from the British Library

Library of Congress Cataloging in Publication Data
Bennett, Tom, 1971–
    Teacher proof : why research in education doesn't always
    mean what it claims, and what you can do about
    it/authored by Tom Bennett.
        pages cm
    Includes index.
    1. Education–Philosophy. I. Title.
    LB14.7.B364 2013
    370.1–dc23
    2012049614

ISBN: 978-0-415-63125-9 (hbk)
ISBN: 978-0-415-63126-6 (pbk)
ISBN: 978-0-203-78229-3 (ebk)

Typeset in Galliard
by Florence Production Ltd, Stoodleigh, Devon, UK

MIX
Paper from
responsible sources
FSC FSC® C013056
www.fsc.org

Printed and bound in Great Britain by
TJ International Ltd, Padstow, Cornwall

Contents

About the author

Tom Bennett has been a full time teacher of Philosophy and Religious Studies for almost ten years. Before that, he ran nightclubs in Soho for nearly as long, because life wasn't weird enough already. In 2010 he was School Teacher Fellow at Corpus Christi College, University of Cambridge. Since 2009 he has written weekly columns, features and articles for the *Times Educational Supplement* as their behaviour expert.

He currently lives in London, where he's thinking about getting a dog.

@tombennett71
http://behaviourguru.blogspot.co.uk/

Acknowledgements

Many people have inspired me to write this book, from the day I started to teach. Ben Colburn of Glasgow University; the anonymous educational vigilante and crime fighter *oldandrewuk*; Ben Goldacre, whose writing got me interested in the possibilities of calling HOAX on the educational cabals of orthodoxy; Gordon Clubb, whose support with my sabbatical to Cambridge allowed me to begin seriously looking into the Matrix reality of teaching; Dr Melanie Taylor of Corpus Christi. Special thanks to Helen O'Shea for editing assistance and optimism.

Generally inspiring people in education: John D'Abbro, Stephen Drew, Vic Goddard.

Many students, who will know who they are.

Many thanks to Gerard Kelly, Ann Mroz, Ed Dorrell, Pooky and Sarah Cunnane at the *TES* for their support of my poor work.

My eternal thanks always to my family: Tam and Betty Bennett, Anthony and Hannah, Florence, Gracie and Alice. And to my wife, Anna, who is a tacit reminder that it is possible to punch dramatically above one's weight.

Introduction

I read this in a national paper recently:

> Anger as 'superhero' school fails to teach special powers[1]
>
> Police are investigating a school in Shanghai after it failed to live up to its promise of teaching children special powers. Dozens of parents fell for the ruse, enrolling children . . . in the summer course at £9,950 (100,000 yuan) a head. Among the special powers . . . to be taught was the ability to read a book in 20 seconds and identify a poker card with the touch of a hand . . . [and] see the answers to exams in their heads on sight of the test paper. This remarkable feat . . . would be achieved by tapping into the right side of their brain. This would enable the children to detect 'waves'.

A real story, honest. It might make you chuckle, but, you know, it's China. China's miles away. That would never happen here, would it?

I'm afraid to say that it can, and it does. Weirdly enough, we have started to believe just about anything in education, as long as it calls itself science. I say weird, because in an attempt to make education more scientific, we have made it less so. And in an attempt to improve it, we have degraded it. These days, education isn't a science; it's an ocean of opinion. The biggest white coat wins.

There is a vast and vibrant field of educational research that is honest, diligent and dedicated in its pursuit of the truth. A quick poll of teaching colleagues reveals that a good deal of formal academic

---

1   www.telegraph.co.uk/news/worldnews/asia/china/9505156/Anger-as-superhero-school-fails-to-teach-special-powers.html. Accessed on 26 March 2013.

enquiry has helped them understand both their own roles as teachers, and also how best to achieve their aims in the classroom and beyond. Dylan Wiliam's research into *Assessment for Learning*, for example, is often quoted as an exemplary piece of investigation that, in its genesis at least, supported the work that teachers do (although it was later corrupted and transformed by an administrative culture that was hungry for metrification and instant answers). Research into the identification of dyslexia; research into effective techniques with autistic children; research into the best way to promote bilingualism . . . I was swamped with great examples of how research, pursued with integrity and precision, has assisted the classroom practitioner with their intuitive and experiential assumptions. It is clear that the fruits of research can be very sweet.

And then there's the other stuff. That's what this book is about.

Education is a human field that longs to be as exact as a physical science, but isn't. Often, no one knows anything. That doesn't mean we know nothing; we desperately wish we had the answers, and that kind of demand won't be denied. Answers are sought, so answers are found. Just as anxious men will pay money for panda penis and spells, so will anxious educators, under pressure to improve results, reach for the magic beans and the magic potions. Cue: educational pseudo-science. Learning styles, thinking skills, multiple intelligences, Visual/Auditory/Kinaesthetic Learning Styles (VAK), Brain Gym® and on and on. Smelly air fresheners to aid memory, flipped classrooms and taxonomies from Mars . . . all promise to revolutionise the classroom, even if the classroom doesn't need to be revolutionised.

Values become facts, which are then taught and propagated in educational training establishments; courses are available on the internet, bought by LEAs and hoisted on the unsuspecting profession, who have little leverage to say no. And as new trainees come through the system, they believe what they were taught in the crib of their profession, and pass it on to their own trainees. I can't remember the last time I met a teacher who knew if Bloom's taxonomy was ever criticised; who knew the evidence that supported VAK; who discovered for themselves if group work really was the best way to learn. Who can blame them? Who has the time?

I was trained on a scheme called Fast Track, which lasted for several years in the early noughties; it cost millions, and part of it – funded by the tax payer I might add – was Neuro-Linguistic Programming, the mystical hoo-ha that rested on the 'science of success' that predicted among other things that you could tell when someone was lying, that you could influence people, and that relied on Brain Gym® as a given. It was extremely interesting; it was also almost completely without scientific grounding, as I saw it.

You'd be hard pressed to find a credible scientist these days who would put their name to it. But back in the day it was all the rage. And someone, somewhere in the Department of Education, pressed a button and said 'Oh man, that looks sweet; where's my Visa?' It's a scandal, and I mean that precisely. This is money that isn't being spent on textbooks and teachers. This is money being hosed up against the garden gate.

And teacher time is wasted on this. And more importantly, kids' time is wasted on it. We are the Golden Goose; we're laying them as fast as we can, but in the attempt to squeeze a few more carats out of our duodenums, the goose is vivisected to see if there's a wormhole to the Dwarven mines inside. There is; it's us – teachers. We're the ones making the gold, but it isn't a process that's particularly amenable to scientific investigation. We know so little about how the brain works, and yet we have the audacity to say we can plan new learning systems based on those scraps of conjecture? This is hubris of the highest order. Unless you can be sure that what you have to replace the traditional methods with are better than the systems and processes that have endured for millennia, I suggest – and I say this carefully – that you take your educational innovations, and park them in the subterranean vaults of your cloaca, where they can harm no one.

You're welcome.

As I explored this subject, what I didn't expect was that the same rag-and-bone approach to belief and evidence familiar to the fringe worlds of quack medicine and lonely people sitting in their underpants, crying as they surfed the net, was so prevalent in education. That not just some, but a lot of what was accepted in education as absolute axiom, as adamantine dogma, was in fact the result of what was, after very little exposure to analysis, very questionable indeed.

I was appalled. I had thought that, given the millennia that teaching had been around, by now we would have (a) a pretty good fix on what good teaching involved and (b) a resistance to accepting, well, any old bull that came along. I was wrong. Education was in the grip of such contestable nonsense that I could hardly understand how it had happened. Where were the gatekeepers, the academic guardians of objective truth that would defend the profession from cant and hoodoo? The more I investigated, the more I found that, sometimes, the very people responsible for researching and supporting good education, the academic community, were the very ones complicit in its disintegration. I also found that their nominal masters, the leaders of the educational political community, were equally complicit, by creating systems that supported this witchcraft. And that schools were complicit in it too, by acquiescing.

As an attempt to turn back the tide, I give you this: Teacher Proof. It's an attempt to say no to some of the ridiculous notions that have poured from the non-laboratories of education in the last 100 years, and an attempt to put the notion of educational research back into context. This is not an attack on all educational research, a lot of which is valuable. But there are an awful lot of people perfectly happy to jump into a lab coat and write articles of such moronism that it almost appears deliberate. And there are politicians equally willing to jump on the wagon if it suits them. And there are media, delighted, it seems, to report whatever makes the best headline about education, regardless of whether it's true or not.

And right at the bottom of this rotten column are the teachers, blown hither and thither on the tides of policy churn, eroded by the ebb and flow, diminished, sapped and deprofessionalised. And below even them are the children who suffer the most, as their teachers struggle to keep up with the labyrinthine hoops through which they are expected to jump.

Where did it all go wrong? What can we do about it?

That's what this book is about.

This book is in three parts – just like the mythical ideal lesson (the three-part thing isn't true either). To begin with I explore how we know anything about the world, so that we know roughly how we come to make claims about what's true and what isn't. There's a bit of philosophy – just enough to get by – and a bit of scientific method. The second part is my teacher's-eye exploration of some dogma and fashionable orthodoxy, either current or recent in schools, that really needs to be parked in the recycle bin. Finally, Part III is a short plenary to make sure no one was on their iPhone during Parts I and II.

And if anyone thinks it presumptuous, that I, a mere classroom teacher, dare to criticise the monolithic edifice of social science, and educational science in particular, well, they're probably right. But I'll stop criticising dodgy social-scientific quack research the day they stop telling me how to teach kids. Which I presume, means never.

I hope you find it useful.

Tom Bennett
London 2012

Part I

How do we know anything?

A brief – I promise – exploration of what it means to say you know something; of how difficult it is in general; and how specifically difficult it is to say we know something in education.

Chapter 1

Quid est veritas?

How do we know anything at all?

How do you know anything at all? I bet you know a lot of things. You know what your name is; probably the day, and that right now you're reading this sentence. Weirdly enough, the very fact that you're reading it means that *I* know you're reading it too, and the odd sensation you get as you realise that this is true, even though I'm writing this in early 2012 in my study, makes you feel uneasy. Don't kill me for my sorcery. So we know a lot of things. But how do you know that you know? Is there any chance – any chance at all – that you're wrong? Of course there is. Unless you are possessed of spectacular perspicacity, you might have occasionally mistaken the day when on holiday, or the date, when asked. I even – and I am far from proud of this fact – forgot my age for about six months, and had to be reminded by my mother. At least I had the rare sensation of feeling a year younger, instantly. And also an idiot.

How do I know anything?

This question (how we know anything, not my age) is not being asked for the first time in these pages. It is one of the great Grails of philosophy, since the day philosophy was first getting planning permission. Although you can trace this debate back to Plato and before, it's useful to start with René Descartes[1], a French mathematician and philosopher in the seventeenth century, who

---

1 Whom, as I never tire of pointing out, was told by a doctor never to rise early *or he would die*. He then went to work for the Queen of Sweden, who made him get up early to tutor her, *and he died*.

rebooted the whole subject in his lifetime. In his *Meditations*,[2] he wrote one of several masterpieces when he considered: how do we know anything, and is there anything we could know beyond doubt?

His starting point was, appropriately enough, his own mind. He noticed that there were many things that he used to believe with utter conviction when he was younger, that he now regarded as being false: both matters of fact and statements of opinion. This is true of all of us. Not only is your opinion about your favourite song probably a little different now to ten years ago, but there are issues even of the natural world towards which you will have very different attitudes. Exhibit A: Santa Claus.

This prompted him to wonder about his present beliefs: were there any of what he believed now that might be overturned in the future? And was there any way to future-proof what he knew? Was there a way to find out knowledge that was incontrovertibly, irrefutably true? We call this the search for Foundational Knowledge. And he was thorough about it. He went about demolishing the creaky old tenement of his beliefs to see if there were solid foundations anywhere he could build upon. To do this he used what is famously referred to as his Evil Demon argument.

Suppose a malicious devil was making him believe he was a French Philosopher with a spectacular nose – it doesn't matter if it's true or not, could it be true? Yes. Could he prove it wasn't true? No. So he was left knowing nothing. He could now doubt everything he thought he knew. What was he left with?

Cogito, sum

He asked the question: is there anything – even by this point of scepticism – that I can still believe to be true? Because if he could, he would have a belief that was pretty robust – a foundational belief. And he believed he did. Even if he was the helpless victim of the evil demon, who was making him believe that he was a pug-ugly polymath who didn't get out of bed until 'after the best part of the day',[3] at least there was something incontrovertibly true: he was thinking. And if he was thinking, there must be at least one thing

---

2   Which was placed on the Vatican list of prohibited books, the *Index Librorum Prohibitorum*, and if that doesn't make you want to read it, then there is no hope for you.

3   Copyright: My mum.

that existed: himself. Perhaps not even his body – he may be a disembodied spirit, for example – but there was some essence of Descartes[4] that was doing all of the doubting. This was the basis of his famous (and famously misquoted) *Cogito ergo sum*: I think, therefore I am. His actual phrasing was closer to the subheading, above.[5]

Already we can see how high the bar can be before we will accept something to be true. This is a common and recurring theme in philosophy: how do we know that we know? The aim of this (epistemology) is to get as far as clear thinking can take us, however far that may be, right up to the very outer limits of what it is possible to say. Fuzzy, it isn't. Descartes used this reasoning to form the basis of a whole lot more philosophical proofs, most of which are far more contestable. But the majority of philosophers agree that his basic groundwork, as laid out in the *Meditations*, is hard (although not impossible) to disagree with.

How do we find anything out?

Returning to our Cartesian discussion, there has been an accompanying, and equally relevant, discussion about this question: how do we actually acquire knowledge? How do we learn anything? This discussion has centred round a centuries-old debate between two camps: the rationalists on one hand, represented by the devilish thinkers of the Continent, and the empiricists, represented by the plucky Brits, showing that the fault lines so splendidly displayed and demonstrated in our differing approaches to what 'food' means and queuing, are also engaged in ideological war on the abstract realms.

Briefly put, empiricists believe that the most valuable, the most reliable source of information about the world is from the evidence of the senses (empiricism comes from the Greek *empeiros*, meaning the senses), and we can find the common sense application of this idea in the term 'common sense'. It's as plain as the nose on your face; I saw it with my own eyes. I have felt your presence, etc.[6] If we can perceive it, we can reasonably say we know it to be true.

---

4 Available at all good perfumers.
5 That's showbiz!
6 I'll grant you that using The Force to know something hasn't yet been accepted in many scientific circles as absolutely beyond reproach as a method.

Contrast this with the rationalists, who as their name suggests, prefer to rely on knowledge gained through use of reason mainly, and point to the notorious unreliability of the senses as a source of anything fundamentally true.

Rationalism

At first it seems a hard claim to make: how can you say you know something just by thinking about it? Well, rationalists such as Descartes thought there were plenty of things that could be known more clearly by reason, for example that I exist (the *Cogito*) for one. But there were many others: in mathematics the rules of maths were demonstrably known without referring to the senses. One and one must equal two, because that is that the definition of those terms, and it would be impossible for the two numbers to come to anything else. Similarly, other truths are known without doubt using reason: 'all bachelors are men' is a truth known without recourse to experience. If someone wheels a bachelor into the room, you know without looking up their kilt[7] that they are male, because that's what the concept 'bachelor' necessarily entails.

So far, so uncontroversial, except it is; everything said so far has been contested, because that's what philosophers do when the other kids are learning to swim and make friends. What else can reason alone help us with? Well, enlightenment scientists (or natural philosophers as they were called in those days, the term scientist not having been created until the nineteenth century) believed and observed that the world around them was reducible to numbers; that everything could be described in terms of mass, velocity, position etc. And that these variables, manipulated by the rapidly emerging disciplines of physics, chemistry and various others, could produce results of terrific accuracy. Want to know how much thrust a rocket needs to reach Moon orbit? Well, you could lick a finger, stick it in the wind and hazard a guess – and watch as billions of tax dollars float down to Earth in a pall of smoke and shards, or you could do the maths. Rough estimates work well – in fact they can work really well – with everyday, human-sized dilemmas – how hard do I need to throw to get this paper ball in the basket? How fast do I need to run to catch the bus? How much pressure should I use on these

7   This isn't a hen party, unless I've miscalculated.

keys? But when it comes to things that are complex, or large, or very small, our human frame of reference becomes swamped quickly. Mathematics can describe and unpack the world for us in a very precise way, which means that rationalism becomes one of our principal tools to evolve as a scientific species.

There was one main problem with rationalism, according to the empiricists. Without experience, it was blind.

Empiricism: in the realm of the senses

Over in Blighty, a triumvirate straight out of a seventies gag: an Englishman, an Irishman and a Scotsman were having other thoughts on the matter. They were the trinity of empiricism: David Hume, George Berkeley, and John Locke. Locke came up with the term *tabula rasa* to describe the human mind. It was, he said, a blank slate, empty of all ideas, except for those that experience provided. In other words, we knew nothing until we had experienced it through our senses. These experiences were then stored in our minds as memories, reflections and so on, and formed the basis of our every piece of mental furniture. If you hadn't experienced the colour red, for example, you would be unable to imagine it.

It sounds reasonable. But what about all those things we could imagine but had never seen: a mermaid, say, or a golden mountain? Easy, says Hume, stepping in: such things were merely the reorganisation of what we had experienced, but photoshopped, cut 'n' pasted into new forms. So if you've seen a fish, and you've seen a woman, and you've seen a pair of clams, *voilà*! The Little Mermaid. It was a simple and neat explanation of how ideas were formed, and how we could be said to know anything.

But hang on, hang on, you might be saying. What about things that we do seem to 'know' automatically at birth: knowing to breathe, knowing to recoil from pain and so on. Ah, said David Hume, that's the difference between knowing how to, and knowing that. The former is instinct, like a bird knows to flap its wings, or a faun knows how to stagger upright. That isn't what we mean by *knowing that* knowledge, or propositional knowledge as it's called. You may as well say that a rain drop 'knows' to fall when it drops.

So: an empiricist would claim that to know something means to be able to make a proposition out of it (a claim that something is true, like 'water puts out fires') and that it must be justified, true and believed. And that justification comes from our senses, which make photocopies of the world, relayed to our brains, which then mop up all that data and become more and more sophisticated. So far, so good. We have a theory of knowledge, and we have a system of obtaining knowledge. This is going to become very relevant for our understanding of science, and later, educational science, and so are the problems.

Problems?

There are always problems.

One of the main problems with the empirical method, which relies on observation, is that observations can often be wrong; mis-interpreted, mistaken, misled. But, as Descartes pointed out, at least we could usually check when we were wrong, couldn't we? And that would allow us to form some kind of reliable, testable picture of the world. Ah, testable; that's the word that starts to bring us closer to the topic of science, which is where this is all leading. Because that was one of the great inventions of humanity, and something that brought us closer to a state of mastery over our environment rather than the reactive servitude endured by most organisms since the primordial soup and sandwich of evolution and competition.

Science: humanity, the great tool-using animal has, if not uniquely, then to a unique extent, discerned the machinations of nature and divined methods to obtain advantage over the other beasts. We're not the fastest, or the strongest, or the longest lived; we don't have fins, or fangs, or luminous antennae to attract prey. We can't detach our mandibles, or change sex, or hibernate, or endure most extreme spectrum habitats. But we are rather good at puzzling out clever ways to cope with it all. And that's based on a system called *induction*.

The Inductive Method

You will – if you've heard of Sherlock Holmes – be familiar with the principle of deduction. I think if I asked most people what it meant, they would say, 'Er . . . working things out. Like Sherlock Holmes and that.' Which is barely right. Because induction and deduction are much misunderstood, and it's worth exploring what they mean briefly here before we start trying to work out what we mean by a scientific method, and more importantly, when something isn't scientific. Like most educational research. See? I'm getting there.

Deduction

Deductive and *inductive* refer to the way you construct a logical argument. Let me give you an example of a deductive argument:

Premise one (P1): All men are mortal;
Premise two (P2): Socrates is a man;
Conclusion: Therefore, Socrates is mortal.

In plain speech, it's this: 'All men are mortal, and Socrates is a man, therefore, Socrates is mortal.' We lay it out like that to make sure we're as clear as possible about what we're saying. Now how do we know that Socrates is mortal? Because if we accept the premises that all men are mortal and he's a man, then he must be mortal too. You can swap the words Socrates, man and mortal with other terms that fit, such as 'Every rainy day I need an umbrella; it is a rainy day, so I need an umbrella.' And so on. The fun you can have with logic.

There's nothing in the conclusion that hasn't already been said in the premises. In effect, all I've done is shift the terms around a bit. And that's the point: deductive arguments are great, because they have the benefit of certainty. If your premises are true, and your argument is valid, then the conclusion must be true as well. Hallelujah! If you want to attack a deductive argument, you either have to prove that one or more of the premises are untrue, or you show that the conclusion doesn't follow from the premises, in which case it wasn't a valid deductive argument in the first place.

Induction

Inductive arguments look similar, but are very different in DNA. Here's an example to begin with:

P1: That man's shoe is plastered with dung.
P2: There is a pile of steaming horse sherbet not two steps behind him.
C: The man has blazed a trail through the nearby equine stew.

Now this seems reasonable; it even shares many features of a deductive argument: premises, and a conclusion that seems to reasonably follow from them. But have you spotted the problem? Pretend you have, and look smug as I explain it anyway. The problem is that it isn't *certain* that the man recently walked through the equestrian excrement in question. Why, there could be similar fewmets in any number of unknown places. Or maybe the shoes were dragged through the stable latrines by his wife in revenge for a bawdy night on the pop and a forgotten anniversary. Or, or, or . . . a million other things.

It's odd that Sherlock Holmes is so well known for his 'deductive' powers, when properly speaking he relied on induction for the most part, and enjoyed a near 100 per cent success rate simply because he was, well, fictional. You don't get the chaps in Scotland Yard being so snooty, especially when they can be caned in court by smart lawyers who know all about induction.

An inductive argument can never possess the incontestability of a correctly constructed deductive argument. Here's a famous example:

P1: The sun rose yesterday.
P2: The sun rose the day before that.
C: The sun will rise tomorrow.

Now on the face of it, that also seems pretty solid reasoning. But you can probably already spot the flaw in it: it isn't certain by any means that the sun will rise tomorrow. Maybe tonight's the night the sun goes bust. Maybe the Earth will be shattered by an explosion. Unlikely, yes, but who knows? The fact is that, just because something has happened a lot, doesn't mean that it will definitely continue to happen the same way. In fact, no matter how many premises you add to this argument (P3: The sun rose the day before P2, P4: The sun rose the day before P3, etc.) you can never be certain that it will rise tomorrow. Why? Because no one has been to the future, and it's unlikely they will. No one knows what will happen: the future is an undiscovered country.

Here's another example: imagine a turkey, reared in a farmyard all its life. Since leaving the egg, the farmer has delivered lunch at exactly 12 o'clock every day. Now, the turkey might not notice this at first, but as the days roll into weeks into months, he begins to notice that at the same time every day, along comes lunch. Eventually (because he's an empiricist turkey with a mind for good inductive reasoning) he concludes the following proposition: 'at 12 o'clock every day I get fed.'

And then one day it's December the 24th (or the day before Thanksgiving if you're reading this in the former colonies of King George), and he doesn't get fed anymore. You get the grisly picture.

That's what's known as 'the problem of induction': no conclusion based on an inductive argument, is ever 100 per cent certain, merely *probable* in lesser or greater proportions.

Why is this so important to science? Because, as David Hume pointed out, just about everything we believe about the world around us is based on inductive – not deductive – reasoning. When I press the ON switch for my TV remote, I believe that it won't explode, or fry me. Why? Because it's never happened before. So gradually I learn to expect that doing so is safe. When I walk down the street, or sit on a chair, I do so in the carefree manner of a man who is certain that the pavement will support me. When I comb my hair, or drink a glass of water, or clap my hands, or . . . or do anything, I do so armed with the subliminal inductive argument that the future will be like the past, that the world is, roughly speaking, predictable, and predictably stable. If it weren't for inductive reasoning, I would have no way to navigate through the world.

But it isn't certain. And often, I *am* surprised by things that I didn't expect. And that's because my expectations are based on my experience, or that of other peoples' experience relayed to me. But there might (and often is) a gulf between the way I think the world is, and the way that she chooses to be. Consider our unlucky poultry, above.

Or in fact, consider any time we come a cropper from inductive reasoning: the days you forbear taking your brolly because the skies don't look so bad, and then suffer as you get drenched; when the traffic is a little worse than normal; when someone acts unexpectedly; when the soaps get rescheduled for the late-running tennis. Life is notoriously, unavoidably unpredictable, and that's without even considering all the really *big* ways in which inductive reasoning has brought us to grisly, erroneous conclusions: witchcraft; superstition; astrology and so on.[8]

Is inductive reasoning useless?

Far from it. Hume observed that it was the only game in town; that, while all of our reasoning about the external world was based on the presumption that the world would obey the predictions of our experiences, and was therefore often very faulty, it was the best we

---

8 Last time I looked, horoscopes still appear in many newspapers, even ones that purport to be credible and hard-hitting. This baffles me.

had to go with. We don't have a better way to define and anticipate the way the world works. And to be fair, it's worked out pretty well so far. See: science, and mobile phones and cars and all that. For the most part, the world seems to operate in ways that can be predicted with a high degree of probability. Certainty, it might be said, is overrated. I might not be certain that my tube home won't suddenly fall into a wormhole and end up on Titan, but frankly, I'll take the bet. Inductive reasoning works. It's useful. It isn't certain, but we can live with that.

One thing causes another . . . probably

We understand inductive conclusions as being probable to different degrees. In common idiom, we say that one thing causes another. In other words, if an event is repeatedly followed by another event then it might be reasonable to assume that they have a habit of following each other.

Example: I have stepped into water many, many times. On none of those occasions has the surface tension been sufficient to bear my dainty weight, and I sink soundly beneath the surface. In fact, I have never witnessed anyone of sufficient weight or relative density to have been sustained by water. And neither has anyone else. Conclusion? Water doesn't support a standing human body. I can say this with a high degree of probability, because I have so much raw data that supports this observation. It doesn't mean it's impossible; it doesn't mean it could never happen; it just means it's very, very unlikely.

Take something else, less observed by the many: if you add Amaretto (almond liqueur) to half a pint of lager, and then top it up with coke and skull it down with abandon, two things will happen: (a) It tastes exactly like a Dr Pepper; and (b) Your legs will get drunk, but no other part of your body. Now it's unlikely you have performed this magnificent experiment, unless, like me, you wasted five years of your life as a cocktail bartender in a novelty American themed restaurant bar. So do you accept the conclusion or not? It's not so easy. On one hand, you might know that Dr Pepper is a kind of marzipan soda, and almonds form the main flavouring of marzipan, so . . . yeah, maybe. Or you might trust me, because you think I'm a pretty stand-up kind of guy. And you might think that as an ex-bartender I know what I'm talking about.

On the other hand, I might be lying; or a terrible bartender; or you might think that there must be more to the delicious flavour of the world's least favourite soft drink than the mere handful of ingredients I described. The point here is that, with less direct or reported experience on the matter, your view as to the certainty of my proposition is far less certain. Maybe you give it a 50/50 chance of being true, or a generous 80/20. Much less than before though. At least you can establish it fairly easily by testing it for yourself (and do: I am completely aligned to the truth here. It isn't classy, but you'll be sickly and numb).

The Black Swan problem

Anthony Flew famously reframed the problem of induction with the problem of the Black Swan. Were you to ask any European in the sixteenth century what colour all adult swans were, you would be hard pressed to find, except among the very witless, a response other than 'white'. Of course they were white. Every swan ever plucked was white. Until, of course, explorers ran aground in the New World, and discovered that Australia was swarming with scores of the sooty, black brutes.

To put it another way, it is impossible (and unwise) to universalise from a specific example. In other words, just because one dog has bitten you, doesn't mean that all dogs will. You can see the problem with the presumption of inductive infallibility. While induction is perfectly necessary for us to survive and thrive in the world, it can also cause enormous mistakes and fallacies: *all* Scots are mean; *no* white men can jump; teenagers are thieves; and so on. It is also the root of some of the least pleasant reasoning known to mankind: prejudice and discrimination.

So, to summarise: inductive reasoning is the only way we can establish anything about the world, even at a fundamental level of operating. It isn't certain, which isn't normally a huge problem, but it can be. Remember this; it's terribly important for how we understand science.

Chapter 2

What is science?

How we understand the physical world

What is science? Science is, at its most blunt, a tool, a method we have invented that assists our understanding of the world. It's a machine for obtaining, or attempting to obtain, knowledge. And it is jolly successful, he said, writing on a computer, looking through a pair of spectacles and listening to Mozart and the Bee Gees on his headphones. It's also a method by which we can make credible claims about how the world apparently routinely works – and just as importantly, how it doesn't work. At its broadest, this is how we can separate astrology from astronomy – one of them provides reliable information about the universe that appears to be routinely justified by experience, and the other doesn't, unless you happen to believe that all Scorpios in the world will experience a broadly similar day. Give me strength.

Note how it relies on experience; science has its roots in empiricism, which is why it is often referred to as empirical science: that which is known by the evidence of the senses. If it can't be heard, touched, tasted, smelt or seen, then it cannot be measured and metrified, and science has a marginal role to play in its description.

The scientific method

Science is designed to:

- investigate new phenomena
- acquire new knowledge
- correct existing beliefs.

Therefore, it is a formalised attempt to maximise the efficiency of the inductive method that we all use on a daily basis. Babies and children use induction to learn about the world: to learn not to touch fire, to gannet chocolate, where to hide from angry, chocolate-deprived parents etc. But, as we have seen, this method suffers from inaccuracy. The scientific method attempts to minimise the inaccuracy, and the faulty beliefs, and maximise what can be claimed.

Scientific discussions revolve around what can be *measured* and *empirically observed*. Given that it is impossible to weigh an intention, the classic sciences such as chemistry, physics, mathematics and astronomy etc. have tended to avoid these matters. The next bit deserves its own box:

> The aim of science is to produce explanations of how things work, which are testable, and which allow us to make predictions about other events.

Basically this means that, if a claim is to be scientific, it must be able to be reproduced and observed by others (in a laboratory or not), and the claim should offer an account of the mechanism by which some process happens, which can then be used to correctly anticipate a similar event in similar conditions. For example, if I apply a Bunsen flame to water, I may be surprised (because I am an idiot) to see it bubble and vanish (let's call it 'boil') when it gets to 100 degrees Celsius. If I propose that this is a routine event, and every time I do the same I obtain the same result, then I can reasonably be said to have a good piece of scientific explanation.

Science normally proceeds on this formula:

- Form a question: does sound travel faster in water than in air?
- Make a hypothesis: yes it does. 'Sound travels faster in water than air.'
- Make a prediction: what would I observe if my hypothesis were true? Well, for a start, perhaps I would hear a noise more quickly underwater than I would on land.
- Test the prediction: gather evidence to see if the real world behaves the same way as your prediction. Get your flippers on.
- Analysis: what does the evidence show? What do we need to do next? And if the evidence proves the hypothesis to be false, what new hypothesis can we suggest?

So rather than just depend on your gut instinct, your prejudice or what feels right, you get a method of establishing if something is probably true or not. Or perhaps more accurately, you get a method by which you can establish if your hypothesis *isn't* true. Why so negative? Because a hypothesis can never be proven 100 per cent true, for the simple reason that induction is limited by its nature – remember the black swan. Unless you have examined every inch of the universe, throughout every moment of time, you can never say 'All swans are white,' merely that 'all swans so far are white'. We say that water boils at 100 degrees at sea level, but what we really mean is that all water so far has displayed this quality.[1]

Properly speaking, what this does is obtain a method of falsifying a theory, i.e. proving it to be incorrect. But the more you test and test and test a theory, the more reliable you can start to assume it becomes. That's why the whole 'I can't walk on water' theory is looking pretty sound so far. I can never falsify it. So far.

Science builds upon itself. The more we discover, the more we record our data, and pass that data on to others, who then don't have to replicate the experiment (if it's been done to death already). This means they save time and effort, and can instead investigate other phenomena. In this way, science accrues, building up like an endless pyramid, getting higher and higher. Needless to say, in the course of a later scientific investigation, a scientist might discover that a previous colleague's work was false, or rather didn't take into account all the data possible (perhaps new data has come to light). Newton's laws of motion worked pretty well for everyday objects and most data from larger objects such as planets. There were some odd aberrations that the theory couldn't explain, but it was pretty good. Then Herr Einstein came along and proposed relativity, which upturned and improved upon Newton. It didn't mean that Newtonian motion was rubbish, merely a rung in the ladder of science. Relativity and quantum physics are two branches of physics that seem to contradict each other, but both of them seem pretty accurate in their respective areas of study: the former astronomical bodies, the latter applying to the realm subatomic.

---

1   Imagine everyone's panic when they discovered that water boils at *different* temperatures depending on how high it is relative to sea level (due to the pressure). They must have had kittens. 71 degrees, in case you fancy an egg once you've ascended Mount Everest.

Better science

So far, so good. We have a method. And if the method didn't work, no one would use it. But they do, and – you know – mobile phones and medicine. Surely, with this wonderful method, we can conquer the world? Well, quite; perhaps we have. As I write this, there are lasers being shone on Moon mirrors placed there in 1969 by Neil Armstrong. By now, a Mars mission has landed that will carry a Curiosity Rover unit that will, itself, carry a laser. You heard me. There will be, by the time you read this, *lasers* on *Mars*. Science, I salute you.

Cargo Cult science

But science has an evil twin: bad science, or perhaps, poorly performed science. The physicist Richard Feynman famously coined the phrase 'Cargo Cult' science. He was referring to an odd phenomenon that had been observed within some indigenous island cultures of the South Pacific. Having little access to contemporary technology, when American water planes started to arrive with goods from around the world, the islanders were understandably impressed, and attributed mystical powers to these foreign devils, and why not? When they left, the islanders formed cargo cults, a religious institution that attempted to bring back the good times by emulating the practices of the army personnel. They would even build fake landing piers, light landing torches and perform rituals that were, to them, aping the gods of plenty from the sky. It's touching, sweet and vaguely tragic.

Feynman believed that there was a lot of science that was like these cargo cults: from the outside they resembled science, and they would probably share many of the characteristics of what we would call science, but at the end of the day they weren't really doing science.

Let me give you an appalling example, and one that doesn't leave me showered in glory. For reasons best described in another book, I had to hastily re-enter my sixth form after a disastrous foray into tertiary education. I chose chemistry because, for about five minutes, I fancied that I might want to be a doctor, and may God be thanked that I changed my mind. In order to pass the paper I had to design and execute a scientific experiment. Because I was a moron, I did what all morons did, and decided that what the world really needed was another sixteen-year-old attempting to extract caffeine from a jar of coffee. Yes, I know, ground breaking. So I did a lot of boiling and evaporating, and distilling, and filtering and *all* kinds of hoodoo, over weeks and weeks, until finally I was left with a beaker containing some residue that may or may not have been purest caffeine. I didn't care. I had inhaled more coffee fumes than I cared for in a lifetime,[2] and I just wanted the damn thing weighed, which I did. Except . . . except that I had forgotten to weigh the blasted thing *before* I even started.

In other words I had no idea what the weight of the residue was, and short of scraping it carefully (and wonderfully inaccurately) into a dish, I never would. I stared at the beaker when I realised my mistake. I thought of how stupid I would look, and how disappointed my chemistry teacher would be, and how I might not be able to get another project done in time. And I did the honourable thing: I made up the data. I worked backwards from the theory, to establish roughly how much caffeine I was looking for, and then fuzzed the number a little to suggest that I was close, and that the errors I had made could be accounted for.

In other words, I was doing Cargo Cult science. It looked like an experiment – I had equipment, chemicals, goggles, a good Bunsen flame, wooden sticks, glass stirrers, a hypothesis, a test, and experiment and even some data. But it was all meaningless. It was a ritual, a shamanic rain dance and, of course, a complete fraud. I was young and stupid; I can live with myself. Publishing my crappy results didn't kill anyone, or knock any satellites out of low earth orbit. But that's how it happens.

When science goes bad

This is just one example of how science can be tortured. There are many other temptations to abuse the method and corrupt the results:

The desire to be published

If you're a scientist, you don't get to do science for free; all that research has to be funded. That means your research has to be in a cool and interesting and – hopefully – lucrative area. That's why, if you want funding for a drug that makes men's phalluses longer,

---

2   Had this been a *Marvel* comic, I would have gained superpowers. I would have become Coffee Man.

you're likely to be beating off a queue of investors. If you're looking for funding to investigate the role of feminist paradigms in Chaucer, then good luck and say hi from me to the guy from the Arts Council when you're rubbing oil into his saddle. This means that the temptation to produce dynamic, exciting results is high. Some succumb.

The desire to make a name for oneself

Nobody cares about you if you're the 'extracts caffeine guy'. They might notice you if you're Baron Von Hammerstein, the first man to regenerate withered members. The bolder, the brassier, the bigger the impact. Scientists, I am reliably informed, are people too, subject to all the vulgar temptations of glory and kudos that everyone else is. Perhaps especially, given that the money can often be so lousy in research, and the work so long and laborious.

The File Drawer effect

This is the well-known phenomena where researchers, having found that their experiment hasn't particularly proven anything at all, or worse, has disproven their groovy hypothesis that they were hoping to cash in on, just file the results away in a drawer, cough loudly, and say, 'Hey, did someone hear that?' This means that negative findings get massively underestimated. Which means that someone might just do the same experiment all over again. This continues until someone gets lucky and discovers that they've managed to find some data that *might* just back the theory up. So they publish. Of course they do! Suddenly everyone starts to believe that the theory is correct, because they haven't seen the enormous amount of negative data to give the lie to the unusual claim.

Aiming for evidence that will support your hypothesis

This is when researchers go out looking for data that will back their claims up, and ignore evidence that doesn't. If you believe that vitamin C cured headaches, you might put an ad in the paper that said, 'Has Vitamin C cured your headaches? Ring us.' Don't be surprised if most of your data supports the theory. This is, of course, very bad.

Misinterpreting the data you obtain

In the analysis phase, it is very easy to oversell the findings, to extrapolate conclusions that aren't really supported by the figures, and to impose your own prejudices on the data. This is to be avoided. Scientists are meant to be careful. I am reminded of the old joke (and it isn't much of a joke really) about three scientists sitting on a train as it passes a field. They see a brown cow. Scientist one says: there are brown cows in this area. Scientist two says, 'No, there is at least *one* brown cow in this area.' Scientist three says, 'No, there is at least one cow in this area, *at least one side of which is brown.*' Good science tries to stay as close to the data as possible.

There are many other temptations to misdirect the righteous path of scientific investigation. I must make it clear that there is no evidence to suggest that this is commonplace or routine. Far from it. I refer you again to all of those mobile phones, medicines and televisions that clearly work. The vast majority of scientists and researchers are dedicated, professional souls who only want to understand the world more clearly, inch by inch, and God bless them. This book is not called 'Science is bunk'. Let me be clear: science is fabulous. I'm passionate about it, and have been since a child, like many children. Science to me is the future; it's Buck Rogers and jetpacks and bubble colonies on the Moon and light sabres. It is the source of wonder and mystery as moving as any aesthetic.

But because it is so useful, so attractive, it is essential that we guard ourselves against its misappropriation; against its imitation by people who have ulterior motives other than the mere search for the truth. Witch doctors, homeopaths, voodoo merchants and snake oil salesmen abound, even in the sciences that I have described. As I write, there are people who give money to astrologers and mediums; who sign cheques to alternative doctors who aren't really doctors, who promise to cure everything from allergies to cancers using nothing more than distilled water, or sugar pills, or exotic herbal tinctures that have no demonstrable efficacy. Who promise they can cure your tinnitus, your eczema, your broken heart. There are products for sale that promise to relieve the pain of rheumatism by the power of electromagnetism (bracelets, it seems).

If people can be fooled by the cargo-cultists of these sciences, which have been tested to defeat so many times that it scarcely seems credible that any sane person would admit their quack theories for one second past the threshold; and yet they do, they do. Cargo Cult science is alive and well. And not just in these obvious charlatans, but also in more subtle form, as passably professional scientists, some of them with authentic accreditation, perform lazy, half-assed research, which is then published in such a way as to create the impression that some really hard thinking has gone into it, when in fact, it's as scientific as Paul the psychic octopus picking the World Cup winners.

And a lot of it ends up in education.

How to spot when a piece of research is from the Cult of Cargo

It says somewhere, 'sponsored by . . .'

This by itself isn't the kiss of death. A lot of research is carried out by interested parties, and it doesn't automatically mean that the research is wrong, or a lie, or badly done. The tobacco companies did some jess fine research into the dangers of smoking (although, mind you, they didn't seem too eager to publish for a decade or so. No one's perfect). But it does give you an idea into the possible biases behind the research project.

It refers to a very small sample

Was I to ask everyone in my smoking room what their names were, everyone would say 'Why, Tom Bennett, sir,' and we would laugh and eat Madeira cake. But I wouldn't, unless I were insane, claim that this justifies the hypothesis that everyone in the world shares this name, because my sample size is one. But in essence this is what some research does, although it might attempt to hide it somewhere in the thirtieth page. Note that small sample sizes don't make a study irrelevant – individual case studies also have an important role to play in discovery, by unpacking the possibilities in detail – but numbers are very important if you want to start extrapolating the many from the few.

There isn't a control of any kind

This is important. If I discover a new metal, *Unobtainium*, and see what it does to pedal warts, I could test it on a thousand people and see how long and how small their warts were after three months (if they hadn't died from made-up-metal-poisoning). But, hold.

How do I know that the warts wouldn't have decreased or reduced on their own? How can I say that the investigated factor (the Unobtainium) was a relevant factor? By having a control: a set of patients who, as closely as possible, parallel the patients given the treatment, but who don't actually receive the treatment. That way you are offered a set of figures with which to compare your data, and you can see if – potentially, hypothetically – there was an advantage to be made by applying the metal.

The control isn't double-blind

There is an odd and interesting phenomenon: the placebo effect. This is a strange interface between the world of intention and expectation, and the world of material effect. Basically, if you give someone a big, impressive (but utterly medically inert) pill and tell them they're going to get better, sometimes, some people do, even when compared with a control. The more impressive the medicine (injections versus pills; pills versus lotions) then the more noticeable the effect. It's not quite in the realms of thinking yourself better, but there are shades of it. A lot of it is possibly to do with the fact that a percentage of all symptoms are subjective, and subject to differences of interpretation: a stoic farmer may bear a leg ulcer and regard it as a nuisance; a foppish education writer may faint at a pinprick. The only difference in each case is the manner in which it is understood.

This becomes important when we conduct controlled experiments, particularly where humans are the host or vehicle of the experiment. We call an experiment where the recipients aren't told if they are receiving a real version of a drug etc. or a placebo version, blind testing. When even the experimenter doesn't know which one he is giving, we call it double-blind testing. That way, the researcher himself cannot subtly influence the patient's understanding of the intended efficacy of the treatment.

Confirmation bias

This is a long-observed effect in research, and one that causes a lot of damage to the progress of understanding in science. Confirmation bias is the tendency people have to favour information that confirms their hypothesis, and discard that which does not. It is because science is conducted by human beings, not robots (give it time, of course), and human beings are not neutral parties to science: they hope; they aspire; they dream. Imagine you are a researcher who is on the brink of an exciting new discovery – room temperature fusion, for example, promising a world of cheap, almost free, clean energy and an end to oil wars and want. The demonic temptation is to start seeing patterns in your data, however tenuous the validity of your theory, so you only publish that data because you're so excited, so hopeful that the data will be proven right by subsequent data. Well, so far, cold fusion is very cold indeed.

Humans are pattern-forming animals. We are terrific at seeing connections between apparently disordered things; we are creatures who see meaning and structure in everything. If you've ever stared at a cloud and seen dragons or into the blank, black canvas of your bedroom ceiling at night and tracked shadowy monsters, you'll know what I mean. If you've come home after a day at work, considered the four or five lousy things that happened to you, and concluded that it's a bad day, then you've formed a pattern. If you're superstitious, if you're religious, if you believe that you can predict the world using inductive reasoning, then you're a pattern user. We all are. We see shapes in the fire, make art out of driftwood, and call people kind or cruel or lazy based on the patterns we form. It is the basis of our art, our science, our very search for meaning and value in life.

It's also an Achilles heel when we see patterns that aren't there. When we deduce, wrongly, from a hidden receipt and a secret visit, that our partner is having an affair rather than buying a surprise present; when we believe that we have a lucky number because we remember all the great things associated with it; when we believe the fortune teller's psychic interpretation of our personalities, rather than seeing it as lucky guesswork, cold reading and universal statements.

Seeing patterns that aren't there is the curse of science, and good scientists try to reduce this effect. Crappy ones write papers called, 'Why sneezing makes you smarter: a study of seven dwarfs.'

The human factor

Because we are all human – even scientists – this bias is significant. Look at the basic scientific method: it starts with a hypothesis. This is, by its very nature, a shot in the dark, however aligned to the facts it seems to be. It is a human judgement, a creative act, a work of speculation that contains DNA of both fact and fiction. Which is exactly how it should be; a lot of science requires a creative mind that sees and goes beyond the merely present. And this is, of course, the first place that human bias can creep in. Victorian scientists were responsible for phrenology, the science of discerning mental and personality traits from the shape of one's skull. This was fashionable at a time when the codes and practices of science were still being assembled, and was a perfect example of how the prejudices and pre-existing beliefs of scientists generated an entire branch of pseudoscience.

It was used for the justification for racial superiority, and therefore colonisation and slavery. It was also used in courts as supporting evidence for a client's propensity to criminality or sainthood. And, of course, it is quite rubbish, absolutely without foundation. Unless you're linking the skull shape 'flattened by a piano' and 'probably dead' then you are in the realms of the Cargo Cult again. I might add that Sherlock Holmes was fond of making phrenological observations, which makes me wonder how he ever caught anyone. Ah, yes! He wasn't real; that's right. Physiognomy was a related quack discipline, where facial characteristics and mental ones were linked in a similar way, which could be seen as simply a way to justify our perhaps innate dislike of ugliness and attach moral qualities to our distaste, thereby justifying it. Besides, you look a bit shifty.

If you've ever been asked a heavily loaded question in a survey, then you can be pretty sure the designers of the survey are succumbing to confirmation bias: 'How strongly do you agree that George Bush was the best president: very, quite, or a bit?' would seem a ludicrously loaded barometer, but it all turns on the way the questions are asked. So too in any natural scientific investigation. If you go out looking for something, chances are you'll find it.

Illusory correlation

This is the tendency we often have to expect – and therefore see – patterns in data. If you present a Rorschach inkblot to someone and ask them if they can see the pretty flower, chances are they will. If you ask someone to track how much better their back pain feels after a placebo pill, chances are they'll notice a positive effect (because of the placebo effect of expectation) and also because they'll notice the benefits more than the times when they don't feel a benefit, or even feel worse.

Cause and effect

Here we go back to the heart of science; the presumption that, in this crazy, mixed-up world, one thing causes another. It's an article of such basic presumption that it almost seems ludicrous to ask the question of whether it exists or not. My fingers hit the greasy keys of my computer; this causes them to move; the movement causes letters to appear on my daguerreotype; this causes . . . etc. etc. An endless chain of cause and effect that can be traced backwards and forwards through time, and sideways through the universe as one cause produces several effects, and those effects spiral off in different directions in a fascinatingly impossibly complex web of relationships between event A and event B.

But does it even exist? What is cause and effect? Or what do we mean by cause and effect?

Hume says habit

David Hume, the empiricist, had a radical idea: he thought that cause and effect as we understood it, didn't exist. Don't put the book down, bear with me; it's a lot more sensible than it sounds. Because he realised that when we talk about causation (i.e. one thing causing something else) we mean that event A (striking a match) necessarily makes event B (an explosion in the petrol station) happen. That B *has* to follow A. That they are necessarily connected, and cannot *not* be connected. At least, that's what we think it is.

He thought the reality was quite different. He observed that, in our experiences of the world, we never actually see 'causation' at all. Oh, we are quite familiar with the events that we *do* witness, but just because one follows another didn't mean that there was some magical force connecting them.

Example: I see a brick thrown at a window. I see the brick just about to touch the window. Then I see the two things touching (I'm a fast watcher). Then I see the window shatter. Then I see the brick on the other side. Normally we would say 'the brick smashed the window'. But Hume pedantically noted that we didn't observe a mystical force of 'causation' – we merely witnessed event A followed by event B. The fact that B routinely and persistently follows A was no proof whatsoever that A caused B. He said that, if we are to be accurate about how we describe such an event, all we should say is that B routinely and commonly follows A, and that this is what causation really means: a 'constant conjunction' as he called it, not the 'necessary connexion' as he said we normally thought. So we can still use the word 'cause' as long as we are aware of what it means.

Where do we get this mystical idea of causation from, the erroneous one? Hume said, in his *Enquiry Concerning Human Understanding*, that it was simply a habit of the mind. When we experience something happening often enough, we expect one thing to follow another, and that belief becomes so strong that we believe that they have to follow, and that they are connected. Imagine Pavlov's famous dogs. Pavlov, you will remember, was the behavioural psychologist who experimented on dogs to see if the mere sound of a bell could make them salivate if he rang one often enough just before they were fed. He found that they would, even when the food no longer came. They had been trained into expecting that one thing followed another, even when they weren't connected in any necessary way at all.[3]

Is this an important distinction? Absolutely. Hume raised a vital point: we have to be very careful when we say one thing causes another. Just as the poor mangled pooches in Pavlov's laboratory of canine mutilation (see footnote) made the mistake (their last, I imagine) of thinking that the bell caused food to come, so too do we routinely attach unconnected events together into patterns of cause and effect that are completely erroneous.

Example: I wake up every Saturday morning with a wet bed and a sore head. Also, empty bottles of whisky surround me. Hypothesis: Saturday mornings give me a headache.

You can see the fast one I'm pulling here, can't you? No one sensible would say that Saturday mornings give me headaches by themselves, and would point to the guilty-looking glass bottles as a more likely culprit. Confirmation bias is an emotional response, or at least an irrational expectation that the world is one way even though the facts may not support it. The judge who sees an ethnic-minority defendant and believes they're probably guilty; the policeman who stops the black man in the wealthy white suburb; the poor man who believes that the wealthy are cruel and selfish. We see the world, often, as we wish to see it. It's a thin, sad way to

---

3   I should point out at this stage that Pavlov conducted his experiments in a grisly way: in order to collect and measure the salivation rate of the dogs, he strapped them to a board and sliced off the flesh of their faces so that he could see them slaver. Don't worry, though, it's *science*. Even if it seems like a doggy version of *Texas Chainsaw Massacre*.

operate sometimes. That said, it can also be the inspiration for the irrational yet essential operant called hope: the belief that things will get better; the belief that we people can improve; the belief that we can survive if we persist against the odds. Confirmation bias has its uses. But as a non-rational framing device, it is marbled with dangers. Witness the parapsychologists who investigate allegedly haunted houses, and report reams of subjectively observed data supporting the ghost hypothesis. Oddly enough, sceptics never encounter anything like this data on their attempts. Maybe the ghosts *know*.

Physiognomy is a good example of this. Time after time, tests have shown that people attribute positive qualities to people who also display culturally desirable facial features. Look at the average Disney film, or indeed any film. How many ugly heroes do we see? Far less, how many ugly heroines do we see?

Correlation versus causation

I am describing, of course, the difference between correlation and causation, a reef of rocks of which every good scientist is wary. Correlation is when events happen to accompany each other, without necessarily being the cause of each other. In my fabulous and shameful example, there is merely a correlation between the day of the week and the pounding in my head. Aficionados of the previously omnipopular series, *Friends*, may recall the episode when scatterbrain Phoebe believes she can change the TV channels by blinking; in actual fact her thick-skulled neighbours are messing around with a seemingly useless switch next door, causing (we assume) the channel changing. Correlation. Every time Miss Marple turns up in a Buckinghamshire village, someone dies. Correlation (we hope. Maybe it *was* her).

It's very easy to misattribute correlation and causation for each other, and often researcher bias is the culprit. People who swear the weather affects their arthritis; people who say that dogs 'don't like me'; people who claim that 'this always happens to me' are all succumbing to an inability to distinguish the repeated co-existence of two events, with causation, when there might be no link at all. See: gamblers, and their belief in streaks of luck, or the superstitious man who fears the evil eye.

But it's also important to realise that there might be *some* relationship between correlation and causation. A high level of correlation may indicate that there is some kind of direct or indirect causal mechanism: for example, wealthy parents tend to have more children that graduate from university with first-class degrees than poor parents. There isn't a simple causal link between wealth and graduation status – money doesn't, after all, make you smart or hard working – but there is clearly an observable indirect causal mechanism at work here: wealthy people live in areas with better schools, or can afford private education; they are more likely to have a strong work ethic and value education; they are more likely to get involved in their children's school work; more leisure time means the possibility of more bonding time with children and so on. It's not as simple as 'putting your hand in flame causes a burn' but it's a ladder of causes, many of which lead to the outcome of academic success.

There's also a tendency to misattribute correlation between two sets of data when the information they suggest is either unusual or interesting – the so-called 'appeal to novelty' effect. Humans like new things, the novel. We tire, eventually, of repeated exposures to the same thing: our fashions change; our tastes move on in music, we get bored of jokes, the same song, the same furniture. Every advert that begins with the Hard-Sell trigger word *NEW!* knows this.

The Hawthorne effect

This is a well-documented phenomenon in social science experiments, where the very act of taking part in an experiment affects the behaviour of the participants. In other words, just by being aware that they are, or some interesting factor is, being studied, can make people act and react differently than they would normally. Tell someone you're giving them a blue pill that enhances concentration, and see to your amazement that respondents comment on increased focus. Or more relevantly, tell children that they're on a special programme that will raise their grades (or even more tellingly, inform the teachers that this will happen) and – stranger than fiction – grades can rise. It's a relative of the placebo effect, and can be explained by the fact that how we expect to perceive a situation has an enormous effect on how we eventually perceive it. This is the source of so many researchers in the classroom miraculously finding that their intervention has been – to some extent – a success. The real question, as with all placebos, is not 'how much impact did this intervention have?' but 'How much impact did my intervention have compared to other interventions, or no interventions?'

The appeal to novelty (argumentum ad novitatem)

This is a fallacy in argumentation in which somebody claims that something is better, or an argument is more convincing, because it is new. Now it seems obvious, to anyone who considers it for a moment, that this isn't true and is, in fact, absurd. Was I to claim that I had designed an entirely new way of chewing my food or draining my bowels, I would be rightly laughed out of the room and into the hands of the 'special room' men. Novelty is not, by itself, a guarantee of veracity. Still, it's an argument that is rolled out time and time again: 'We need some new staff', 'Your ideas about schools are from the 1950s', 'Have you read the new book on Lizard Parenting? It's *new*.' Etc. New, schmoo. Scooby Doo got a relaunch in the eighties, with the damnable sidekick Scrappy. Was that better? No. The twenty-first-century learning movement (see later) is particularly fond of this fallacy.

It has been observed that researchers are often victims of this problem; when data suggests something surprising, they seize on it, and overestimate its importance, to the cost of other, perhaps more reliable but boring data. If I had performed my caffeine experiment more carefully, I might still have obtained surprising amounts of the stuff whenever the Moon was full. Rather than consider that my career lay in fields other than science, I could be dazzled by this novel correlation, and launch off into other experiments and hypotheses that explored the radical and exciting possibility that my coffee pot was some kind of werewolf, or were-cafetière, if you will.[4]

Better science

The way we attempt to immunise ourselves against this effect in science is by randomised trials; by large samples; by exposing our research and findings and complete methodology to the scrutiny of others, who may not share our biases, and can point them out in the process called peer review. It also means letting people know about the research you did that *didn't* support your hypothesis. It also needs the following features:

---

4 I know many teachers who become quite feral in the absence of coffee. Perhaps more research is needed. Can I have some money?

Replication

Can the results be repeated by other researchers, working independently, using the same methods?

External review

Publish the whole process: the hypotheses, the experiments, the method, the data, the analysis, and let others in your field judge what you have done.

Data sharing

Make sure that *all* the data you collected is available for others to scrutinise. In other words, let them take over at the Analysis stage, and draw their own conclusions from the raw, unprocessed information your experiment has resulted in.

If your research doesn't do this, then you expose yourself (or your research) to accusations that what you've done doesn't really prove your original hypothesis; that you merely hope it has; that you have simply dressed up your prejudices and instincts in the form of data. In other words, you've done Cargo Cult science.

Falsifiability

Finally, one of the methods proposed by Karl Popper, among others, is that for a hypothesis to be meaningful, it has to be falsifiable. This means that there must be some way of proving it wrong. So the hypothesis 'all swans are white' could be proven wrong by the single instance of a non-white swan. We don't actually have to find such a beast, just know that we could, so the hypothesis is at least meaningful. This automatically excludes most religious claims ('God is love') because we have no way to prove it wrong, but this isn't a problem. Science has a clear locum: hypothetical models of the physical world. Any attempt to use it in any other field is to misunderstand what the method of science is used for. Relax, faithful. Science and religion have little to say to each other. Falsification leads to a reduction in bias because it formalises the attempts to prove oneself wrong, and leads to a greater understanding of the frailty any hypothesis contains.

Feynman made this clear at his commencement address given in 1974 to Caltech:

> There is one feature I notice that is generally missing in 'Cargo Cult science'. It's a kind of scientific integrity, a principle of scientific thought that corresponds to a kind of utter honesty – a kind of leaning over backwards. For example, if you're doing an experiment, you should report everything that you think might make it invalid – not only what you think is right about it; other causes that could possibly explain your results; and things you thought of that you've eliminated by some other experiment, and how they worked – to make sure the other fellow can tell they have been eliminated.
>
> Details that could throw doubt on your interpretation must be given, if you know them. You must do the best you can – if you know anything at all wrong, or possibly wrong – to explain it. If you make a theory, for example, and advertise it, or put it out, then you must also put down all the facts that disagree with it, as well as those that agree with it. There is also a more subtle problem. When you have put a lot of ideas together to make an elaborate theory, you want to make sure – when explaining what it fits – that those things it fits are not just the things that gave you the idea for the theory, but that the finished theory makes something else come out right, in addition.
>
> In summary, the idea is to try to give all of the information to help others to judge the value of your contribution, not just the information that leads to judgement in one particular direction or another.[5]

Science as practised by men and women of character and precision is one of the greatest methodologies within humanity's reach. But the previous pages have shown that there are considerable obstacles to reaching this ideal, or even coming close. Awareness of the sharper end of the practice shouldn't lead to a general scepticism, where any and all claims made by science are derided, but should instead lead us to a greater caution before accepting any hypothesis as valid. Indeed, this caution should be a scientific caution. As David Hume nearly said, it's the only game in town.

5   'Cargo Cult Science', adapted from a commencement address given at Caltech (1974). http://calteches.library.caltech.edu/3043/1/CargoCult.pdf. Accessed on 26 March 2013.

Natural sciences and the social sciences

These problems are difficult enough in the natural sciences: chemistry, physics, biology and similar. These are fields of study where the subjects tend to sit still, don't have opinions of their own, and are amenable to repeated experiments of a near-identical nature. When we get to Social Science – of which educational science is a limb – it gets much, much worse. Read on, *if you dare*.

I think it's important to say that I'm hardly the first person to come to these conclusions: social science has not escaped previous opprobrium. My position could broadly be described as Positivism; this was the theory that the only meaningful things that science could and should describe were empirically verifiable; it posits the existence of an external world that is objective and not mind-dependent. In other words, there's a real world that we can observe and agree upon. Social science gets a beating from positivism because it talks so much about matters of values, perspective and subjective belief. While we can agree on the mass of a brick, we can't find such easy consensus in describing the fairest way to distribute resources, or even the colour of a rainbow. Just how deep *is* your love?

Social science isn't a huge fan of positivism, because it holds that many of the things we observe and record are themselves products of subjectivity. In essence, true objectivity is impossible, even for the scientist. The scientific method itself contains a number of unprovable assumptions and values: something is true only if it can be expressed numerically, and so on. It has been criticised for only valuing what can be weighed, and for having a reductivist view of the universe.

This misses the point. Of course, we do experience the world in a subjective way. And of course, it is probably impossible to obtain certainty in any proposition, apart from deductive syllogisms and analytic statements. But science doesn't make any claims to certainty – merely probability. And good science actively seeks to disprove its own hypotheses; in effect it says, 'This might be true, until proven otherwise.' Social science – at least some of it – seems to dispense with that level of self-awareness and scepticism; it simply says, 'This is true because I believe it to be so.' That might be a valuable realisation for aesthetic matters and questions of value and art (maybe, although many claim that moral truths are objective) but science has one great trump card to play: when it's right, it works. Your engine turns; your text message sends. Our global belief in an external universe that follows a series of predicable routine is evidenced every time we brush our teeth, drink coffee, and clap our hands. As Samuel Johnson said, 'I refute it thus.' *kicks stone*

Social science cannot be exempt from the same level of rigour and reliability if it wants to make factual claims about the world; if it seeks to assert that anything is true in an objective sense, then it needs to provide reliable objective evidence. Christopher Hitchens put it best when he said something that should be carved in stone like the Ten Commandments above the door of every social science department: 'That which can be asserted without evidence, can be dismissed without evidence.'[6]

Social science (and I mean educational science) makes claims that intervention X causes educational outcome Y. That means it makes claims about physical organisms that exist in three dimensions that are composed of atoms.

Philosophy and science both converge in their expectation that the world isn't quite as simple as that, of course. Einstein observed that at the cosmic level, the Universe follows some very strange laws indeed that seem counter intuitive – time speeds up, slows down, mass turns to energy and so on. Quantum physicists such as Bohrs discovered that, at the sub-atomic level, matter also obeys equally absurd behaviours: simultaneous dual existence, travelling back in time and so on. The world is clearly not as simple as our human perspective permits. But that doesn't matter to this level of enquiry; at the human level, the universe follows numerous laws of almost certain predictability. In other words, if anyone wants to claim that because nothing is certain we can believe just about anything (as social science often does), then I welcome them to display similar levels of uncertainty the next time they cross the road or run for a train. Then you'll see the real belief system kick back in.

Critics of positivism make a fair claim when they say that to some extent, we create our reality. But there are levels of doing this. Were I to stand on a rail track, and sprint as fast as I could towards an incoming bullet train, my friends and family could retrospectively assess that my act was either heroic (if I was saving a child from the collision) or mental (if I were simply seeing what would happen); in that respect we construct the reality. But on a very different level of reality, and in both cases, I would be strawberry jam on the ground, drawn out in a skid mark five miles long. No amount of subjectivity

6   www.slate.com/articles/news_and_politics/fighting_words/2003/10/ mommie_dearest.html. Accessed on 26 March 2013.

affects that. And that is the level of reality I'm discussing; I suggest it's the level of reality that most people are concerned with. That may make them thuggish, naïve brutes in the eyes of some theorists. It also makes them correct. I do not 'construct' (as the constructivists think) the reality of what happens at school. I inhabit it. I may construct social meaning and so on, but I cannot create physical conditions; I may consider my lessons to be like flying, but I cannot fly. I may burn with ambition, but I cannot spontaneously combust. If kids are failing their exams and taking drugs, a perverse subjectivity could hail this as some kind of positive thing, but I see kids with no qualifications and a drug addiction.

If you make a factual claim about the world, I expect you to provide factual evidence. Otherwise it's flatulence.

Chapter 3

What a piece of work is man

The rise of the social sciences

social science
> *n.*
> *1. The study of human society and of individual relationships in and to society.*
> *2. A scholarly or scientific discipline that deals with such study, generally regarded as including sociology, psychology, anthropology, economics, political science, and history.*

If the scientific method was a relatively recent addition to the repertoire of human experience, social science has practically just turned up to the party[1]. There have been precedents through history of emergent social science, because ideas spring from the soil and seed of their predecessor ideas, and social science is no different. But it was in the last few centuries that it started to gather enough interest, recognition and academic traction to call itself a separate field, or collection of branches.

The new sciences of physics, chemistry and so on had not only shown promise, but had delivered on that promise. The world had been transformed by the appliance of science, and industry, agriculture and both the public and private spheres started to display the frightening and exhilarating churn of modernity. The sciences were a success; the world was unfolding before us. How much more could be achieved if the method of science could be applied to the matter of humanity and not just the world of the inert? The social sciences were born: the study of humankind. I bet they thought by the twenty-first century we'd have seen world peace and universal

---

1   No doubt with a filthy bottle of plonk from ASDA.

enlightenment, the flying cars and light sabres of political and philosophical endeavour.

Dream. On.

The sixteenth to eighteenth centuries saw thinkers such as Adam Smith, Thomas Hobbes, Jean Jacques Rousseau and J.S. Mill using reason, rather than revelation, to establish the correct way in which humanity should be governed. For Hobbes, the pitiful state of humanity in a pre-social state was the result of our innate selfishness; our reason combined with selfishness provided the spur and method of our salvation, and social contract theory was formed – the idea that we should all bind ourselves to each other in law in order to enjoy the consolations of communal endeavours. By the eighteenth century, what we call social science was called moral philosophy: theology, ethics, jurisprudence. Other branches of science were called natural philosophy.

These days the social sciences have branched off from the trunk from which they emerged, set down roots of their own, and developed into an entirely different organism. Whereas the scientific method is broadly established and agreed within the natural sciences, there is, as yet, still no agreement about what would constitute a methodology consistent with all the social sciences. This, as we shall see, is part of the problem.

Another problem we shall encounter is that natural sciences tend towards the idea of an objective, agreeable set of conclusions and data that can broadly be described as positivist. However, when we step into the theatre of the social sciences, we will find that what the truth means often depends very much on who experiences it: relativism. Attempts to marry the two approaches can lead to distress.

What we call social sciences can often be broadly described as the following: anthropology; archaeology; criminology; economics; history; sociology; education; law; ethics; political science; and my favourite, psychology. Emile, Karl Marx and Durkheim are generally considered to be the ancestors of this field, and if you want to go leave flowers on their graves in thanks, you are free to do so.

The aim of social science has always been to systematise and regulate the attempt to understand the difficult realm of human interaction, and to create some kind of scientific framework by which we might be better understood. And with that understanding, should come benefits. At least that's been the goal. But human beings have proven to be rather more resistant to the conventional scientific approach. Why?

The nature of the questions asked

In the natural sciences, we seek to find the answers to questions that often have a fundamentally quantitative answer: how much fuel does a rocket need to reach Mars? What is the mechanism by which haemoglobin oxidises? And so on. The object of social science is often far more stubbornly qualitative: what laws will maximise liberty in a democratic society? What are the best ways to teach children – rows, columns or human pyramids? Such pursuits are as much to do with the definition of the terms themselves as they are with the hypothesis. And definitions – and meanings of definitions – are extremely relative. What do you mean by liberty? Such things are fluid, subjective and dependent on context. Even forming a hypothesis in the social sciences is fraught with philosophical debate.

The nature of the qualities being assessed

If I want to hypothesise that a grain of salt is heavier than a grain of sand, then I can at least work out how this is done: I weigh the little granular fellows. If I want to find out how to increase the creativity of a child, I am paralysed with questions of definition before I've even left the starters' blocks. What is creativity? Is it even a thing? You don't get those kind of 'is it real?' questions in the sand/salt debate. Everyone pretty much agrees they exist. But 'creativity'? I can find ten different opinions on what that is just in my classroom. Weigh *that*, homie.

The nature of human experience

Namely, that human experience is *lived*. As soon as we start trying to measure qualities such as happiness or well-being or offence or any other thing that exists as a perception and has no quantifiable existence of itself independent of being observed (try to imagine, if you will, a feeling of happiness that no one is currently feeling. Where does an orgasm go when it's finished? Don't answer that). Have you seen any national Happiness indices? A conceptual bag of bones and fairy dust, supported by good intentions and men with clipboards who can't sleep at night.[2]

2   Or shouldn't.

The difficulty in designing tests

What is it that social science investigates, around which tests have to be devised in order to collect data on the original hypothesis? Often: people. But people are very slippery customers to catch under a microscope (don't try this). Just getting enough of them to provide data is hard enough – we're busy in a way that rocks of anthracite will never know. They're also often quite unreliable. If I asked a hundred people how many partners they'd slept with, the men would provide figures so enormous that it would exceed the available partners on the planet, a problem that would be exacerbated by the average response from women, which would further compound the impossibility. If I asked men how blessed the trouser pixie had been to them, what kind of response do you think I'd get, after the obligatory sore face? People – as Gregory House likes to observe – lie. They do it for all kinds of reasons. And when they're not lying, they're mistaken. Or they've forgotten. We make, frankly, rotten providers of data, at least the kind that keeps research on the level.

The impossibility of an appropriate control

Say you want to test the hypothesis that Glade air fresheners improve exam results (I am not making this up; this is a thing I have been told). I could, I suppose, be a real scientist and take one of my classes, deliver them a syllabus, and then compare them to another class who get the identical syllabus *plus* the magic smellies. That's science, right? An experiment and a control? Like hell it is. Apart from the obvious sample size problem, we have the experimenter bias problem (I might be geared up when I teach the class with the plug-ins because I expect them to do better) and there's a bigger problem. The control isn't a control at all. It's a Cargo Cult control.

Why? Because when I want to test the hypothesis that temperature is the main factor when water boils (and not, say, the scent of roses in the air or otherwise) I can obtain a control fairly easily: more water. Same salinity, same volume, same lots of things. When I want to devise a control for a group of students, it's impossible to get anything close to something so similar. Unless I devise a technique for snatching the exact same students, duplicating them and then teaching them separately, I'm doomed to teach different people.

And, of course, the problem with that is that I'm no longer comparing like with like. I'm comparing one class with another class.

Every single person in that sample is a human being (one would hope), and the thing about humans is they're so devilishly different. One teaching technique might press all the right buttons with a particular student, but drive another to distraction, for millions of reasons that are almost impossible to ascertain. Let's say that the class with the plug-in smelly gets on average half a grade better than the 'control' class. Before you start installing one in every room, you realise that class A was composed of more bright, hard-working students than the non-smelly class. Ah. Perhaps that might have something to do with matters.

In fact, even if you did have the exact same people to create a control group, you still face the problem that people, because they are driven by complex psychologies, desires, delights, aims and goals, can react in completely different ways to a stimulus one day than to the next. On Monday, the smooth music of the Bee Gees might have me jiving down the corridor to the bathroom as I whistle a tune. On Tuesday you might find me hurling my iPod like a discus in frustration, because I slept badly, because I realised it was raining, because I'm a psychopath. Whatever. Not only can you never put your foot in the same river twice, you can't even put your foot in the same river once.

Richard Feynman, in interview, once expressed his maddening frustration with social science in this way:

> Because of the success of science, there is, I think, a kind of pseudoscience. Social science is an example of a science which is not a science; they don't do [things] scientifically; they follow the forms – you gather data, you do so-and-so and so forth but they don't get any laws, they haven't found out anything . . . You see, I have the advantage of having found out how hard it is to get to really know something, how careful you have to be about checking the experiment, how easy it is to make mistakes and fool yourself. I know what it means to know something, and therefore I see how they get their information and I can't believe they know it, they haven't done the work necessary, haven't done the checks necessary, haven't done the care necessary. I have a great suspicion that they don't know, that this stuff is [wrong], and they're intimidating people.[3]

3   From Feynman, *The Pleasure of Finding Things Out* (1999).

There's a phrase in that which is apposite: 'I have the advantage of having found out how hard it is to really know something.' That's because Feynman worked in a field – theoretical physics – that sounds fuzzy to the layman. He was one of the scientists who worked on the Manhattan project with Oppenheimer, developing the first atomic bomb, and there was nothing fuzzy about their work. If they tried to fudge a result, or leave a data field hanging, then the bomb wouldn't go off. It was that simple. There can be no more effective or dramatic punctuation separating the demands of the nuclear physicist from the social scientist.

What have the social scientists ever done for us?

Well, quite a bit. I'm not trying to convince anyone that they are useless. This is not a binary debate: natural science good, social science bad. But it is important to understand the kind of problems that social science tries to tackle, and the kinds that its natural counterpart does. It is important to discern the methodology of either in order to distinguish them from each other, and to see that mistaking one for the other leads to enormous complications. Social science is the attempt to understand the world of humanity and the social spheres. There is no one methodology that applies satisfactorily to all of them. It uses many methods with which to attempt to capture data: questionnaires, surveys, interviews, case studies, observation, numerical analysis and so on.

> While physics and mathematics may tell us how the universe began, they are not much use at predicting human behaviour because there are too many equations to solve.
>
> Stephen Hawking[4]

It uses these because, as the above quote from Stephen Hawking illustrates, natural sciences can't provide us with the same level of accuracy or authenticity in the sphere of human behaviour. Human behaviour isn't amenable to the same kind of reductions and processes that we can use in, say, chemistry, where concepts such as the bonds

---

4   www.time.com/time/magazine/article/0,9171,2029483,00.html. Accessed on 26 March 2013.

between atoms are fairly well understood and relatively easy to break down and analyse in isolation.

But humans don't work like hydrogen bonds. There are so many factors that appear to govern our behaviour that to reduce them to one of two variables is to lose sight of the complexity of the picture. On an average day, I may start with cereal and coffee. But it would be self-evidently absurd to say that I was guaranteed, or even likely, to do so on any specific day, because there are an almost limitless number of factors that influence my decision, from the music on the radio, to my attitude towards my waistline, to my tastes, to what I had for dinner the night before, or the programme I watched on processed sugars and so on. Even if you claim (and this itself is contestable) that human behaviour could theoretically be predictable, that is very different from saying that it can in any instance be predicted.

Much of what we seek to explain using social science is to do with qualities and abstracts that are themselves human creations. When I ask the question, 'How best do I promote equality of opportunity in my classroom?' or 'What's the best way to teach?' I already beg the question of what each of these concepts mean, and those meanings are ultimately found in the subjective nature of human experience.

This is why social science seeks to capture data that is itself relativistic; because the intended outcomes of that data occupy the same sphere.

So what's the problem?

There is and there isn't a problem. There is nothing wrong with social science per se: it is nothing less than the attempt to comment and understand humanity better than we already do. Philosophers like J.S. Mill, when they were building their theories of morality, and political ethics, were conducting what they saw as social science, developed and deduced from first principles such as 'we all seek pleasure and we all avoid pain'. And taken as a theory, liable to peer review and open to discussion and analysis, this is fine. We can (and should) contest J.S. Mill's or Jeremy Bentham's utilitarianism. Social science is a commentary upon human experience; it is the Talmud to the Torah of the natural sciences.

It is useful because it attempts to understand and tease apart the complications and apparent paradoxes of human existence. It is food for thought; it is contrast; it is theory and practice; it is an opposing viewpoint; it is a framework. It is nothing less than an attempt to understand how we best integrate the hard sciences into their natural destination, the human community. It is a complex and complicated blend of the subjective and the objective in order to understand ourselves more clearly.

But what it isn't, is science. It's not science, because it isn't readily amenable to the scientific method. Ergo, it isn't science. This is very important, because the distinction is clear and it is vast, and frankly, the vast majority of the public cannot see this distinction. They see any report, or research, or investigation by the men in white overcoats as science, and when somebody claims that, for example, immigration is the solution to the pension crisis, or that group work is the best way to teach pupils and they point to 'all of the science' that's been done, there is a tendency for people to assume that all science occupies identical spheres of validity.

But social science is not science. It borrows the success of the natural sciences, it wears its wig and apes its ancestor, and people . . . well, people buy it. Worse, when they hear social scientists pronounce one day that musical instruments in primary school lead to improved mathematical ability, and the next that more PE helps literacy, people start to lose faith with the whole institution of science as it begins to blur and melt in their view.

Worse, many social scientists seem to ignore or forget the distinction between the fields. I'm the eternal amateur, like I say, and even I, in the course of my pursuit to try to understand the role science plays in the classroom, constantly come across examples of social scientific research so bad that I can scarcely believe someone wasted the paper on it.

Here are the most common mistakes I find in social science research:

Poorly phrased hypotheses, or titles

This is when you have a title that nearly reduces you to tears of mirth or sadness, depending on how strong your stomach is: 'How does emotional intelligence best increase performance in postgraduate studies?' 'Using Brain Gym® as a tool to promote multiple intelligences', that kind of thing. Papers loaded with so many assumptions and presumptions that you would need a crowbar to separate them all from each other. This is why scientists weep when they look at these kinds of papers. If they tried to get funding for 'The causal relationship between fairies and dream catchers', there would be a riot in the Sorbonne. But some social scientists launch into their grand expeditions with, it seems, not a care in the world.

Papers so obviously designed to prove their point that the reader feels clobbered if they presume to disagree

This is one of the most common errors. 'Research from the Academy of Flutes,' the article will start, 'shows that flute usage, or flutage, adds on average two grades to a pupil's GCSE outcomes . . .' and so on. 'We asked 200 Cambridge professors from the university flute society if they felt that flute playing was useful to their overall well-being. 110 per cent said yes . . .' and so on.

Research that is unfalsifiable

Also common. Claims that 'capitalism is inevitable, but so is communism', may impress them in the shipyards, Mr Marx, but there's no way of showing this to be false, unless you want to wait until the end of time and see every civilisation ever.

Analysis that reaches past the data

This is the work of the devil; when a paper takes the opinions of, say, 100 schoolchildren, and presents it as a fait accompli that these opinions are representative of the whole population. Or worse, that then claims this evidence shows that 'children are not being listened to enough', and so on. Which leads me into my next – and least favourite – social science trope.

Mistaking facts and values

If I interview 100 teachers and find out that 90 per cent of them would like longer summer holidays, that is a *fact* – that 90 per cent of them think that. For a paper to then suggest that 'this means teachers should have longer holidays' is an absurd leap from fact to value; the writer is peddling the latter, which is fine – have all the opinions you want, but don't dress them up as research. I think that dogs should shut the hell up when I'm trying to sleep, but I haven't kept a dream diary to back this up.

Social science is often not science. It is investigation; it is commentary; it often illuminates and helps provide valuable light and guidance in human affairs. What it does *not* do is offer reliable predictive powers, nor irrefutable explanatory mechanisms for processes. Merely commentary, case study, opinion, and subjective analysis.

And that's fine. If we don't conflate the two.

Why?

Lots of reasons. One is the quality of some of the research itself. Leslie K. John of Harvard Business School said that '1/3 of all academic psychologists admit to questionable research practices'.[5] For example: stopping data collection at convenient points, when the desired results had been found, and omitting other tested variables. One third! No wonder it gets a rep. There have been a variety of scandals uncovered in social science research that shows how problematic this is for the integrity of the whole subject. Note how difficult it is for scientists to duplicate, and therefore test the claims made by previous researchers in social science. Which makes open release of ALL data even more important, and when this isn't done (as in the Dutch scandal) then it's simply a case of, well, making it all up, and then you can say anything and science is dead.

But if you thought that was bad, wait until you read the next report.

The Tooley Report

In 1998 James Tooley and Doug Darby wrote a report for the Office for Standards in Education in England and Wales (Ofsted), called *Educational Research*.[6] It was written in response to a speech given by Professor David Hargreaves in which he criticised educational research for being 'poor value for money, remote from educational practice, and often of indifferent quality'. As you can imagine, this went down like surf and turf at Gandhi's funeral. In response, Ofsted commissioned the Tooley Report, as it is now known, and it did

5   http://bps-research-digest.blogspot.co.uk/2011/12/questionable-research-practices-are.html. Accessed on 26 March 2013.
6   www.ofsted.gov.uk/resources/educational-research-critique-tooley-report. Accessed on 26 March 2013.

nothing to calm the storm. Instead, it confirmed what Hargreaves had said: a lot of social science was rubbish.

It took a broadly representative sample of 264 research articles from four prominent and popular educational academic journals, with care taken to randomise the sample reasonably well. Its findings would appal anyone who cared about the quality of research in educational science. Hargreaves' words remained unminced when he claimed that there is a 'considerable amount of research that is frankly second rate which . . . is irrelevant to practice . . . and which clutters up academic journals that virtually nobody reads'. The Tooley Report supported this. It stated that there were considerable problems in the following areas:

The partisan researcher. The researchers had agendas so obvious you could spot them from space. This was found in the way the research had been interpreted (e.g. saying the data said one thing when it meant another), the presentation of the research (e.g. by putting the research in the context of supporting or advocating this policy or another), and in the argument of non-empirical research (e.g. by being critical of say, one government's reforms while remaining neutral or supportive of a more preferred party or government). The Tooley Report said that 'not all research was partisan in this way. A minority of articles showed a detached non-partisan approach'. A minority . . .

Methodological issues. This was to do with the conduct of the research itself. Sampling biases were noticed in many articles, and there was little triangulation (i.e. verifying data from different sources to confirm that they were saying the same thing. For example, if you want to find out if an institution has problems with racism, you could ask the first person you see. But then if you were sensible you would triangulate this with other sources of data (work-hiring records, dismissal records etc.) to see if this was corroborated. There was also a lack of reporting of the sample size. Can you imagine? Some papers didn't even say how many people they interviewed, or polled, or tested or whatever. One? A million? Answers there were none.

Non empirical research. This was research that was broadly in fields of contentious discussion or debate, which were not portrayed as being part of a greater debate, but were instead argued incoherently, illogically or simply relied on the opinions of others, in a game of academic Chinese whispers without primary sources being quoted.

The focus of research. This is the irrelevance bit. The Tooley Report found that many of the papers seemed to have little relevance to the practice of education. While research can be said to have an intrinsic value in itself, and issues of utility are sometimes secondary to the point of simply seeking, it would be surprising to see so much research for so little purpose. Also, there was little evidence of replication of experiments: researchers rarely referred to previous research done by prior social scientists in the same field. They simply started their own experiments, as if in an academic bubble, where nothing done before or since has much relevance.

Sobering stuff. The problem is that the Tooley Report, which is itself a piece of social science, was a terrific example of good practice – it bloody well had to be; it was like picking a spelling fight with the man who invented Scrabble: don't put a foot wrong, or else. It laid out its methodology clearly. It presented all of its data. It triangulated. It published in an open forum. It attempted to randomise the sample, and so on. Best of all, in its conclusions, it was careful to admit that its sample could very well be unrepresentative, and made only tentative suggestions on the basis of them. But I think we all knew what they were thinking: educational research, pull your socks up.

Chapter 4

Educational science and pseudoscience

And so, to education. The social sciences have proliferated in every sphere that humans can occupy. There are now people currently studying for PhDs in sober universities, basing the laser focus of their endeavours on such subjects as the Masters of the Universe toy range and the symbolism inherent in Britney Spears' oeuvre. And there is nothing wrong with this. Why shouldn't we gaze into the navel of every moment and discern our truths there, however diaphanous? There is a perfectly good argument for the pursuit of knowledge and understanding for its own sake, regardless of apparent utility. Not only because often discoveries are made in such ways that revolutionise the world, but because they are intrinsically valuable – knowledge pursued for its own sake, devoid of aim or ambition beyond itself.

However, there is a broad but existent line that we need to be aware of. There is a world of difference between making factual claims about an empirically verifiable world, external to us, agreeable in its details and discernible to multiple observers, and making value claims about such a world.

Facts and values

This is a distinction that is often overlooked in social science; it is practically compulsory in the field of literary and aesthetics. Science assumes (and openly so) the following:

- there is a world, external to us
- it is mind independent
- it exists even when we don't perceive it
- we can agree about it, given the correct access
- it is objectively real.

This is often called Realism. It is, broadly, the philosophy that most people in the world hold, whether they are aware of it or not. This is the realm of facts; propositions that can be made, justified and known. 'Today is Friday'; 'Most London buses are red'; and so on.

Then there are values. These are propositions that, while they relate to the external world, do not necessarily promote anything other than a relationship between the proposer and the object.

Examples:

> Private schools are unfair.
>
> No one should be allowed to smoke in public.

They express an attitude, a subjective point. No matter how finely you slice a private school, you'll never be able to distil it sufficiently to discern justice or fairness, or lack thereof. Of course not; these are not physical qualities. Some philosophers would describe them as secondary qualities, that is to say, known only in the mind. I would call Bernard Bresslaw pretty tall, but to an elephant, he's tiny. Big is relative.[1]

That seems as plain as you can get. But to some working in the field of social science, it seems a slippery fish to seize. Research in education, as with most fields of social science, is sodden with assumptions, values and bias even before they pick up the clipboard. As the Tooley Report showed, one of the significant problems with education papers is that they seem designed to prove something the researcher already thought. That would get you few Brownie points in the natural sciences (By Zeus, let us prove that the world is balanced on a great donkey of sorts!), and that was exactly the kind of thing that many were doing prior to the Enlightenment.

Causal density

Simply put, human behaviour is incredibly complex. Unlike physical objects, we occupy a mental space of reasoning, intention, desire and free will. Two men could be equally angry, but the anger of one could prompt him to an act of kindness; the other, an act of

---

1   Although in *Hawk the Slayer*, we are assured that he is indeed, a giant.

bloodshed and cruelty. You cannot say that event A causes event B because human thinking simply defies this level of reductivism. There are too many causes to take account of; besides which there is the further problem that we can't say with any veracity that we have even considered all the relevant factors that might generate some kind of causal relationship. I might have a cheese sandwich for lunch because I saw a billboard that reminded me of a sandwich I had as a child and I might not even be aware of it. We're tricky beggars.

So are we totally unpredictable? Of course not. Hume observed that, of course, people followed broad principles in their behaviour; if they didn't we would be in trouble, because then people would be completely unpredictable, when clearly they are not. I know broadly how people will act, especially if I know them well; I say that this man is kind; this woman is reliable; this child is irascible, and so on. It's called character.

And what about people in plurality? Well, the same applies; there are things that we can broadly say about people that we know to be true: if I pull a gun in a cinema and fire rounds into the ceiling, by and large people will flee. If I start handing out fivers in Times Square, I'll draw a crowd. If I keep my word, people will trust me. All of this is true, as long as we remember these two points:

1   The more general the observation of human behaviour, the more likely it is to be true. It is only when we attempt to use psychology, sociology or anthropology, economics etc. to predict the behaviour of a specific individual, or make too specific a prediction for a group, that we encounter problems.
2   Even these tenuous predictions lack the higher levels of probability enjoyed by natural sciences, because of causal density. There are simply too many factors in human behaviour to make anything more than the broadest claim that we have considered the main ones.

Social science in schools

The great experiment of the social sciences began in the closing years of the nineteenth century. What many people often forgot is that, in the UK at least, widespread education didn't become a thing until well into the twentieth century. You may hear the oft-repeated moronism that modern schools are hampered by the DNA they share with the Victorian school system. Well that's odd, because there wasn't one. Until the 1910s, there wasn't even a requirement for the state to provide any education. Most children still learned from their families the tools of their trade, or learned at the hands of private tutors if they were the very wealthy (not even the 1 per cent). There were alternatives of course: you could send your child for a religious vocation, or there were the occasional charity schools, usually run by local churches, but these were uncommon.

To say that science hadn't even poked its head into education in those times was an understatement. Methods of instruction were as conventional and as appropriate as the subject demanded. If you were learning to become a blacksmith, you watched, practised and improved. If you were learning catechisms, you were drilled. Anything else was what would broadly be called traditional methods: rows and columns in classroom, an almighty educator at the front and plenty of copying. Ah, the Golden Age.

So the next time some humourless techno-zealot whines about Victorian classrooms, feel free to correct them. There weren't any. Also: the Victorians – what did *they* ever achieve, eh? Oh.

When I was training to be a teacher, we had to write a formal essay investigating a topic of our choice. I like essays, and I like a bit of research, so I enjoyed it. I looked into the topic of how should G&T children be taught in the classroom. Here's how I approached the task:

- I had a broad opinion of what I thought.
- I read broadly around the topic.
- I selected other papers that supported what I already knew.
- I summarised them, threw a little of my DNA in there, and interviewed some pupils with the most scandalously biased questions I could imagine.
- I wrote the damned thing, and did fine.

It wasn't going to win any awards, and it was way far from the standard any academic journal would touch, but whenever I see a paper written in the field of education, I now think of the Tooley Report,[2] and I nod my head sadly. That isn't to say there isn't a lot of exceptionally good writing being done, and many people who are absolutely dedicated to its dissemination and distribution. Just that

2   www.ofsted.gov.uk/resources/educational-research-critique-tooley-report.
   Accessed on 26 March 2013.

there is an enormous amount of stuff out there that, in its own postgraduate way, mimics my errors and prejudices just as surely as if they were looking over my shoulder as I distilled imaginary caffeine from a non-existent beaker, taking notes.

It's interesting to note that neither I, nor any other student I knew who underwent teacher training, was given any substantial guidance in how to conduct a trial, write a research paper, or approach the matter in anything approaching a scientific manner. The attitude this reveals about the threshold of verifiability required for a paper to be acceptable is concerning. Of course, you might reasonably argue that a teacher doesn't need to be conversant with such levels of double blind scrutiny in order to teach, but I would argue the opposite – that in a field dominated by quasi science and quack theories, it is more important than in most professions.

It's also interesting to note that so many educational research papers are written with such a cavalier attitude towards impartiality, transparency and integrity, that it is clear that there is an enormous deficit in scientific method in this field. I once attended a conference where an esteemed historian was asked how he would improve education in this country. His answer: 'Close down all the faculties of education.'

This is an extreme reaction. But its pompous, dare-to-dream quality allows us to at least ask this question in return: what are education faculties for? What is all this research supposed to achieve? If we can agree that it must either have the aim to improve education, or the aim of simply discovering knowledge for its own sake, and at the very least not to actually harm education, then we have to say that it is not doing a very good job as a field. What significant gains have been made? What have we learned that has advanced the field in the last fifty years that we did not know before?

My opinion is this: there are few things that educational science has brought to the classroom that could not already have been discerned by a competent teacher intent on teaching well after a few years of practice. If that sounds like a sad indictment of educational research, it is. I am astounded by the amount of research I come across that is either (a) demonstrably untrue or (b) patently obvious.

In a way, this is also a criticism of what we have allowed the teaching profession to become. If we had the nous to question the research we are given on a daily basis, then perhaps much of it wouldn't find such a purchase in the classroom. Instead we gobble it up and hold out our plates for more. But as I have already mentioned elsewhere, the teaching profession cannot be blamed a great deal for this situation. We have collapsed under the weight of expectations from above; we have suffered with impossible expectations; the generation of teachers working today (or trained in the last ten years) are barely taught anything other than the latest dogma and cant. Newer teachers I talk to are astounded by any presumption that these paradigms might be questionable.

And what's worse, some of these teachers will then enter the field of tertiary education and earn academic plaudits for papers with titles such as 'Which thinking skills are best developed in emotionally illiterate pupils?', which will be coolly passed by tutors as reasonable topics for analysis. And not a single child's life will be better. And somewhere down the line, a school leader, a local government official or a minister, will catch the scent of the research, be taken by its bold, revolutionary flavour, and create an edict that somewhere, in some school, in a classroom with real children, this is how it must be done. And the teacher will look up from their marking and ask, 'So what is it you want me to believe now?' And if you're like most teachers, you won't have the foggiest how to respond.

What I'm going to do over the next few chapters is attempt to redress that balance. I'm going to look into a few theories that have been passed down the line over the last few years and see how they stand up to a little bit of scrutiny. Some of them are no more, and some of them are still very much part of the furniture for teachers in the UK at the time of writing. It doesn't matter how out of date or achingly hip they are. What's important is that we (and by we, I mean anyone in the teaching profession) are aware of how easy it is for a value or hunch to become a hypothesis that, untouched by credible testing, can escape the laboratory and run amok in the real world. The next time you come across one of these escapees, I hope you know what to do. In each chapter I'll also give you my own practical advice on what to do in each situation, and what the best evidence points towards.

Because there *is* good research being done, there are useful, credible studies that can assist the understanding of education, how children learn and ways in which we can ensure they are safe, well taught and tended in our care.

But even more important than all that is the experience of teachers, the great collective ocean of understanding that is treated as mere anecdote by many in the research industry, which is ironic when you consider how much is published that simply reflects intuition and personal prejudice dressed up in 10,000 words with references. That ocean of experience is hard to access, however; while most teachers are trained in the context of in-school tutors and mentors, the rot has set in so firmly in some schools and training institutions that dogma is often quoted as solutions to specific problems when what is required is personal experience, transmitted by expert professionals, one to the other.

Here's what I believe; this informs everything I have learned in teaching after a decade:

> *Experience trumps theory every time.*

There *are* rules of the classroom: broadly predictive mechanisms that are useful in directing and educating a room. But as I have said, the diversity of human experience ensures that few specific, micro-management techniques persist in being universally efficacious. An example would be: children are deterred from poor behaviour by sanctions, and generally are encouraged by rewards.

But because people (and children) are complex, multi-layered, complex beasts of illogic, emotion, background, reason and possibly free will, they are not predictable in anything more than broad brushstrokes. The best comparison is with the weather. I already mentioned that even the next meteorological forecast is confounded by time periods of expectation greater than a few days or weeks. But that doesn't mean to say that we don't have a pretty good idea that summer will, in general, be hotter than winter. That's how we should view teaching and learning. I know that in summer I'll need shorts, and in winter I'll be rocking duck down. On a daily basis I have to look out the window and play it by ear. But I know my wardrobes.

So too in teaching. There are nuts and bolts to running a room and conveying facts and skills that are universal. And then there are things you'll have to do for individual pupils on a case-by-case basis. That's the skill, the joy, the torment of being a teacher. The broad brushstrokes can be learned from a book, although their implementation takes a lifetime to learn. Teaching is akin to an art or a craft as well as a technical profession. Just as a carpenter can learn what techniques exist formally transmitted in written form, but he doesn't get the hang of the craft until he actually has to get out there and build something; so too do teachers learn their craft in, and almost entirely in, the classroom. Teaching is a verb, a doing word, and is not amenable to the Petri dish, the slide, the clipboard.

It is a relationship between one adult human being and a room full of children, with no exact precedent or control in the laboratories of academia. I sometimes think that when some educational scientists investigate the actions and reactions of human beings, they forget to observe real people at all, and simply load up their version of *The Sims*, and see what they do. And then, if they disagree with their hypothesis, they simply ignore it and keep testing until they get the result they want. And who's to know? Who's to contradict?

Let's see if we can do any better. They say it's a lot easier to criticise than it is to create. Good. Let's criticise for a while. Besides, teachers like me have been creating since the day we set foot in a classroom. It's called learning to be a teacher, and experience trumps theory every time. If research contradicts your experience, use it as an opportunity to reflect on what you already do and think you know. If you can spot where the research went wrong then you can take that as a failed attempt to falsify the data of your own experience, and therefore your own theories and hypothesises are strengthened.

Let's look at a few theories. Get your knuckledusters.

Part II

Voodoo teaching

In the next few chapters I'll discuss a variety of theories that many teachers will have encountered. Some of them are dead; some of them still walk. What's interesting is to simply take a general claim in education, and then do a bit of simple investigation: see what references they provide, and then attempt to follow those references back to their references, and on the way, look at the strength of the research quoted. It is a sobering journey, I assure you.

This is my method, and it is a teacher's-eye method: I start with an educational fashion, and I simply start working backwards to see what research is quoted to justify its claims. Then I have a poke at the research, and see where that leads me. That's all. Where possible, I've looked for meta-studies that take as much research into account as possible. In other words, I'm not just looking for something that backs up my hunch. I'm actually trying to find good quality research that backs up the claims made by Brain Gym®, and NLP, and everything else.

Unfortunately, it isn't easy to find any. Quite the reverse.

Voodoo teaching

Chapter 5

Multiple intelligences
If everyone's smart, no one is

You will have heard, of course, that people do not have one simple level of intelligence, from stupid to smart; they have many varying types of intelligence. This idea was put forward by the psychologist Howard Gardner in 1983 as an alternative to the traditional idea of IQ, or a singular type of 'smart'. The idea was seized upon by the educational academic community and, certainly by the time I entered the profession, it was one of the pillars of modern education. As we shall see, how are the mighty fallen.

Previously, researchers into the field of intelligence referred to Intelligence Quotient (IQ), which was related to a common factor described as g. High levels of g correlated to high levels of what would commonly be called intelligence across a broad range of cognitive tasks: memory, processing and so on. But, of course, the problem with this definition of intelligence is that it is resolutely polar: you have it or you do not. It also anticipates that children would be broadly smart at most things, or not at all. It also carries the considerable conceptual baggage of suggesting that one's intelligence may be fixed, which means that students with varying levels of g would have varying levels of potential, above which it would be theoretically hard to rise above.

Along came Gardner. He hypothesised that there was not just one intelligence, g, but many:

- spatial
- linguistic
- logical mathematical
- bodily kinaesthetic
- musical
- interpersonal

- intrapersonal
- naturalistic.

Plus two more that he added later:

- spiritual/existential
- moral.

Of which more later. These intelligences explained why children could be good at one type of task (e.g. working out maths puzzles quickly) and not at others (stumbling over poetry, or misunderstanding how plants work). It also offered an exciting new model for teachers: instead of regarding some students as smart and some dumb, and consigning them to pigeonholes their entire academic career, rather than writing off children for not having the capacity to flourish at school, teachers should instead regard every student as having different intelligences, different capabilities and different ways in which they could excel. Everyone was special, in other words.

Not only that, but it offered a revolutionary way of teaching children; educators were encouraged to appeal to their existing intelligences and design learning tasks that played to these strengths in order to encourage development in other areas. For example, a student who scored highly for musical intelligence but poorly in mathematics could be assisted in learning maths by developing ways to communicate mathematics through the language of music; perhaps by linking notes to numbers and imagining the symphonies that resulted.

It was certainly bold. Up and down the teaching cosmos, teachers were encouraged to create geography tasks that involved students discussing their feelings about soil erosion, and music teachers attempted to convey Mozart through the medium of mime. It was, for a time, the learning theory that devoured the world.

But it didn't take long for cracks to emerge in this elegant and intuitively appealing theory. For a start there were the categories themselves.

Which intelligences?

Some of the categories seemed to make sense: children were good at maths, or good at English and sometimes both. So they might be seen as relatively easy to include in the taxonomy. But as we progress farther and farther along the list we encounter more controversy. Intra versus inter-personal? The overlaps seem as profound as the differences. And what about music and maths? There has often been a strong link evidenced between both of these aptitudes, possibly due to the very mathematical way that music, in its acoustic nakedness, can be described. And surely there are skills in linguistic ability that map with the conceptual realm of the spatial? And so on.

And that's before we even get to the upper end of Gardner's Multiple Hootenanny. If alarm bells aren't ringing by the time you get to Naturalistic intelligence, then I suggest you need to check your clappers.[1]

Naturalistic intelligence means the general intelligence of being able to appreciate nature and how it connects and operates. This is one of his most contested fields. Was he reading *Lord of the Rings* at the same time? It sounds like such a subjective collection of abilities and capacities that most of us (the author included) wouldn't have even thought to describe them as intelligence at all. We might as well describe 'good with card tricks'.

And then, of course, there are the big bears: existential intelligence and moral intelligence. I *think* I've studied and taught ethics long enough to be able to say with confidence that these two are highly, highly contested as even having any level of existence at all. Moral intelligence: what does that mean? Is someone more morally intelligent than another? Does that mean kind, virtuous, dutiful, loyal . . . what? It is a collection of values and opinions so loaded with subjectivity that it seems indescribably cocky to attempt to shoehorn it into any metric of intelligence.

So the whole taxonomy appears to be suspect. What else?

The ontological problem

Simply put, this is the argument that Gardner has used the term intelligence when what we might more meaningfully use is the term 'abilities' or 'capacities'. It is fairly uncontroversial to say that someone is good at sports, or some sports. But to then take the word intelligence and adopt it in this context seems like a waste of a perfectly good word that means something that people broadly agree

1   As the LEA coordinator said to the SENCO.

on. I suspect that what Gardner was trying to do here was – and this is conjecture – to attempt to defy the hierarchy of abilities that placed academics at the top and sportsmen at the bottom. It was, I believe, an attempt to wrest the pecking order into a more egalitarian sphere. Well intentioned it might have been, but Gardner makes the fatal error of stretching a concept so thin, so wide, that it means so much that it begins to mean nothing. If everything is intelligence, then nothing is. Or to put it another way, if everyone is special, then no one is.

The academic response

This criticism of Multiple Intelligence (MI) theory was advanced as early as 1983 by Robert Sternberg, 1985 by Scarr and 1994 by Eyesenk. It might surprise a great many educators to know that, even among the intelligence community in which Gardner worked, his MI work is not even slightly recognised. Gardner hasn't provided us with any kind of test for these multiple intelligences, you may be delighted and dismayed to hear. You hear that? *No way of testing them.* There are *many* on the internet of course, where you can also find mail-order Harvard degrees and *Space Monkeys.* You may have even seen one of them. Ever done one of those circles that look like a dartboard, and self-assessed? I hope you had fun.

Furthermore, Gardner himself admitted that he had no fixed definition of his intelligences (which is why, presumably, he added to them later on with nine and ten. Give him long enough and he would have come up with 'Programming Dishwasher Intelligence' or something). Instead he said: 'At present it must be admitted that the selection (or rejection) of a candidate's intelligence is reminiscent more of an artistic judgement than of a scientific assessment.'[2]

So just to be clear, he admits that this is an aesthetic taxonomy, not an objective definition and guide. Some would describe that as 'opinion'. He also writes: 'I balk at the unwarranted assumption that certain human abilities can be arbitrarily singled out as intelligence while others cannot.'[3]

He may balk, but without something more empirically founded, one man's dismay remains a personal matter.

2   Gardner, *Frames of Mind: The theory of multiple intelligences* (1985).
3   Gardner, Howard (1998). 'A Reply to Perry D. Klein's "Multiplying the problems of intelligence by eight"'.

Where's the evidence?

Confirming what Gardner himself suggests, even the many peers engaged in similar research have struggled to find a meaningful way of identifying these alleged intelligences. Indeed, the more work is done, the more scientists appear to find evidence that g exists in some way as a reasonable hypothesis for a general level of intelligence. Of course there are disputes and investigations about where g originates from – the role of nature, the role of nurture – and these are all fine questions to pursue. But more importantly, no MI. Gottfredson (2006)[4] argues that MI are 'unsupported by many tests'; others have contended with Gardner's claims that IQ tests are restricted to measuring linguistic and logical mathematical abilities – Kaufman argues that they also assess and involve what Gardner would call spatial ability.

In her assessment of the papers that supported the existence of MI, Sternberg found that there were no papers that supported it,[5] and previously, in 2000, Allix[6] reported no empirical papers that did so. Gardner and Cornell conceded in 2004 that there was 'little evidence to support Multiple Intelligence theory'. Boy, he really is quite the cheerleader for his own theory. See his next book: *They called me mad, they said I was a fool, but they are the mad ones, it is they who are fools* etc. He also said he would be 'delighted were such evidence to accrue'.

I *bet* he would. He added: 'MI theory has few enthusiasts among psychometricians or others of a traditional psychological background' because they require 'psychometric or experimental evidence that allows one to prove the existence of the several intelligences.'[7]

Many neuroscientists don't think the brain could physically work in the way described by MI theory. Steven Stahl reviewed previous studies that purported to support MI theory and found that of seventeen positive studies cited by a well-known practitioner of MI, fifteen of them were doctoral dissertations, thirteen of them came from the same university, and only one had been published in an

4   Gottfredson, L.S. (2006). Social consequences of group differences in cognitive ability.
5   Sternberg, R.J. (1991). 'Death, taxes, and bad intelligence tests'.
6   Allix, N.M. (2000). The theory of multiple intelligences: A case of missing cognitive matter.
7   Waterhouse, Lynn (2006). 'Inadequate Evidence for Multiple Intelligences, Mozart Effect, and Emotional Intelligence Theories'.

academic journal. And thirteen of them actually claimed to support something else other than MI theory.[8]

So there we have it. Even Gardner admits, in a kind of coughing-in-his-handkerchief-holy-smokes-is-that-the-time-gotta-run way that the evidence is ambiguous. And yet many schools still accept MI theory as Mosaic tablets from the mountain top.

I'm amazed by this. People who would normally be called free thinkers, open minded, hard-to-fool, wolf this up like ice cream, and then replicate it for other teachers and children. So why is it so indelible?

My suggestion is that it simply appeals. The idea that everyone can get better at something, that we're all special, that we all have magical gifts, and that there's a cute way to teach anything to anyone, grabs the heartstrings. It's something that caught a wave, an empathic, benevolent tide that wanted to believe that nobody was stupid, and we were all smart in different ways. It's kind, and it's well meant. But it's as daft as Daffy Duck.

Another reason I think it's found traction is because, like many Cargo Cult theories, it has at least one foot in common sense. We're all good – or could be – at different things? Sure! That sounds about right, and I'd argue there might be something to that. And as to the teaching style thing, the idea that we can use surprising contrasts of material and method to achieve interest, engagement and – best of all – focus, is by no means perfectly daft. If you can convey Shakespeare through the medium of roller derby, then be my guest. But the idea that this is the panacea to poor learning is witless. There's a reason why some disciplines are best learned in their concomitant ways: Shakespeare through grading performance and analysis; art through practice; football through exertion and team play – because these are the basic modalities of the activity; these are the skills of the subject. I often teach some RS through watching films, writing scripts, rapping, whatever works for that class at that time. But the heart of my learning is the activity of religious study – reading, speaking and being questioned about the subject. Sometimes I get speakers in. Sometimes I get them to make something appropriate at home, or revise, or drill, or create as I see fit.

But these are all activities aimed at some greater purpose: a greater understanding of the subject. I don't do it because I think we're all

8   Stahl, S.A. (1999). 'Different strokes for different folks? A critique of learning styles'.

special soldiers with fairy gifts. All subjects are hard work, if done well; I teach them all study skills and get them to repeat them in class. I don't do it because I think they've all got different abilities, like the Legion of Super Heroes; I do it because I think they're all human, with different levels of displayed ability. I differentiate so that everyone can learn at a roughly appropriate pace, and so that no one feels dumb.

But the only dumb thing here is to assume we all have different brains.

On a closing note, I'd like to add that, as recently as 2012, I was still sitting in INSETs delivered by an unnamed 'learning expert' who rattled off MIs as one 'great tool for engaging children and imbedding deep learning'. It was all I could do to stop myself yelling at the stage. But I'm a patient soul. Also, a quick survey of websites devoted to MI tells me that this theory is still propagated by people who will happily take your dollar, even though the evidence (or lack thereof) is freely available for all to see (not even hidden in obscure academic journals, as is usual). They usually add the caveat that 'this is a learning *aid*', which is certainly one way to avoid making a definite claim. One website even had a link to MI tests with the dandy disclaimer that 'these are not scientifically validated, and if you want tests that need to be such, we suggest you look elsewhere'. Where, Narnia?

There is no evidence for multiple intelligences that I could find. The next time someone tells you they exist, ask them to produce data to support it. I'm still waiting.

Chapter 6

My NLP and Brain Gym® hell

I'm writing this in 2012. In 2004 I was being carefully moulded from the lumpen clay of a night club manager into the super teacher[1] whose writing you now hold. My teacher training involved a scheme called Fast Track, which was funded entirely by the Department of/for Education.

It involved residential training courses where we spent days in the Welsh countryside learning how the brain worked, how to influence people, how to tell if someone was lying, and essentially how to read minds. If you remember the claims in the introduction to this book, you might think this all sounds a bit familiar; that's because it actually was. In 2004 we were being trained to read minds, control the weak willed and hone our minds to perfection. In 2004. That isn't a long time ago.

The training was called Neuro-Linguistic Programming (NLP), and it was *all the rage* at the time. At the time I was very taken with it; after all, this was sponsored by the Department of Education; it was part of a government funded scheme. Surely it must be true?

The claims NLP made were, and are, extraordinary. I'm not joking. It claims that you can do all the things I described above. And almost without exception, the claims have been shown, by a deluge of research so enormous it would swamp a continent, to be completely without demonstrable basis. NLP, as it was sold to me, was a complete stew of viscera. Without basis in credible science, and without demonstrable effects.

It emerged, perhaps unsurprisingly, from the self-help mysticism of the seventies. Richard Bandler and John Grinder, two psychologists

---

1   Warning: contents may vary from description. See website for terms and conditions.

(one with a PhD, I might add) developed what has been called the 'science of success'; they theorised that by emulating the micro-gestures of successful people, others could imitate their success. Their first book, published in 1975, was called *The Structure of Magic*[2] and I am not making that up. Without wishing to go into inter-minable detail, they believed that there was a link between the brain (the neuro part), bodily movements and language, and that by paying close attention to these, many wonders could be achieved. For example, by paying attention to the way someone spoke or acted, you could emulate these behaviours, achieve rapport with the subject, and then create similar gestures that could then be used to influence the subject. Some of the claims made about NLP are quite incredible; I once spoke to a certified master practitioner who said – with a straight face – that he could make someone opposite us in a bar get up and walk over and buy us a drink . . . without saying anything to him. Needless to say, he declined to demonstrate.

It also makes claims that by watching people's micro-gestures you can find out if they are lying, and what they're really thinking. You may have heard of this bit: if someone is looking up, for instance, they are supposed to be accessing their visual brain, which means they are recalling something; upper right means they are creating a lie, and so on. Complete rubbish, but it certainly sounds good.

The whole 'achieving rapport' thing was achieved by watching their tiniest gestures and copying them; this led to the odd situation where you would be crossing and uncrossing your legs in time to the subject, who was probably worrying if you were taking the mickey. The funny part came when you saw two NLPers sitting with each other, both desperately trying to copy each other. And if you were really good at it, you were supposed to be able to achieve this kind of rapport by copying the blink rate of the subject. I'm not making this up.

Of course, there is, as with most contestable theories purporting to be science, just enough truth in it to convince, and just enough trappings of science to make it sound plausible. For example, it's long been observed that people who are really into each other do sometimes fall into similar ways of sitting and so on. And if you've ever watched two people on a car-crash date, you'll see plenty of body language that says 'Please *please* go away and leave me to my life of single misery, preferable to a moment more with you.' So the

2   Bandler, R. and Grinder, J., *The Structure of Magic:1*. 1975.

rest of it sounds like it might be true. I remember long hours standing inside my circle of power while I visualised the last time I felt powerful and confident, before popping an imaginary lasso into my pocket. I'm serious.

It's also meant to have use in the field of psychoanalysis, making claims to be able to cure phobias, and so on. You can use it to build up confidence, get over heartbreak, motivate yourself and others, and so on. It really is all very marvellous. It's the real-life *How to Win Friends and Influence People*. As teachers, we were told that it would be an invaluable tool for persuading and leading staff, running classrooms, motivating students and so on.

Except of course, it isn't. There's barely a scrap of science to support anything in it. It's been extensively reviewed and researched by people, wondering if all these fantastic claims are actually true. Soon after its invention, books, videos and courses started to appear; this was hot stuff, and people wanted some of that success magic. But by the 1980s, more sober members of the scientific community[3] were putting it to the test and concluding that

> . . . a host of controlled trials had shed such a poor light on this practice, and those promoting the intervention made such extreme and changeable claims, that researchers began to question the wisdom of researching the area further and even suggested that NLP was not a testable theory.[4]

Christopher Sharpley tested to see if the hypothesis that your eye movement gave a clue to your 'sensory preferences' (which, of course, brings us back into the learning style game again), and found that it did not.[5] Heap (1988) also came to the same conclusions.[6] Daniel Druckman (1990), working with the US National Research Council, found that there was no evidence for the claim that tracking eye movements could enable any kind of influence over another.[7]

3 Devilly, Grant J., Power therapies and possible threats to the science of psychology and psychiatry.
4 Sharpley C.F., Research findings on Neuro Linguistic Programming: Non supportive data or an untestable theory?
5 Sharpley, C.F. (1984). 'Predicate matching in NLP: A review of research on the preferred representational system'.
6 Heap. M. (1988). Neurolinguistic programming: An interim verdict.
7 Johnson, S.J. (1990). 'Enhancing Human Performance: Issues, theories, and techniques'.

And on. And on. And on. There is an embarrassing wealth of research, which repeatedly and routinely fails to find any efficacy for the techniques described by Bandler and Grinder. I can also match these findings with my own experience as a classroom practitioner. At the time of learning about it, it seemed wonderful; mainly, I think, because it promised so many wonderful things. It seemed to be too good to be true and, of course, it was.

How have NLPers responded? Well, partly, they just ignored it. Remember, I was being trained in its magic ways in the early part of the new millennium, decades after it was exposed as having a wobbly (read: almost no) scientific basis. Once a movement has started, you can throw as much real science at it as you like. Once people want to believe something, they'll believe it. And people with no concern for scientific veracity, or no doubt to suspect the veracity of what they had been told, passed it on to others, in an enormous game of Chinese whispers. This is how rumours start, especially when those rumours serve a purpose.

This is connected, I think, to the magic bean syndrome; people want to believe that there are magic ways to solve complex problems, that science can reduce the difficulties of human interaction into a series of learned, demonstrable tricks that can change the world. Would it surprise you to find out that it can't?

Other practitioners were more bold: NLP practitioners and academics Tosey and Mathison have argued that the experimental approach is not always appropriate for researching NLP, instead proposing that NLP should be researched phenomenologically. Gareth Roderique-Davies (2009) stated that 'Phenomenological research is free from hypotheses, pre-conceptions and assumptions, and seeks to describe rather than explain.'[8]

See? It's not NLP at fault: it's *science's* fault. Give me strength. Now we need magic science to investigate magic science.

The term 'Neuro-Linguistic Programming' has been characterised as pseudoscientific. Witkowski (2010) writes that 'NLP represents pseudoscientific rubbish, which should be mothballed forever.' Roderique-Davies (2009) states that 'neuro' in NLP is 'effectively fraudulent since NLP offers no explanation at a neuronal level and it could be argued that its use fallaciously feeds into the notion of scientific credibility'. Witkowski (2010) also states that, at the

8 http://en.wikipedia.org/wiki/Neuro-linguistic_programming#cite_note-Heap_1988-58. Accessed on 26 March 2013.

neuronal level, NLP provides no explanation at all and has nothing in common with academic linguistics or programming. Similarly, experimental psychologist Corballis (1999), in his critique of lateralization of brain function (the left/right brain myth), states that 'NLP is a thoroughly fake title, designed to give the impression of scientific respectability.'[9]

Everything I've read about NLP suggests that it has as much scientific plausibility as *Avatar*, and that in my opinion, it has as many demonstrable effects as a homeopathic pill. Of course, there will always be people who swear by it, but they have no way of showing that it is repeatable, or demonstrable in any meaningful way, or cannot simply be explained by the placebo effect or the Hawthorne effect. I mean, I left the course with a beginner's level certificate in NLP; a few more days of courses on it and I would be qualified to *teach* the stuff. Funnily enough, every single one of the teachers on my course (thirty or forty of us) passed it too. Isn't that marvellous? You'd think for a minute that perhaps it lacked some kind of assessment rigour. No, surely not.

I'll mention Brain Gym® in passing, because it has a lot to do with NLP; we were trained in the Dark Arts of this too. It's an idea, similar to NLP, that moving in certain ways can assist reasoning and retention, learning, motivation and thinking. Now that *is* a very definite claim. For example, I was encouraged, along with my class, to rub my 'brain button' (just under my collar bones, if you're getting interested) before a new activity, to activate my 'cognitive centres', which I think meant my brain. I still have my notes from the sessions. They are a perfect hoot, I assure you. I was also told to 'take a swig of water' before every lesson or session, and hold it against the roof of my mouth in order for it to be absorbed more quickly into my brain. This must be some new way that water gets into my body – most of us just swallow it, but I'm sure there's something to it. There's also the lovely assumption that without a good glug of water, my brain will be dry.

I won't go into too much detail of this, because Ben Goldacre[10] has so effectively demolished this in a chapter of his book *Bad Science*. In fact, it was this book that started me thinking about science in education. It was, as you can already see, a can of worms.

9   http://en.wikipedia.org/wiki/Neuro-linguistic_programming#cite_note-Heap_1988-58. Accessed on 26 March 2013.
10   Goldacre, Ben, *Bad Science*, 2008.

Chapter 7

Group work
Failing better, together

In the mid-2000s, an earthquake rocked education that promised to revolutionise the way teachers taught and children learned. It was a strategy that claimed it would:

- improve learning
- develop social skills
- develop empathy and altruism
- deepen learning
- improve test scores and retention
- develop complex learning strategies
- create independent learning
- enable lifelong learning.

The last time I saw claims like that, they were on the adverts page of a *Marvel* comic next to Charles Atlas and the X-Ray specs. It is, of course, group work. In 2006 several reports appeared that seemed to support the use of group work as one of the best ways to learn. It was widely reported at the time that group work, or collaborative learning, was also widely misused as a strategy at schools; students often sat together, but infrequently learned together in a meaningful way. There were many other reports at this time, and many more afterwards, all saying the same thing; if you want children to learn – *and I mean really learn* – then you gotta get them in groups.

But Chris Keates, General Secretary of the NASUWT, said the ideas sounded 'unrealistic'. 'They have got to look at the context teachers are working in,' she said. 'It is a mistake for people to say "we have done this piece of research – this worked and it is the way it'll work all the time."'

Very, very early on in my career, it was one of the pieces of absolutely infallible dogma I had been told to adopt as a consistent and coherent way of driving learning.

I'm going to confess that me and group work have history. In the first few years of my teaching I was formally observed by a man with a clip board and too much time on his hands. The lesson wasn't a symphony, but you could make out the tune, and everyone knew what notes to play. We even ended on time. It was a decent lesson. But I was rocked by the result: unsatisfactory. When I queried it, I was told that because there was no group work, the students couldn't really be learning very much. I promise you, verbatim.

When you're green and raw, and you don't have the guts to question things, that kind of thing is like a smack in the kisser. I went down like an old man with a walking stick on a greased floor. It ruined me, as professional criticism often can; my lesson wasn't just average and bland – it had failed. I was failing them.

I'm now going to confess to even more previous with group work. (See, me and group work go a *ways* back, he says, adjusting his cigar and looking into the sun like Clint.) As a school kid, I was the subject of an apparently mad experiment by one of my secondary teachers. There were a couple of wild men in my class called Rab and Skully, who only came into school to avoid the probation officers. No teacher could control them, even in my relatively polite school, and they bubbled and brewed for six or seven years before falling into progressively more anti-social crimes, and I believe they both ended up doing time in the big house.

Well, I always got paired with them. I am not fussing with you here. I was an enormous geek; I corresponded to every nerdy cliché you can imagine: shy, intense, bum-fluff moustache, full school uniform, bucket hair, acne, thick glasses, poor at sport. Those of you of a certain age will feel for me when I say that when Sue Townsend was riding high in the paperback charts with Adrian Mole, I was simultaneously 13¾. So there is a God, and he is not a Good God.

Every week, twice a week, in what was, I imagine, a pretty fair imitation of the punishment undergone by Loki, trickster of the Viking deities, who was imprisoned in Tartarus upside down, with venom from the fangs of the Midgard Serpent perpetually dripping into his eyes until the end of time.

Well he had it easy. Group work. With the *mentals*. At first, it was just a weekly gobbing in my face. Then they used rulers; then they tired of them. Eventually, we were given the half-term project: design and build a mosque out of polystyrene bricks, using a hot wire to cut the pieces into shape. This, for a month. Four weeks of watching design sheets being turned into enormous comedy spliffs, of the smell of melted polystyrene, chips in my hair and, at the end, a pile of white crumbs and a grade F.

That's my enduring memory of group work.

When I look at the claims made of group work by advocates, I wonder when they got back from Toon Town. Because I know that, in a real classroom, there are many variables working against the success of any group activity:

Disguised inactivity. Bluntly, in a group, lazy kids get a chance to really spread their lazy-ass wings and reach heights of doing absolutely nothing. If you give a task to three or four people, it takes the couch potatoes about half a second to realise it's time for a cuppa and a fag, because there will usually be one or two others who will design the logo/poster/remix of the Ten Commandments. Their indolence is hidden behind a cloud of other people.

Unequal loading. Related to this is the problem that while every student might participate, the participation might be as uneven as a trapeze artist with a balloon in one pocket and a cannonball in the other. Some will contribute as slowly as continental plates scrape past each other; others will tap dance like a dressage horse through every sub-task just to save face.

Developing social skills. Oh, they'll develop social skills all right. They'll talk each other's backsides off in a competition for who can discuss the task least. Playtime has come *early* in this scenario. Some kids can't believe their luck: Sir just gave them an extra twenty minutes to catch up with who's dating whom and who's untouchable at that exact instant. Result.

Unfair assessment. When I give a kid a thumbs up (Tom Bennett 'likes' this) then it's a clear mono-directional relationship. When I tell a team that their polystyrene mosque is an abstract marvel, or a splendid waste of four weeks, it's an unfair commentary on anything other than the fact that the group didn't do well together, as if I had suddenly put Peter Kay in the Jamaican 4x100m relay and then given them grief for coming last.

This is my experience of a lot of group work and, believe me, I was doing it for some time.

One of the great advantages of the practice, the research assures us, is that it's a great way to engage children. Well that seems to be true, if by engage you mean 'give them a chance to do less for a period of time, and catch up with each other'. Of course many kids will leap like salmon into that river; it's brilliant. Loads of kids really *really* do like working in groups – witness the phenomenon when you have a group of agreeable, biddable kids who get on with each other and want to show what a great bunch of pals they are by making the best poster. I've seen it happen a lot. But this appears to put the strategy benefit before the horse; the point of group work is that it is supposed to develop and encourage these skills of interactivity and motivation. But in the examples where it seems to work best, these qualities and skills have to pre-exist the activity. Which seems to make the whole thing pointless.

But what does the research say? Plenty.

We can see the modern incarnation of group work emerging from the wombs of such theorists as Vygotsky and Piaget. Lev Vygotsky, the Russian psychologist, has been a major influence in the past few decades. He believed that social interaction precedes development; action is the basis of forming thoughts, in a child-centred understanding of how we learn. Pupils are in the roles of problem solvers, and teachers are there as facilitators; this is the famous transition from the sage on the stage to the guide from the side. Language, used by children, is a tool used in order to think. Talk, for Vygotsky, is a learning tool. He believed that the use of talk – group work, discussion – in the classroom would help to reduce the pupils' 'zone of proximal development' or the gap between where they could be and their current stage of learning. 'What a child can do today in cooperation, tomorrow he will be able to do on his own.' (Vygotsky 1962, p. 7, see 'Learning to teach'.) 'The students are responsible for one another's learning as well as their own. Thus, the success of one student helps other students to be successful.' (Ibid.)

Proponents of collaborative learning claim that the active exchange of ideas within small groups not only increases interest among the participants but also promotes critical thinking ' . . . there is persuasive evidence that cooperative teams achieve at higher levels of thought and retain information longer than students who work quietly as individuals. The shared learning gives students an opportunity to engage in discussion, take responsibility for their own learning, and thus become critical thinkers.'[1]

According to Vygotsky (1978), students are capable of performing at higher intellectual levels when asked to work in collaborative situations than when asked to work individually. Group diversity in terms of knowledge and experience contributes positively to the learning process. Bruner (1985) contends that cooperative learning methods improve problem-solving strategies because the students are confronted with different interpretations of the given situation. The peer support system makes it possible for the learner to internalise both external knowledge and critical thinking skills and to convert them into tools for intellectual functioning.[2]

And my personal favourite from the aforementioned article:

> For collaborative learning to be effective, the instructor must view teaching as a process of developing and enhancing students' ability to learn. The instructor's role is not to transmit information, but to serve as a facilitator for learning. This involves creating and managing meaningful learning experiences and stimulating students' thinking through real world problems.

Well that's me screwed then, isn't it? Because I don't believe that. My role (note: I'm not a teacher anymore, I appear to have become an instructor) isn't to transmit information? How extremely odd, because that's exactly what teachers have been doing for thousands of years. Suddenly we don't do this anymore? I must have missed the memo. 'Stop telling them things they don't know.'

This is a common trick in social science research: to say, 'This technique only works if the teacher–instructor does X and the pupils all do Y,' as if to say that if you *don't* find that this method works in your classroom, it's *your* fault. Far be it from me to suggest that maybe the reason it doesn't provide the benefits promised is because it's not that simple.

I must emphasise that I'm not anti-group work, and that I use it myself. I enjoy it, especially with sixth formers, who do some brilliant work with it. I'm neither scared of it, not am I anti. I use anything that works for me, and I'll try anything that looks like it works for other people. But the insistence that group work is the best way to

1   Anuradha A. Gokhale, 'Collaborative Learning Enhances Critical Thinking'.
2   Ibid.

develop higher-level thinking skills, and that it has an appreciable improvement effect on students overall, is just untrue. The paper I just quoted (which was aimed at further education) had forty-eight participants. That's *forty-eight*. I could fit them in my tiny garden. That is barely evidence. If I had a bouncy castle in my back garden I could probably whip up forty-eight guests. Should I surmise that British people jump up and down most evenings? Maybe. Maybe not. Not from this evidence.

OK, that was an easy one, I didn't even have to look at the methodology or anything. But it's strange that people put so much effort into these things and yet make such formative errors. There are no credible predictive or universalisable conclusions to be drawn from such a study. It doesn't even contribute to the greater mass of evidence, because – you guessed it – you can't build on this research unless you were to somehow involve the exact same participants and make sure 100 other contributory factors could be ruled out. It is quite simply impossible to use this study in any way other than as a prompt, a thinking point.

I turn to another paper at random:

> There is an ever increasing need for interdependence in all levels of our society today. Providing students with the tools to effectively work in a collaborative and cooperative environment should be our priority as teachers. Cooperative learning (CL) is one way to provide students with a well-defined framework from which they can learn from one another.[3]

That was from the very opening paragraph, first line. There's an *ever increasing need*, is there? Really? First sentence: unproven, unprovable conjecture, opinion and subjective values of the author. It doesn't really bode well for the rest of the paper. Can you imagine Niels Bohr[4] starting a paper with 'There is an ever increasing need for the value of Pi to be 3.13'? I fancy not. But in social science papers? Ppphhhh. Fill your boots. Some writers feel they have carte blanche to assume anything, and proceed from that point.

One paper I read from 2006 talked about 39 test groups, and 33 control groups; the size of each group is unspecified, but let's be generous and say four, which would give us around 250 kids. It isn't

---

3   Folake Abass, Cooperative Learning and Motivation.
4   Father of Quantum Physics.

looking huge already. But looking more closely, occasions where adults dominated were removed from the final data. Because? Because it doesn't suit the findings? Why shouldn't it be included? Doesn't it offer, potentially, evidence that might show that deeper learning and social skills hadn't happened because of the group work? Of course, it might mean that the adult intervened for safety reasons or something, but it isn't stated. And that just isn't good enough, surely? Otherwise, removal might appear arbitrary to an outside observer. Me, for example.

The study was focused on video-recorded evidence of group work after months of training, both of teachers and students. Of course, permission had to be obtained for filming, and when it wasn't, the pupils were removed from the test subjects. Can you imagine a sample of iridium, or a beaker of iodine giving or not giving its permission to be included in an analysis? Students knew that they *might* be filmed that day. Teachers probably did. Groups of students were then given group tasks designed to display problem-solving ability, cooperativeness, etc. So the tasks themselves were factors in the process; what might the researchers have found in tasks that weren't designed to show the quality tested?

Researchers then had to watch selections of the clips, and decide to what degree students were on task and engaged, and what kind of quality of engagement they displayed. Now these are tremendously subjective properties, and could vary from researcher to researcher, from day to day, depending on a million factors, subconscious and not. To its credit, the researchers were, at this point, unaware of which groups were control, and which were not. That's good. That sounds more like science.

And what did they find? It may stagger you to learn that the test groups displayed better group work skills than the ones who had not been through the training process. I'm not kidding. What they did was something that is common to a lot of social science: using proxy indicators. What are they?

Proxy indicators

It's easy enough to measure height or temperature. We have tape measures and thermometers that cope splendidly with such tasks. But how do you measure something more abstract like learning? I mean, how deep *is* your love? We don't have spirit levels for them yet. So what we do is try to capture the next best thing: something that we *can* measure, that we think will correspond with the quality we're interested in. So, for example, we can't see electrons, but we know that whenever you get them, you have voltage and amps and electricity, and wheels can move, so we know when we've got them. So too with learning. They haven't built a learning dipstick yet (thank God) so we broadly judge it by something that we know requires learning to have happened: exams. IQ tests are a bit more controversial, but they work by the same principle; someone has more of it if they can perform well at the spatial, linguistic and mathematical psychometric tests.

In this experiment, what did they use as proxy measures? I've mentioned that they noted degree of engagement, quality of interactivity and numerous other factors, such as sustained levels of discussion. These things could at least be observed by the researchers with their eyes – back to empiricism again. They found that at the end of the experiment, test groups of pupils had longer discussions, maintained their groups better, blocked each other and so on far less than the control groups.

This somehow proves that group work is better learning? Or it could prove that groups trained at group work get better at group work. Or it could prove a million other things. Or nothing. That's the problem. We don't know. And neither do the researchers, who are involved in a large-scale project designed to show that collaborative learning is just dandy, and – holy smokes! – would you believe that they succeeded?

The paper generously mentions that the Hawthorne effect may be a factor, but then fails to explore it beyond saying that they tried their best to keep it to a minimum, and they reckoned that it hadn't much of an effect. Cheers. So they've proven that students undergoing the programme probably get better at the kind of things the programme is designed to teach.

The website accompanying the paper claims that 'Experimental research on small groups and psychological theory emphasises that effective group work in classrooms has enormous potential in terms of increasing children's motivation and learning.'

That'll be those theories that are essentially untestable, right? Just checking. So, we start from an unproven premise and look for ways to confirm it, with an aim to rolling it out across mainstream schools (you won, incidentally. Congratulations. We're swimming in bloody group work).

One paper investigating group work produced this statement: 'The majority of pupils and teachers have little preparation for group work and have doubts about and difficulties implementing group work in classrooms.'

I love that last bit. You *bet* we do. It's sweet how often this type of phrase can be read in academic literature about teachers, when they remember to mention us at all; look out for the phrase, 'Teachers reported that this strategy was extremely problematic', or something similar, before the paper then goes on to bulldoze (or simply ignore) these qualms by describing how the ideal teacher would enable the fabulous theory, and any negativity was just teachers being heavy and reactionary. I'm serious: 'Patients reported that their heads hurt after being hit with a claw hammer, but the evidence suggests that this method of trepanning will allow evil spirits to leave, thereby ending headaches' etc. Theory trumps evidence and expertise, and findings that contradict already set conclusions are ignored, and more amenable ones sought instead.

> Closer examination of teachers' experiences show that they appear sceptical about the benefits of allowing students to work together (Bennett and Dunne, 1992). Teachers cite loss of control, increased disruption and off task behaviour as main reasons for avoiding group interactions in the classroom (Cohen, 1994). When spread across a number of groups working simultaneously, teachers are not easily on hand to resolve conflicts or to support group task management and decision making. There is also disbelief in the capacity of students to work together (Lewis and Cowie, 1993) particularly the less able, beliefs that group-work is overly time consuming and in particular that students lack the communication skills to engage effectively in group interactions.[5]

One of the recurrent themes in the literature about group work was the claim that students and classrooms would benefit from group work *if* they were trained in the skills necessary to interact as groups. This is the cart before the horse; if effort is put into ensuring that children can behave well enough to participate meaningfully in group

---

5 Baines, E., Rubie-Davies, C. and Blatchford, P. (2009). 'Improving pupil group work interaction and dialogue in primary classrooms'.

work, then that same effort can be directed towards teaching them just as well in non-group environments.

In 2005, the BBC and the *Guardian* reported that schools were failing to implement group work effectively. This research, backed up by a much larger study of 4000 students over a year in Key Stages 1, 2 and 3, seemed to testify to the same claims made elsewhere: pupils working in groups collaborate more, learn more, socialise more and are more motivated to succeed. But motivation was measured by the proxy of self-evaluation questionnaires, which, as we all know, is a notoriously bad way of ascertaining the truth, as I found when I asked 1000 men if they had erectile problems, how many sexual partners they'd had, and how racist they were. People lie. And sweetly, people sometimes write what they think you want to hear. It doesn't mean they *were* lying, just that this isn't a great way to prove that someone means what they say. Even the Key Stage 3 results weren't clear about this. Behaviour was measured by researchers, with all the problems described above in ensuring authenticity and validity of data.

One complaint I found in several papers was that the collaborative strategies worked well when the research groups were conducting them in classes, but when adopted by regular teachers, beneficial effects slipped away due to teacher unfamiliarity with the techniques. These bloody schools eh? Just not *doing* it right. Classes are messy, made of humans. If group work doesn't work for a teacher, it might not be the teacher's fault; maybe it's the strategy not being effective for that group, that teacher and that lesson. And that's what professional judgement is for.

The problem with even larger studies is that they aren't actually measuring anything other than the effect of themselves being in the classroom. The Hawthorne effect is extremely hard to displace from findings in any situation like this. Students and teachers might actually perform well simply because they are involved in the special environment of a laboratory scenario; they might also respond to the simple process of operating in a structured routine way, rather than a more spontaneous one. Who knows? No one. That's the problem.

The same papers often noted that data collected between schools could be of varying quality and structure due to different collation techniques used between sites.

So some of these large-scale experiments don't even compare the same methods of data collection; they vary between schools, classes and age groups, in order to measure increased attainment? What's worse is the previously mentioned problem of controls: a true control would be the same kids, in the same circumstances, except for the subtraction of the intervention under research. But that isn't possible. You're comparing children with different children. You can bluster as much as you like about keeping the demographics as clean as possible, but it's a huge problem. The differences between two children can be enormous. You can't control it. It isn't like two beakers of identical water, separate only spatially. If you compare one class with another, you're comparing oranges and lemons. If you're looking for results you'll find them if you're not careful. If you're involved in an organisation that exists to promote group work in classrooms, don't be surprised if you find loads of research that confirms exactly what you stand for.

No wonder Feynman used to despair about social science. He knew what it meant to say you knew something. Compared to this diligence, sometimes the white coats of psychology can seem – to me, anyway – haphazard.

More research then: Johnson and Johnson.[6] One of them is the co-director of the Cooperative Learning Centre, so I'll take a stab at where his interests lie. Action Research: Cooperative learning in the science classroom (Johnson and Johnson, 1986) is an often-quoted text in this argument, and the foundation of many a paper I came across.

> The fact that working together to achieve a common goal produces higher achievement and greater productivity than does working alone is so well confirmed by so much research that it stands as one of the strongest principles of social and organizational psychology. Cooperative learning is indicated whenever learning goals are highly important, mastery and retention are important, a task is complex or conceptual, problem solving is desired, divergent thinking or creativity is desired, quality of performance is expected, and higher-level reasoning strategies and critical thinking are needed.[7]

This contains what I think is one of the fundamental misassumptions upon which this project rests: that everything is done better in

---

6 That must have been a hoot when they teamed up. Can you imagine the laffs they had?

7 An Overview of Cooperative Learning, Roger T. and David W. Johnson, 2009. Originally published in: J. Thousand, A. Villa and A. Nevin (eds), *Creativity and Collaborative Learning*, 1994.

groups. There is, of course, an enormous amount of evidence that people can usually achieve more working together than alone, and you don't really need a whole lot of chaps with clipboards to tell you that. But the problem is that this doesn't mean that all endeavours are best achieved in a group. I can think of many: writing; reading; working out maths in your head; designing a magazine cover; writing a poem, a melody; falling in love; going for a walk; sipping a Rusty Nail and watching the smoke from your cigarette curl up into the darkness above you as you sit on a Roman veranda. Just because some endeavours benefit from cooperation doesn't mean that all endeavours do. Learning is not shifting boxes.

Then there is the confirmation bias of students involved in any large study: tell a teacher that they're involved in an experiment that will raise attainment, tell kids that they are too, and watch the placebo effect start to take hold. It can be argued (by me, for example) that if a teacher makes an effort to undertake any structured scheme involving routine, then it will often have a positive effect, because kids like structure and order.

I feel like I'm taking crazy pills here. There are hundreds and hundreds of articles supporting group work as having myriad benefits for the pupil, classroom and teacher; in the course of this chapter I've read a few dozen, so that you don't have to. Over and over again the same basic flaws; dripping with subjectivity and value judgements as the very basis of research; skipping from fact to conjecture to fact without blinking or blushing, and then photo-shopping any data they do generate into something unrecognisable from the evidence, such as it is, like a magician's dove appearing from a silk scarf.

This isn't evidence; this isn't proof. This is narrative; it has more in common with the content of a diary than it does with science. And I return to the point I'll stress throughout. *That's OK.* There is nothing wrong with poking your nose into a few classrooms and speculating about what does and doesn't work. But don't stick a hat and a raincoat on a scarecrow and call it the groom. And don't deceive your audience that what you have said is in any way science, because it isn't.

The verdict on group work

This isn't to discredit group work, just because some have hitched their wagons to it; it's a perfectly sound approach in the classroom for many activities. My experience in teaching and teacher training shows me that there are several good reasons to do group work.

- In situations where tasks are impossible to achieve without it, for example, football or an orchestra.
- To vary the type of classroom activity, moving from a period of individual book work to a short session of cooperation, in order to stimulate the pupils by the ancient method of mixing things up a bit. A change is as good as a rest and so on.
- Fun. Lots of kids like working in groups; this is often for all the wrong reasons, but it's often for some very good ones too. I know some kids who eat up group work with a spoon, and would lick it afterwards if you asked. There is nothing wrong with injecting as bit of fun into an activity by putting them in teams or getting them to cooperate with each other in a way that they find pleasant. As long as you remember that fun is an extrinsic aim of education, not an intrinsic one. We're not entertainers, and this isn't a bouncy castle, and I say that because I take their education seriously, and won't waste a moment of their time when they could be learning.
- Oddly enough, all the reasons that advocates of group work also espouse: improving their ability to cooperate, reason with each other, listen to other's opinions and so on. I think that these are valuable goals for child development, and I'm happy to use group work from time to time as one way to support that. But while I think that group work can support these things, there is an enormous danger sign flashing in my head: my job is to teach them the subject I teach, not to develop skills that, frankly, I'm not an expert in developing, even assuming that such things can be taught, which I'm not sure about. And I'm honest enough to admit that, unlike many advocates of group work, I don't know how to teach such things, but as an adult I hope that they pick it up somehow.

And furthermore, group work is only one way of developing such things, and group work is not a universal strategy because there is no such thing. The claims that advocates make are simply unproven, and possibly unproveable.

The problems with group work

There are many, most of which I've discussed; the main one is that it allows some/many/most kids to freeload, while a minority carry the big stones. It simply isn't good enough for advocates to say,

'Well, if you were to do it properly, it would work,' because that's not true. I'm a pretty sturdy teacher, with classes that, on happy occasions, I get along with brilliantly. Even with near perfect relationships and well-trained kids, it's a recipe for off-task behaviour, particularly in less able kids, particularly with disaffected kids, or lazy kids, or unpopular kids, or a million other reasons. Any strategy that requires me to execute it in a near perfect manner is simply not fit for purpose, like a car that can only be driven by a Formula One expert.

Another issue is that there is a basic flaw in the theory, especially among those who claim that group work not only develops skills and thinking abilities (hard as they are to either define or measure) but are also better methods for conveying knowledge. There are many ways that people have advanced this theory, through techniques such as jigsawing, where pupils are split into groups and given 'seek and return' missions with specific learning goals. That's fine, but it is incredibly time consuming; half a lesson can easily be consumed in the conveyance of a group of facts that could be far more efficiently conveyed in five minutes and a demand that pupils revise and take careful notes.

But that's not the main conceptual problem; the main one is the self-evidently intellectually bereft idea that children learn best from other children; that they are the sources of all the information that they need. This isn't a bad idea when it comes to getting them to think about alternatives and ideas and values opposite to their own, because one student's opinion about something is just as good as another's for learning about justifications and difference. But when it comes to factual conveyance, it is pointless to put two equally uneducated people together and say, 'Teach each other.' That's what a subject expert is for. For every subject there is an enormous body of content that is beyond dispute, even within the humanities, and that is one of the main tasks of the teacher, to introduce children to the best of what has already been discovered and thought of. If we don't do that, we break the link between children and the legacy of the ancestors. You might as well start from scratch. That's not something I want to do with my kids. I want them to build on what I and others have learned, and hopefully to surpass us. I refuse to hobble them by forcing them to discover everything for themselves all over again. That's just cruel. It also condemns them to cultural and intellectual illiteracy, as if the characters of *Lord of the Flies* really had been stranded on a dessert island and forced to reinvent society and science. I shudder.

And there's another problem with group work, often completely overlooked by more experienced teachers who advocate it: group work is hell for newer teachers, absolute hell. The temptation for children to be off task is simply too great for many of them, and I witness new teacher after new teacher go screaming down in flames before a class of kids who are all facing each other and not the class front or the teacher. It's an invitation to misbehave. Many of the studies I have read have been conducted in schools that could be best described as pleasant, with groups of students who are best described as amenable.

But group work in a difficult class, with more than a couple of hellraisers, in a tough area, with a new teacher . . . it's carnage. You won't see much independent learning and collaborative thinking then, because they'll be too busy setting up Facebook pages called 'The teacher is a prat' and eating each other.

But that is a common problem: people with little experience of the real workings of a classroom telling teachers how they should really be doing it because, you know, Vygotsky said that kids learn like this.

When did this happen? When did armchair educators start thinking they could tell us how children best learned? People who have barely seen a child? It's absurd, and it's faintly tragic, because just in the last few years I have seen good, potential teachers leave within the first six months of their training year because everything they've been told wasn't good enough, or true enough, to help them get past the first few hurdles.

The message

Use group work when you feel it is appropriate to the task you want them to achieve, and at no other time. It isn't dogma, it isn't a panacea and it isn't the Messiah. It's one strategy among many. And it's a fine one; not because Johnson and Johnson say so, but because teachers say so. As long as you use it when you feel it is appropriate, and not before.

Chapter 8

I'm with stupid

Emotional Intelligence

For almost two decades, the educational world in the West has been populated by a concept that is now so commonplace it is practically slang: Emotional Intelligence (EI). This has been defined as 'abilities such as being able to motivate oneself and persist in the face of frustrations; to control impulse and delay gratification; to regulate one's moods and keep distress from swamping the ability to think; to empathise; to hope.'[1]

I've just quoted Daniel Goleman, because he, more than most, has been responsible for the popularisation of Emotional Intelligence in his 1995 number one bestseller *Emotional Intelligence: Why it can matter more than IQ.* More from Goleman later.

This is now common in UK schools and schools in the USA; programs such as SEAL (Social and Emotional Aspects of Learning) have been rolled out for years. Some schools even have SEAL written into their schemes of work, indicating neatly where students have been encouraged and coached into developing their Emotional Intelligence. I have seen lesson plans that devote columns to it; Ofsted routinely mention it in their school evaluations. Schools now routinely include mention of Emotional Intelligence and connected terms such as social literacy and social intelligence in their prospectuses, proudly demonstrating with how much vigour they promote, monitor and nurture such a thing. Any teacher who has taught a PSHE/PAL lesson in the last seventeen years has probably been working his or her way through a programme based on Emotional Intelligence. It is very, very hot right now.

But, some exceptions notwithstanding, there appears to be little evidence to support it. I am unable to find evidence that Emotional

1   Goleman, 1995, *Emotional Intelligence: Why it can matter more than IQ.*

Intelligence even exists; and that even if it does, it can be taught meaningfully in a formal school environment; and there is no credible evidence I could obtain that EI – which among other things, claims to enhance learning – actually does any such thing.

Let me explain how this piece of theory escaped from the laboratory and into the classroom. I'll start with the aspect of EI that most UK teachers will be familiar with: SEAL, and then take a look at the zoo from which it came.

SEAL

SEAL, or Social and Emotional Aspects of Learning, follows in the tradition of Goleman. It was introduced in the UK in 2005 as part of a national strategy. The aim was that children would, as Goleman said, learn better if schools attended as much to their Emotional Intelligence as to their IQ scores; that learning could be assisted when students were also coached and directed towards better ways of feeling, relating and valuing. In the words of one advocate: 'Research has shown that well designed programmes that promote social and emotional skills have shown to have a positive impact on pupil's attitudes and behaviour.'[2]

For example:

- Pupils have higher self-esteem and confidence.
- Pupils are happier and get on better with each other.
- Pupils are more engaged in learning so fewer disengage with school.
- Quieter pupils become more assertive and confident.
- There is better behaviour in the classroom and improved attendance.
- There is less bullying.
- There are lower rates of truancy, offending and drug misuse.[3]

Those are quite some claims. You get these kinds of claims simply by clicking on any link you fancy on Google after a simple search for SEAL or EI. One thing about pseudoscience in education: there are often quite a lot of very committed zealots out there who are

2 Weare and Gray, 2002; Zins *et al.* 2004.
3 http://schoolswork.co.uk/blog/entry/seal-what-is-it-and-how-can-it-help-me/. Accessed on 26 March 2013.

determined to tell you that, Yea! Their way is righteous, and here, at last, *here* is the solution we've all been looking for. Funnily enough, much of the time they also want to sell you their magic bullets/beans at considerable cost. Magic bullets aren't cheap, it seems. If you really want a chuckle, go to the website www.emotionalintelligence.com where you will be treated to some brilliant claims about EI, before being invited to get on the EI magic bus by buying the products. Two days training? $4,000. A bargain! Get me two! $3.95 will get you a foam brain – and I am NOT fussing with you here – so that you can: 'Set one on your desk or shelf to remind you to practise your emotional intelligence skills; include them in group exercises and training activities to help facilitate participation in discussions.'[4]

I will. Right after I plant these magic beans and drink my smart drink, rub my brain buttons and plug in my mnemonic air freshener. And join a cult. For *God's* sake. Everyone wants to pick your pocket, it seems. I stress that I am sure that the people involved are honest and well-intentioned. I just think they're wrong.

Shall we have a look at the papers quoted? Oh, go on then.

A paper by Weare and Grey (2002), from the University of Southampton, was financed by the DfE at a time when the DfE was more sympathetic to such ideas (see later for details). From the introduction:

> In January 2002, the Department for Education and Skills commissioned Southampton University's Health Education Unit to undertake a study examining how children's emotional and social competence and wellbeing could most effectively be developed at national and local level and identifying those broad approaches which show most promise.[5]

Note that the genesis of this study already includes the assumption that children's emotional competence was something that existed, and could be modified in the school environment. It wasn't questioning the existence of EI, or its amenability to instruction; it was asking which programme would be best to do this. Now this isn't something you could begin to get away with in the natural

4   www.emotionalintelligence.com. Accessed on 26 March 2013.
5   http://southampton.ac.uk/education/research/projects/developing_childrens_emotional_and_social_competence_and_wellbeing.page. Accessed on 26 March 2013.

sciences. But you can in social science, because, well, no one can catch you out, because no one can prove you wrong. It would be akin to beginning a biology paper with 'What are the best ways to breed fairies?' If you wrote that, they'd throw nuts at you. In educational psychology? You get a national strategy.

So we begin with unproven assumptions. Anything else? Well, like most Cargo Cult papers, it lays out its methodology with relative clarity: a review of the literature; interviews with experts; and case studies with five good LEAs in this field. What does that mean?

A review of the literature. This means that the veracity of this paper rests on the veracity of papers that precede it. This is quite right; the only way we put rockets on Mars is by building on the work done previously. But in social sciences, instead of standing on the shoulders of giants, we find a spot that fits our feet and try to hang on. Apocrypha has it that Bertrand Russell, the famous philosopher, mathematician and atheist, was challenged by a woman who claimed that the world balanced on the back of a giant turtle. When he asked, not unreasonably, what it was that sustained that turtle, she said, 'Oh you can't get clever with me; it's turtles all the way down.' Well, quite. In social science, it's turtles all the way down. In Terry Gilliam's *The Adventures of Baron Munchausen*, the titular protagonist attempts to lift himself up by his own pigtail, a feat he accomplishes until he realises that it is quite impossible. I read papers in educational science and I feel the same. I'll look at the pigtails hanging this up in a minute.

Interviews with experts. Which experts? Oh, experts in Emotional Intelligence and emotional literacy. Which is like trying to establish good practice in astrology by asking Russell Grant and Mystic Meg. Or writing the *Encyclopaedia Britannica* entry on the Big Bang by speaking to fundamentalist creationists.

Studies with good LEAs in this field. How do we know they're good in this field? Isn't that what the paper is trying to establish? Or have we already decided not only what EI is, but what the best ways of promoting it are? In which case the paper is circular and therefore redundant. Brothers and sisters, I'm barely off the first page.

> The literature review was not a 'systematic' review in the sense that texts were not subjected to rigorous criteria for inclusion. However, the key databases were searched for relevant texts,

and key organisations and individuals consulted for further suggestions. Particular use was made of selected systematic reviews. The experts in the field represent some of the major organisations and agencies working in the field of emotional and social competence and wellbeing. The LEAs were selected on the basis of recommendations by the project steering group, and the application of criteria to ensure diversity (p. 5).

See? 'We picked what evidence we used to support our study by asking people who already believe in this stuff.' What evidence do the authors rely on that this policy has any efficacy whatsoever?

There is sound evidence from the literature, mainly from the US, that work on emotional and social competence and wellbeing has a wide range of educational and social benefits, including greater educational and work success, improved behaviour, increased inclusion, improved learning, greater social cohesion, increased social capital, and improvements to mental health. However, evaluation in England is not well-developed (p. 6).

Which is big of them to say. 'Sound evidence', eh? So people keep saying. Undaunted, I plunge in up to my elbows like a vet. Oh, and in case you thought this paper was anything other than a poorly dressed-up piece of advocacy posing as research, it says in the key findings, 'Many of those working in this field believe that a higher priority should be given to the promotion of emotional and social competence and wellbeing at national, LEA and school level.' (p. 6) Which isn't surprising; I have a man that knocks on my door on Sunday morning and thinks I should be at church more.

Finding number 11 makes me suspect that the whole thing is an ironic masterpiece penned by Chris Morris:

11. Promote teachers' competence and wellbeing. There is good evidence that teachers cannot transmit emotional and social competence and wellbeing effectively if their own emotional and social needs are not met. At the same time, there are indications that teachers feel very stressed at present. (p. 7)

So part of the machine responsible for designing yet another enormous, monstrous exercise in futility and time wasting are a bit concerned we're stressed, are they? I have a suggestion for them, but I don't think they'd appreciate it.

Data from LEAs and schools was gathered from interviews, self-evaluations and such. Which sounds like a complex way of saying, 'What do you think then?' Brilliant. And you thought science was difficult.

OK, so what evidence do they rely on? Let's have a look. By now you should feel like Leonardo di Caprio in *Inception*. We're going deeper into the world of dream. One more level. They discover this literature, not systematically, but by contacting relevant organisations and asking for direction, and by entering key terms such as emotional literacy in the databases of websites that archive such things. You know, I normally cuff my sixth formers when they Google something and pick things from the first page. That might just be me.

> Particular use was made of some key systematic reviews and systematic databases of work in and around this area (Catalano et al, 1995; Durlak, 1995; Durlak and Wells, 1997; CASEL, 2000; Lister-Sharp et al, 1999; Wells et al, 2003; Shonkoff and Philips (eds) 2000; Catalano et al, 2002). (p. 13)

And in the paper's definitions of the key term Emotional Intelligence, it has this to say about its magnificent research credentials:

> 'Emotional intelligence' is the term most popularly used in the US. It is attributed to Salovey and Mayer (1990), who gave it quite a limited, technical and value free meaning . . . The work of Salovey and Mayer coincided with that of Gardner (see for example Gardner et al, 1995) who argued that the whole concept of intelligence was much wider than is generally supposed . . . Goleman then popularised and used the term 'emotional intelligence' in a much looser way than Mayer and Salovey, to include all kinds of skills and competences, including social ones. (p. 15)

We're getting close to the mothership now: Salovey and Mayer, and popularisation by Goleman. So I guess we should go there.

Daniel Goleman is the player here: his book has been a number one best-seller, which is unusual for an academic piece, but less so for a piece of well-written advocacy and pop psychology. In it, he describes his horror at the emotional ineptitude in modern society. 'A spreading emotional malaise can be read in numbers showing a jump in depression around the world, and in reminders of the surging tide of aggression – teens with guns in schools . . .'

And so on. Now that's not science, but it's a perfectly reasonable view of one man's interpretation of how society rolls. Sure, it has much in common with any Golden Age meme, leaning back to past eras of glory, but everyone is entitled to their opinion. To then link this with a rise in emotional illiteracy, well . . . that's a jump. That involves a lot of assumptions about the way the world was then and the way it is now. I'd like to see the data by which we can compare and make that statement. As many have pointed out, the current generation of older grandparents have a Golden Age rooted in the days of carpet bombing, Hiroshima and Auschwitz. Their grand-parents grew up in a Utopia of child labour and desperate poverty, now unseen in the West.

And it's not the soundest of baseboards from which to launch a grand theory. He refers to the fact that recent science has taught us more than ever about the way the brain works; perhaps more astonishingly, he claims that 'science is finally able to speak with authority to these urgent and perplexing questions of the psyche at its most irrational, to map with some precision the human heart'.

It's poetry. But science it isn't. His main idea is that Emotional Intelligence is of greater importance than traditional views of IQ, and that schools should be doing more to try to educate children to be emotionally intelligent. What does he mean by Emotional Intelligence? To 'rein in emotional impulse; to read another's inner-most feelings; to handle relationships smoothly' – as Aristotle puts it the rare skill 'to be angry with the right person to the right degree at the right time, for the right purpose and in the right way'.

This appeal to Aristotle is very significant; it's a reference to his theory of Virtue Ethics; it's a fine examination of what we mean by morality and I recommend it to anyone. But one of the key difficulties is this idea of 'rightness'. What is the right amount of, for example, anger? And when? How do we know? Aristotle's idea is that, as one matures, through reflection, observation and instruction and maturity we get to understand this 'doctrine of the mean' as he calls it, and we'll act accordingly. It's a bit like realising the quickest route to the shops: once you understand it, you'll just do it, and recommend it to others.

But this is a theory built upon foundations (or turtles) of pure value; the right amount of anger depends on the person you ask. When I managed nightclubs in Soho, there was a large pimp called Boxer who believed that the appropriate level of anger to carry throughout the day was 7 out of 10, even when he was buying a pint of milk. Many men with sore faces felt that this level of anger was inappropriate. Who's to say? Boxer felt it gave him meaning; it defined him. Now, you won't find many people who agree with Boxer, but you'll find enough.

Another criticism of Aristotle – and Goleman – is that any attempt to teach the 'right' level, or the appropriate emotional response, is simply going to be a reflection of the prevailing dominant instructor. Many people live their lives in ways we would consider inappropriate, or excessive, but we might also discern some value in the way they react: artists such as Hendrix, or Van Gogh, or Jim Morrison certainly weren't paragons of emotional calm or balance, but it can be argued that their very imbalance was the fuel of what we might call their individual genius. It's very subjective.

Can you feel this? Criticism from other research

Other criticisms have come from the academic communities: Eysenk (2000) claims that Goleman has misappropriated the way that researchers normally study intelligence. Locke (2005) also claims that what Goleman is referring to here is a skill rather than an intelligence. The essence of this criticism is that psychology, for any of its flaws, already has accepted paradigms about how to measure and analyse intelligence: imperfect, but a best fit, and not simply plucked from the air. Goleman's influential opus blurs the distinction between Emotional Intelligence and other forms of the word, and simply conflates similar sounding, but distinct ideas.

Landy (2005) claims that EI doesn't offer any substantial predictive capability, and there is little correlation between alleged EI and other measures, such as test scores. In the main, this potentially shows that what EI proposes to measure is more closely a measure of personality type rather than any kind of aptitude, skill or awareness.

Roberts *et al.* (2001) suggests that EI is actually measuring conformity, not intelligence, expressed as an indication of how closely an individual demonstrates externally desired reactions and intentions. To suggest that this is intelligence, rather than merely a faculty of survival and accommodation, is to ask too much of the concept.

Brody (2004) claims that EI may simply measure knowledge rather than ability or aptitude; that scoring highly on EI tests simply shows that someone has acquired a set of learned appropriate responses which are then recalled and demonstrated. Much like a stranger to a new land might act inappropriately at first (offering the wrong hand to shake, not examining a business card closely enough), these are mere objects of content to be learned and recalled later. On this score it isn't an ability at all.

Many of the complaints against Gardner's theories of multiple intelligences, and the ways in which these might not actually refer to intelligences, can be applied to Goleman and Emotional Intelligence too. In my own teacher-training bible, I was reminded that:

> In unit 4.3 you met Gardner's multiple intelligence theory . . . this clearly has application when considering how individuals learn. Similarly emotional intelligence . . . is also of interest to teachers.[6]

There are many more conceptual and empirical problems with the EI project. Suffice it to say that it is unsupported as a general theory as a means to assist learning, and there have been no projects based on it that have demonstrated anything like predictive, repeatable and measurable benefits. But it feels right to many. It sounds good. It appeals to our belief that children can be improved, and that we can tame their characters to make them more fit for a world. And they probably can, some of them, sometimes. But perhaps not by us, and as far as the evidence goes, not by appealing to EI.

The view from the classroom

Do we want to be arbiters of children's emotions? One moral flaw in the EI argument is that it presumes a level of authority over the individual that we might genuinely balk at accepting: authority over their feelings. Who am I to tell someone else to feel? How long, for example, is it appropriate to grieve? If someone loses their life's companion, and then starts to drink, or mope, or hide from the world, we might hope and advise them to get busy living again, but really, who gets to decide what the appropriate reaction is? If someone subjected people I love to torture, I hope I would have the integrity to avoid rampaging in revenge on them; but unless you've been in that situation, what is appropriate? I have the right to tell children, within prescribed limits, how to behave in school, as a matter of practicality, safety and efficiency. But should I be able to tell them how to feel? When I am not even sure myself what such a thing would mean?

6   *Learning to Teach in the Secondary School* (Capel *et al.* 2003) p. 235.

This level of assumed expertise is perhaps one of the biggest flaws. How many of us would say that we were experts in human interaction? That we understand the moods of others to an expert level? That we knew the appropriate emotional response to any given situation? Some schools have begun to teach lessons in happiness, as if the solution to such things had been cracked, codified and reduced to a learnable structure. Good luck to them. How many instructors in such things would say they were happy? On a scale of ten? And what would such a scale mean anyway, when happiness is an internally experienced, intrinsic, subjective quality. What is my six compared to your four? How would we know? This is the realm of the aesthetic and the moral; it is certainly not the realm of the scientist.

There is no evidence that Emotional Intelligence is something that even exists, because there is no agreed definition of what it means. There is certainly no evidence, as Goleman claims there is, that it is the polar opposite from IQ, and that it is something separate from it. Many critics have pointed out that EI, as Goleman defines it, is simply a skill, a correspondent of general intelligence and perceptiveness; I have high EI when I can recognise behaviours that signify emotional states in others, and I have good reactions to those emotional states inasmuch as I react in a way that seems to benefit myself and the other person concerned.

There is no evidence that it can be taught formally. Even the DfE has rubbed its eyes and woken up from the dream.

Seal clubbing

In 2010, the DfE commissioned another piece of research, SEAL Programs in Secondary Schools, by Humphrey, Lendrum and Wigelsworth (2010). Five years on and oh! how things have changed. The aim of this research was to evaluate the impact of the SEAL programme on measureable outcomes. Its findings were hard reading for anyone interested in SEAL: it said that implementation of SEAL had been 'mixed', with resistance from some schools (fancy that). The assessment of impact was even more damning.

> Finally, in terms of impact, our analysis of pupil-level outcome data indicated that SEAL (as implemented by schools in our sample) failed to impact significantly upon pupils' social and

emotional skills, general mental health difficulties, pro-social
behaviour or behaviour problems. (p. 2)

Which is social science-ese for 'Three hours in the oven, it's a turkey.'
Want more?

In relation to school-level outcome data, our analyses indicated
that SEAL (as implemented by schools in our sample) failed to
have a positive impact, although the results were less straight-
forward here. Analysis of school climate scores indicated
*significant reductions in pupils' trust and respect for teachers,
liking for school, and feelings of classroom and school supportiveness
during SEAL implementation* [my italics]. (p. 3)

Everyone's a winner, I'm sure you'll agree. At the time of writing
(2013), support for the SEAL programme has melted like snow,
but attitudes persist. The language, the vocabulary of Emotional
Intelligence lingers on in much school discourse; it only takes a brief
search of the internet to find scores of thousands of mentions of it
in relation to schools. A cursory search of school websites and
prospectuses will find EI trumpeted as a major part of the school
ethos or vision. Ofsted reports are still heavy with the language of
EI. This perhaps indicates that once adopted systematically as part
of a new dogma, even the removal of formal recognition fails to
remove all traces of the roots, once they have taken hold.

Another problem, as with many pseudoscientific projects, is that
part of their endurance relies on the fact that they have two crucial
elements: a basis, however tenuous, in some empirical evidence, and
an appeal to values that many of us already hold.

Just enough science to stick

This is a term I use to describe when a theory, no matter how loose
or unevidenced, has a filament of evidence that connects it to the
senses, and prevents it being seen as pure hocus-pocus. Astrology,
surely one of the least evidenced theories of human behaviour and
destiny, is seen by the majority of people as completely bogus, but
many people read their star signs every day. Not just screaming
mentalists, but people you would trust your children with, albeit for
short periods of time. Of course, much of this is probably based on
pure neuroticism and fancy, but it is not uncommon to hear people

describe it as 'having something to do with the gravitational pull of distant stars' on the human body, which is, of course, composed of water. It's thin, unappealing nonsense, but the attempt to root the justification in science is there. So too with homeopathy, and as far as I'm concerned, its nonsense theories of like curing like, which has some correlation (although none demonstrably true) with the concept of immunisation, provoking a body to reject smallpox by first preparing it with cowpox, for example.

EI is not without evidence; in fact, Goleman is a psychologist, not a fairground conjuror, and uses neuroscience heavily to support his claims. But this is the educational equivalent of the shampoo advert's 'science bit', where the men in white jackets pop up to reassure us that the fragrant, expensive detergent has some kind of penetrative and restorative effect, rather than simply being a kind of Fairy Liquid for hair.

There is plenty of evidence to suggest that children learn when they are in one emotional state as opposed to another. Mere experience can supply us with as much: when agitated and unhappy, I am unlikely to absorb or retain much information, or attend particularly efficiently to my lessons. Similarly, if too enthused, if too obsessed and agitated, I might suffer in a similar manner. Most trainee teachers could probably tell you that occupying a calm midpoint between these two would be a good place to start, emotionally, to maximise the learning environment. But these experiential homilies are a far field from the assertion that training children into, for example, group work, or into acceptable emotional modes is either possible or desirable. As the DfE research shows, above, there appears to be no benefit to be accrued from such programs as SEAL.

An appeal to the values

Commentators such as Willingham (2012) have long observed that we frequently cling to beliefs that confirm our pre-existing set of values; that we often filter out evidence that contradicts our dogma, and actively seek or emphasise evidence that confirms them. This is, of course, another example of confirmation bias; we find what we seek, and we are blind to what we are not, like a wronged partner ignoring obvious signs of adultery because the truth is too painful, or a paranoid racist seeing minority villainy in every headline.

Emotional Intelligence is an appealing theory because it fits nicely with many fashionable and tempting values; that there is a correct way to handle one's emotions; that there are appropriate ways to demonstrate and process those emotions; that education is the answer to many of society's problems; that the breakdown in the family unit can be remedied with formal instruction by the state.

I'll demonstrate with an example from *Star Trek*, so that you know I have no shame. In the much vilified *Star Trek V: The Final Frontier* (subtitle: Kirk versus God), our veteran action hero is up against a messianic alien who enslaves people with a kind of Vulcan brain-washing. 'Share your pain with me,' says Sybok (for it is he) before he slips them a cognitive Mickey Finn. He tries the same wheeze with the barrel-chested/corseted Kirk, who bats him off. 'I want my pain!' he hams. 'I NEED my pain. My pain is what makes me who I am!'

Ah, the Tao of Kirk. Who is to say that pain is unnecessary, or to be dealt with in sanctioned ways? I have, in my short life, managed to make more moral and practical errors than one would think possible, and from these I rightly recoil. Sometimes the memories of my failings keeps me awake at nights, thinking of the times when I let people down, or failed to help, or even harmed others. Some might say that this level of retention, years after the events, is unhealthy; that my reaction is inappropriate and pathological. I worked in clubs in Soho for a decade; it was thrilling, but I look back now and consider much of my time wasted when I could have been knocking off educational thrillers like this. It's the memory of that waste, the memorial to my mistakes and failings, that provides me now with the enthusiasm to do better, like rocket fuel. When I feel like being selfish, or slacking off, or turning away from others, the jagged ice cube in my gut stirs, and like an ulcer, reminds me it exists. Jean Paul Sartre believed that morality was an entirely personal affair, and that what was right for one person might be right only for that person, at that time, and from their perspective. You don't need to embrace this form of extreme moral relativism to acknowledge that there may not be a right way to feel about anything. And there certainly isn't a way, therefore, to teach it.

Star Trek seems to have a fondness for this nugget of wisdom: in 1966's 'The Enemy Within' written by Richard Matheson (who also wrote the astounding *I Am Legend*, so repeatedly butchered by film makers), Kirk is split into two Kirks by a transporter accident – one good, but indecisive and insipid, the other cruel, but passionate and vigorous. Faced with Spock's conjecture that they can just bin the bad one, Doctor McCoy chides his Vulcan colleague by reminding him that 'they need each other – one side can't survive without the other.' And so it is. Like Robert Louis Stevenson's *Jekyll and Hyde*, perhaps two cannot survive without the desperate, wounded veins of tragedy and defeat that marble our character; perhaps, like Kirk, we need our pain. Who knows? The point is that it is not a settled matter that we know how people should feel, respond and apprehend each other. Such matters are not for administrators to circumscribe and describe.[7]

I find it interesting that people who would normally baulk at any form of state-sanctioned repression or interference with their civil liberties are so happy to adopt a strategy that amounts to cognitive eugenics, involving the wholesale disintegration of the individual's right of intellectual autonomy for the sake of a spurious and unproven utopian garden of personality. What space is more sacred than the one between our ears? Who but the most illiberal of tyrants would demand that we not only conform in action, but acquiesce in volition as well? Like the teacher who mistakenly demands, 'Say sorry and *mean* it,' there is no greater indignity than to attempt to engineer with a human's mind.

Does this show that emotions have no part to play in the educator's considerations? Of course not. As a teacher I have to be attuned to the emotional states of the class; agitated or despondent, I need to be on the heels of my feet, ready to respond to the heartbeat of the class. When a favourite teacher passed away some years ago, I had to be aware enough to suspend formal instruction and discuss the ramifications of loss with some pupils. When a student returns from a serious illness, or a bullying incident, or is reintegrated after some felony, I have to keep a third eye open to the circumstances and plan accordingly. When I see my class getting worked up over a task, or not worked up enough, I need to be able to respond and generate emotional states in them that are more conducive to learning.

But this is an experiential skill; it is not something that can be taught formally, either to the teacher, or to the students. Their emotional states are their own. As a teacher, I have absolute authority

---

7   In case anyone gets their knickers in a twist: not that I am not attempting to prove my argument by referring to *Star Trek*, although I'd love to give it a try, I'm *illustrating* my argument. I'm happy to expose my own argumentation structures up to analysis, but not if I get there first. I learned that from reading social science research papers that prefer to pretend they're Moses coming down from Mount Sinai with the Ten Commandments.

to expect certain behaviours, this way or that, because this is the basis of their safety and their access to their educational entitlement, whether they know it or not. But their emotions? What the Hell gives me the right to tell them how to feel? How do I know? I am a teacher of Philosophy and Religious Studies, and, I fancy, a passing competent one. But I am not a counsellor, or a therapist, or a Soviet brainwasher. Perhaps with training I could become one of these, but I have no wish to, and there is no evidence that I should aspire to it either.

The best way a teacher can influence the emotions of their students is by two methods:

1   Be a role model yourself. Conduct yourself in a way that you feel best exemplifies adulthood and maturity. That means in your dealings with the children, their parents and other staff. Let them see how you think it's done, rather than instruct or mentor them into such states.

2   By insisting on good conduct from your students. You are the justiciar of the classroom; children look to you to ensure fairness and equity. So don't shy away from this responsibility; be honoured by it, and govern them with wisdom and fairness. If I can jump back into Goleman's inspiration, Aristotle, he famously claimed that action flows from character – the type of person you are determines the kind of actions you commit. This sensible and intuitive piece of wisdom has a correlate: actions can flow back to character. If you habituate children into acting a certain way, then you at least give them the possibility of developing good habits that they can choose to adopt or discard; habits such as punctuality, self-restraint and civility. That's as far as you can go down the route of emotional intelligence.

Emotions aren't intelligent; emotions aren't rational; it is no more irrational to look at the 9/11 bombings and feel hatred than it is to see the same scene and weep for pity at the cruelty of the world. As Hume and many other moral philosophers have observed, you cannot generate a value from a fact. The mere instance of an event does not provide you with a moral clue one way or another. Some see the harrowing of Hiroshima as the Armageddon of human compassion; others approve of it as the best bad option available; some even rejoice in it.

While I have my own approach to such matters, what right do I have to dictate levels of appropriateness, other than by the intuitive attempt to inculcate social mores into children? Because we are all responsible for that, we are all – to some extent – role models for children; they see; they copy. The least we can do is give them a good example. That's the least, and sometimes, the most we can do. So we may as well do it, and nevermind a state sanctioned course in moral Pilates that has no more evidential basis than Chinese medicine.

Maybe we need our pain.

Chapter 9

Buck Rogers and the twenty-first-century curriculum

Have you been told recently that your children need to learn skills appropriate to the twenty-first century? Perhaps you have also been told that the way they learn has changed? Additionally you may be required to think about the way you teach, and amend it to the dizzy new plateaus of this brave new world. Now *this*, you hear a lot. One of the contemporary shibboleths (and one that doesn't look like it's going away soon) is that students need to be prepared for a dazzling future of uncertainty and change; that the challenges offered by our dizzying century means that schools can no longer teach the things they used to in the ways they are used to. And schools, educators and policy makers are listening to this mantra. The DfE has made it clear: 'They [parents] also want schools to equip their children for tomorrow, not yesterday, giving them the up-to-date skills and knowledge for success in a rapidly changing world.'[1]

We even have the *ubergroovy* Free School movement picking up the baton:

> To prepare our students for success in the twenty-first century we are creating a school that will support them to develop the skills, attributes and leadership qualities required. This means the very best learning environment ... And finally it means rigorous assessment to ensure that we can support your child in a targeted way as they master all of these 21st century skills.[2]

1 'Your Child, Your Schools, Our Future: Building a 21st Century Schools System', DfE 2009
2 School 21 website, http://school21.org/primary/21st-century-learning/culture-and-expectations/Page: ethos. Accessed on 26 March 2013.

Grr, baby, *very* grrr!

> Though there are timeless skills and knowledge important for
> success in any age (language literacy, problem solving and
> initiative for example), what was needed to be a skilled person
> in nineteenth century agrarian society (including brawn power
> and using horse power) differs dramatically from the expertise
> needed to be a well-educated and capable twenty-first century
> citizen (including brain power and using 'hertz power' –
> computing and digital tools).[3]

That's also from the Wikipedia page (and boy, does that just
remind everyone why Wikipedia, brilliant as it is as a free resource,
will never replace the Encyclopaedia Britannica). I'm not kidding
though; it's all the rage. You cannot have a conversation about education these days without somebody mentioning twenty-first-century
skills, or twenty-first-century learners, or a twenty-first-century curriculum.

So far I've attempted to look at educational initiatives that are
backed up by spurious attempts to use science as justification. With
the twenty-first-century advocates, it's a little bit different; they
usually don't claim that there is some kind of scientific justification
for the project. They just say it's true, self-evidently, apparently. But
they do rely on evidence of sorts. Let's see what shape it's in.

> [Our aim is] to promote cross-cultural understanding – equip-
> ping young people with key 21st Century skills needed to live
> in a world of diverse faiths and beliefs.[4]

Michael Barber at the 2000 Rotterdam Conference, for instance,
argued that:

> The explosion of knowledge about the brain and the nature of
> learning, combined with the growing power of technology,
> create the potential to transform even the most fundamental unit
> of education – the interaction of the teacher and the learner.
> Moreover, huge social changes, such as growing diversity and
> population mobility, present educators with new and constantly

3   http://en.wikipedia.org/wiki/21st_Century_Skills. Accessed on 26 March
    2013.
4   Tony Blair Faith Foundation US, front page (about). www.tonyblairfaith
    foundation.org/page/about-face-to-faith. Accessed on 26 March 2013.

changing circumstances. As a result, the characteristics which defined the successful education systems of, say, 1975, are unlikely to be those which will define success in the future.[5]

Let's start with a popular source of this theory: *21st Century Skills: Learning for Life in our Times*, by Bernie Trilling and Charles Fadel. The authors have some big credentials: they chair the Partnership for 21st Century Skills, which produces white papers, skills maps, policy guides and other resources; they're global directors of the Oracle Foundation (where they direct the Foundation's ThinkQUest – you heard me – go *team*); they work with Hewlett Packard and Cisco Systems (a Californian multinational that manufactures computer networks). You will be pleased to know that the Partnership for 21st Century Skills has on its strategic council, among others, representatives from Adobe, Apple, ASCD, Blackboard, Inc, Cisco, Crayola, Dell, Hewlett Packard, Intel, Microsoft and, funnily enough, Crayola and Lego.[6]

Nothing wrong with that of course, although I might[7] point out a few issues with such heavy industry representation in a minute. As an aside, Charles Fadel's mini-biog at the start of this book mentions that, as an avid reader, he has auto-didactically learned cognitive sciences disciplines (sic), evolutionary psychology, comparative linguistics and others. Blimey, when I used to write CVs, I just put 'My hobbies are . . .' Next time it's 'I have auto-didactically learned . . .'

21st Century Skills: see 'talking like Mr Spock'.

I must point out that the authors are not teachers; their backgrounds are Silicon Valley. But I'm sure they have the very best of intentions. As Jay Matthews, writing in the *Washington Post* about this book, says:

> I am trying NOT to write off the 21st Century Skills movement as a sham, but its leaders don't make it easy.

> The premise of this book is that the world has changed so fundamentally in the last few decades that the roles of learning and education in day-to-day living have also changed forever.[8]

5   (OECD, 2003: 115).
6   I note this with some joy.
7   I will.
8   http://voices.washingtonpost.com/classstruggle/2009/10/21st_century_skills_a_suicide.html. Accessed on 26 March 2013.

OK, so we have a premise; upon this foundation, everything else is built. If there are cracks in this part, then the rest of the skyscraper doesn't stand up. So let's find some kind of justification for this statement. And that's where the hard part begins; everyone seems to agree that the world is moving jolly fast, the future is unclear, so we need our children to be taught differently, and different things. But why do they agree?

One way to attempt to prove this is to appeal to previous pasts. In the book, the authors set four questions: they call it the 'Four Question Exercise'. (See what they did?)

1   What will the world be like 20 or so years from now when your child has left school?
2   What skills will your child need to be successful in this world you have imagined, twenty years from now?
3   Now think about your own life and the times you were really learning, so much and so deeply, that you would call these the 'peak learning experiences' of your life. What were the conditions that made your high performance learning experiences so powerful?[9]
4   What would learning be like if it were designed around your answers to the first three questions?

According to the authors, the answers to these questions, no matter where they go, is remarkably consistent: 'It's high time that learning becomes more in tune with the demands of our times and the needs of today's students.'

Says who? *Everyone*, say the authors, breathlessly. That's not really evidence, is it? That's conjecture about the future, and not just that, but reported conjecture. I really hoped there was more to it than this, so I ploughed on. Incidentally, the answers that, apparently, *everyone* comes up with to those questions can be summarised as follows.

• The world will be 'smaller', more connected by media, global economies, strains on basic resources, concerns about terrorism, security, more diversity of cultures, and so on.
• Children will need twenty-first-century skills to meet this: learning skills, creativity, problem solving, communications, working in groups, digital literacy skills, flexibility, adaptability, responsibility.

9   (To be honest, reading question 3 always make me a little bit sick in my mouth, but anyway.)

- Best learning happens when challenge is high, coming from internal passions and loving teachers who inspire them.
- Schools should be composed of groups, doing group work, using technology, solving problems, working on things children care about more and helping children to develop creativity and innovation.

This sums up twenty-first-century learning nicely. But so far it isn't based on anything more than speculation. Nothing wrong with that, but as any oracle will tell you, predictions about the future stand or fall on one thing – do they come true? The normal method for discovering this answer is by witnessing it as it happens. But, as Shakespeare and others have commented, the future is an undiscovered country. Where's the evidence for these claims?

Anyone can make general, speculative claims. Man, some days, it's *all* I do. The trick is not to make too many factual claims: for example, on page 7, when they say that employers wasted 'over $200 billion a year . . . finding and hiring scarce, highly skilled talent, and in bringing new employees up to required skill levels through costly training programs.' There isn't a reference for this, but it does sound an *awful* lot of money to lose down the back of the sofa. Unfortunately, I can do this too: 'Companies saved $300 billion last year by developing their own in-house talent which aided retention, morality and loyalty.' See? It's easy. And I just saved them $300 billion.

It really is a new orthodoxy: current methods of instruction aren't sufficient to equip our children for this brave new world, and what we teach them also needs to be transformed. It's a global movement, and much like liberalism and capitalism, has become the ideology that ate my civilisation. It's so ubiquitous it's invisible. Even Barack Obama is in on it:

> I'm calling on all our nation's governors and state education chiefs to develop standards and assessments that don't simply measure whether students can fill in a bubble on a test, but whether they possess 21st Century skills like problem–solving and critical thinking and entrepreneurship and creativity.[10]

10 President Barack Obama, Remarks to the Hispanic Chamber of Commerce, March 10, 2009. www.whitehouse.gov/sites/default/files/rss_viewer/education_standard_factsheet.pdf. Accessed on 26 March 2013.

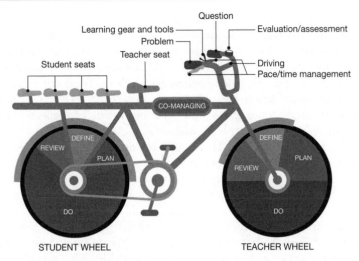

Figure 9.I The Learning Bicycle[11]

This is like reading that a favourite uncle wears a gimp mask. Here's one of the more famous quotes endlessly recycled by proponents of this idea, from Richard Riley, secretary of state under Bill Clinton: 'We are currently preparing students for jobs that don't exist yet . . . using technologies that haven't yet been invented . . . in order to solve problems we don't even know are problems yet.' (Trilling and Fadel, 2009).

Hang on – jobs that *don't exist yet*? What, like a janitor at the 2046 Olympics? A light sabre inspector? This is madness. As I'll discuss in the next section, this appeal to the terrifying unfamiliarity of the future is a sham nestled in a half-truth. Of course no one knows the future, but to say that we have no idea what jobs there will be is rubbish. Take someone who designs iPhones; he or she might have a job that didn't exist in 1995, but back then there were mobiles, and people who designed things. Before that there were phones, and people designing other things. Today's jobs rely on skills that already exist, which is handy, otherwise nothing would be invented. We don't predict the future. We create it!

The book talks about the shift from the industrial age to the 'knowledge age' like this was an accepted phenomenon, and we didn't

11   Charles Fadel, reprinted under Wikimedia republishing permission. Use of this author's work in no way conveys approval by the author.

require mining, agriculture and industry any more; like two-thirds of the world weren't still based in a rural economy. I might go to the steppes of Mongolia, hang out with some tribesmen and ask them how they feel now that the world is a knowledge economy.

But this isn't getting me anywhere. Where's the beef? Where's the evidence, other than some fairly Americancentric navel gazing about the world that sounds groovy and true, but is simply a reflection of the author's peculiar fetish for innovation.

The Learning Bicycle. This is one of my favourite illustrations, not just from this book, but any book. It's a perfect example of something I encounter frequently in social science: an attempt to, presumably, clarify and exemplify a complex theory by illustrating it in a graphic, amenable way. This may be in order to appeal to the visual learners. Unfortunately, I also find that these graphics often fail to accomplish what they set out to do. Although sometimes they do bring a smile to my face. I have literally no idea what this bicycle does. I'm certain you wouldn't be allowed that many passengers.

Fortunately, we only have to wait until we get to Chapter 8 before we get some evidence. Actually there are a few graphs before that, like the one *New skills for 21st Century work*, which claims to project that today's jobs require more and more complex communicating and thinking skills. A graph! Helpfully, we get a reference: Levy and Murnane (2004), in their book *The New Division of Labor: How Computers Are Creating the Next Job Market*.[12] They project that the jobs that will be created in the future will be based on things computers can't do – problem solving, lying, that sort of thing i.e. complex communication skills. Which sounds good, until you consider that the American Bureau of Labour Statistics predicts that, during the same period, the job creation will be in the unskilled McJob sector.[13,14]

So it's still conjecture. Who knows? Evidence from the future is, I hope I need hardly say, not evidence at all. Where's the evidence that current teaching methods are unsuitable, that current content is stifling education, and that the only way to escape the gravity of this disaster is to get real groovy, real fast?

12 Remember, there is no such thing as American English; there is English, and there are mistakes.

13 www.bls.gov/. Accessed on 26 March 2013.

14 www.gse.harvard.edu/news/features/murnane06012004.html. Accessed on 26 March 2013.

Chapter 8 was the promised spot, but turning there leads me to conclude that they lost a bit at the printers. No evidence or research to justify the claims that are made that I could find. Instead, what we have for the first seven chapters is an analysis of history, particularly recent history, and a conclusion that the way we teach isn't fit for future purpose. This is both disappointing and exhilarating. Disappointing because the aspirations of the twenty-first-century learning movement seem absolutely from the heart; they really want some very lovely things: kids learning, happy and fulfilled, and ready for the future. Exhilarating because, as I'm fond of quoting endlessly from the Hitch: 'What can be asserted without evidence can also be dismissed without evidence.'[15] The aims of the twenty-first-century learning movement might be noble, but they seem to be unsupported by evidence.

They are presented as fact, when in fact they are advocacy; they are partisan; they are lobbyists. And while I make no claim about the integrity of any of its activists – I am sure that everyone involved in the movement is perfectly without moral stain – it is interesting to note that the funding for many in the movement, and prominent members among the movement, are drawn from the IT multi-nationals and business communities that stand to benefit the very most by the transformation of the classroom into a junkyard of new technology and costly new training programs.

The cult of 'Shift Happens'

Let me digress slightly and look to an internet phenomenon that has been extremely influential in the 21st Century Skills movement. Have you seen 'Shift Happens'? Around five million people have seen the 2006 viral PowerPoint by Karl Fisch[16] that describes how scary and weird the future will be, and how we'll all have to learn Esperanto and live in tree houses to cope with it all. I saw it years ago at a staff meeting, where it was used as a starter. Very stirring, full of portentous predictions about the future, and terribly big numbers about how many geniuses China had and so on; and the music was terrific. But even then I had my doubts, despite the ontological certainty it possessed.

15 Hitchens, C., 'Mommie Dearest', Slate, 20 October 2003.
16 www.youtube.com/watch?feature=player_embedded&v=ljbI-363A2Q. Accessed on 26 March 2013.

Then I realised what gave it potency; it was the music – the music made it, in the way that good music can often rescue poor drama (see the ending of any *Holby City*) or imbue any situation, however trivial, with pathos (see *X-Factor*'s horrific misappropriation of *Carmina Burana* whenever some strung-out twinky gets to the last round) and gravity. The excellent piece, *The Gael* (by Scots writer Dougie Maclean, and adapted by Trevor Jones) is used to great effect at the end of *The Last of the Mohicans* – a perfect example of music and motion working in synchronicity, multiplying each other.

To my mind, 'Shift Happens' is high on style, low on content – it takes a stirring piece of music (which Fisch's collaborator said he added 'to keep people awake', which is telling) and treats the viewer to a mixture of mundane statistics and spurious observation posing as deductive syllogisms. Take away the dramatic soundtrack and there's little factual there. I'll summarise:

- Gosh, aren't there lots of people in the world?
- The world is changing.
- Everything we think we know will be useless in about five minutes.
- Shift Happens!

And this is meant to be a good thing?

And that's it. It's the video that popularised the mantra 'According to the former Secretary of Education Richard Riley,' – dramatic pause – 'the top 10 jobs that will be in demand in 2010 didn't exist in 2004!' Now that is the oddest thing I've heard for a long, long time. For a start, it assumes a knowledge of the future that I normally associate with the Delphic Oracle or St John of Patmos. Really? How do you know? Add to that the Marx-Brothers logic of what it actually says: the jobs don't exist yet? Where does he think that jobs come from? As many other commentators have noted, sure, maybe 'iPhone App designer' didn't exist as a career option in 2006, but the job didn't spring out of nowhere – it emerged from existing careers and disciplines: design, programming, etc. To say it's a 'new' job that 'didn't exist' before is moronic – the job of sweeping up after the 2088 Mars Landing doesn't exist yet, but when it does I suspect no one will faint in terror at the modernity of it all.

'We are currently preparing students for jobs that don't exist yet . . . using technologies that haven't been invented . . . in order to solve problems that we don't even know are problems yet . . .'

And so it goes on, serious as a chastened child, sticking its bottom lip out and frowning. If anyone has the time and energy, could you put this video up online, but this time with the theme from Benny Hill on behind it? Then we can all have a good laugh. Although it's not all giggles; there's even a slightly ominous 'If we don't get our acts together we'll all be gobbled up by Indo-China' thread running through it, which seems to be a rather gauche piece of slightly xenophobic fear mongering. We don't want those brown and yellow people catching up with us, do we?

It doesn't help that it chips in lines such as 'If MySpace were a country, it would be the eleventh largest in the world.'

Really? *clutches heart* And if the streets were made of trifle we'd all have to buy wellington boots. Lucky they aren't, eh? And funnily enough, MySpace isn't a country, so that's that then, and neither are: 'all the left-handed people in the world', 'all the people who watch *Doctor Who*', or 'all the people who missed the tube on the way home last night'.

'It is estimated that a week's worth of the *New York Times* contains more information than a person was likely to come across in his entire lifetime in the eighteenth century.'

I have absolutely no idea how you would come about a statistic like that – what is information? How can you quantify it? As I sit here at my desk, I am bathed in a constant stream of experiences, from the light entering my eyes, to the feeling of the chair on my righteousass. Is that information? How do I break that down into quantifiable units? Does a fact about the weather in Madagascar count as information, but the sound of a crow outside my window escapes quantification?

Or my favourite:

'The amount of new technical information is doubling every two years.'

Really? How on earth do you know that? What's the measurement? It gets better:

'For students starting a four year technical or college degree this means that half of what they learn in their first year of study will be outdated by their third year of study.'

Elmer Fudd could knock this one down. Outdated? If you mean 'learned at a previous date,' then, sure. If you mean 'irrelevant' then, er . . . not sure. So if I go to uni and study the laws of thermodynamics because I want to become a scientist, they no longer apply by the time I leave? Boyle's Law? The laws of motion? Yes, I remember when we had to throw them out the window and start again; after all, they're hundreds of years old, surely annihilated by the paradigm shifts that have taken place several hundreds of times, according to 'Shift Happens'. Oh, wait, they're still applicable. Funny that.

It goes on. Apparently Nintendo spent a jillion dollars on R&D, but in the same time period, 'the US government didn't even spend half this much on research and innovation in education.' Oh no! Barricade the pet shops! Frankly, that last stat delights me – the idea that innovation is the transformative key to our industry, or the idea that research will act as its salvational mechanism, is appealing but dangerously wrong.

And it would be easy to ignore; but this type of thinking, fuelled by this sort of sexy, brave-new-world advertising, has infected the way we view education and harmed how we view the role of education, and the most effective ways of education. For a start, it generates the myth that what we teach children (content, facts, etc.) is less relevant, because everything's changing so frightfully fast; so why bother teaching them anything? This leads to the second danger: the idea that if content is irrelevant (we can Google it after all) then what we should be teaching children is versatility, the ability to think on their feet, the ability to think creatively and adapt to the chaotic culture and fluid job market that our children will enter. Why, it'll be barely recognisable! Who needs history or formulae when the inheritors of tomorrow will need all their wits about them just to inhabit the cybersphere?

'Shift Happens' came out in 2006, and some of its predictions could be tested in 2012 (in a manner not dissimilar to *Back to the Future*, which predicted a variety of dystopian/utopian crypto-cultures that would be with us by the staggeringly distant . . . 2015. Great Scott! Hover boots any day now). And having lived through the specified eras, I can confirm that . . . well, it's not all that different, really, is it?

The idea that we live in a radical, fluid epoch in history where nothing is certain, and the future is impossible to predict . . . well, isn't that how it's always been? That's the problem of inductive infer-ences – you're never certain, and we rely on the reassuring semi-certainties of past experience and the Einstellung Effect to paddle our canoes into the future, or back to the future, perhaps. Kids need to be educated just as much in maths, English, humanities and arts as they always did. The minute we stop doing so is the point at which we will be de-educating ourselves back to the Stone Age. Let's not do that, eh?

RSA Animate: how one cartoon changed the world

Another popular video easily found on the internet is the RSA animated cartoon of Sir Ken Robinson's speech to the Technology, Entertainment and Design (TED) exhibition. TED exhibitions are extremely groovy indeed. Originating in San Francisco, they can cost $5K just to turn up, and are a mixture of the world's leading innovators and thinkers (it says here on the website). In many ways it's a fine thing bringing together artists, scientists, poets and futurologists, except that 'futurologist' isn't really a job is it? How do you get to be a futurologist?[17]

Sir Ken Robinson is the spokesman of revolutionising educational paradigms, which he does before breakfast, after which he moves on to inspiring – I don't know – children on the Moon or something. He is enormously popular – one of the new academic supercelebs created by the unifying power of the internet, and proving it's not all LOL cats, *Schadenfreude* and perversion. He exists as part of the brainy internet elite created by the information superhighway; famous for his inspirational speeches and TED conferences, he has achieved a fame and influence that would have been hard to imagine prior to the web – which *is* one of the cultural game changers that we can recognise as significant.

I find it impossible not to like Robinson; I have been sent his 2010 RSA lecture (put to excellent animation by this video) many times by well-meaning friends who know that I am interested in all matters pedagogic. He is charming, erudite, quick-witted and has a wonderful sense of timing that makes him a rarity – an entertaining academic. But like 'Shift Happens', I'm worried about the content behind the music, and while I agree with him on many things, there are many ideas he promotes that, while well-meant in root, bear potentially dangerous fruits.

He talks about our educational system as having emerged from the cocoon of industry, and being based on a factory model, which

---

17 Now THAT'S an example of a job that hasn't been created yet.

he says like it's a bad thing. The image of schools as factories is a powerful one, and – correctly – makes us recoil to imagine children as drones in a hive, divided in their labour and alienated from their produce. So far, so Marxist.

But we also need to consider the question, 'What is a better way to educate millions and millions of children?' The only answer that can be provided is: 'In large numbers, together, in schools. Those schools will require classrooms. And in those classrooms they will study subjects taught by specialists, because while all knowledge is undoubtedly interrelated, it is hard to find people who understand more than one specialism.' Hence, the modern education system.

There is nothing nefarious or soul-destroying in accepting this: yes, it would be great for children to receive genuinely personalised learning. But what nation could afford this? And besides, who is to say that such a way of educating wouldn't bring its own attendant problems. Until everything becomes free, the best, the most efficient way of teaching children is in the context of the class, in the school paradigm. Of course, Ken correctly identifies that there are lots of ways we can play with this model: why do we teach children in chronological cohorts (apart from the obvious reasons), when many countries allow progression only after ability has been confirmed, for example?

The claim that modern education was designed for a different age is wrong – for a start, the education system that we know is frighteningly modern; the curriculum, some of the subjects, most of the qualifications, a lot of the teaching practice, and even the varieties of schools, are almost entirely the product of the post-war era, and even formal state schooling itself was only instituted in any meaningful way right at the end of the nineteenth century. This isn't an old system – this is a child, and pretending that we're simply slavishly following the paradigms of the ancients is an absurd claim, absolutely at odds with the truth. Therefore the claim that it isn't fit for purpose just isn't true. There are many things wrong with education, but that's not the same claim as 'the whole thing needs to be tipped on its head and made to limbo dance'.

One of his principal objections is that creative thinking has historically and currently been marginalised in society and education, and there's some truth in that. (Although not when you consider that the top earners in society, discounting media moguls and businessmen, are often entertainers, artists and creatives. But I digress.) It's true that education is tilted heavily towards English, maths and science, and the structural appreciation of those faculties. But the last time I looked, the curriculum was also stuffed with drama, music, dance, writing essays, poetry, design, textiles, expressive arts, and on and on and on. If creativity is being given a raw deal I think it could be a hell of a lot worse.

And even in the so-called academic subjects, where on earth is the prohibition on creativity? I don't know of any subject in any of the academic disciplines that don't cater for, or require, a creative component. All humanities subjects need the student to synthesise ideas and promote their own arguments; English appreciation and literature involves the systematic reproduction of the creative process in order to criticise it, and that's when the students are themselves not writing essays or poems. The suggestion that the contemporary curriculum is somehow the death-knell of creativity is nonsense. It's a bona fide saviour: millions of children exposed to a spectrum of art and opportunity that our grandparents would have drooled over.

Also, the idea that schools somehow drive creativity out of a child is laughable. Robinson's hypothesis is this: a 'study' (ah, studies, my favourite. Ultimate Truth Alert!) shows that if you ask a kindergarten child what a paper clip could be used for, 98 per cent of them achieve a 'genius level' number of answers. But as they get older, the percentage reduces, which proves – according to Robinson – that the dastardly education system turns creative geniuses into simple-minded, mouth-breathing morons. Or . . . perhaps as children get older they realise that there's a fabulous use for a paper clip that really, really makes sense: to bind loose sheets of paper together. Oh yeah, sure, it can be used as a miniature radio receiver for Stuart Little or some bloody thing, but frankly, there are better things out there that do that too. A paper clip makes a great paper clip. That's not a deficit in the imagination of a child – it's an asset for them to quickly associate intended function with form. That way they get their papers sorted out much more quickly. If you spend all your time trying to figure out a novel way of making fire, we'll all freeze to death while the innovators rub their heads together furiously.

Sir Ken Robinson is a fantastic speaker and passionate advocate of the creative arts, and he deserves enormous credit for standing up against a good many inequities in education. But I tire of someone who has never been a classroom teacher telling me what classroom teaching is like, or how children should be taught. If I can paraphrase – I suspect – Christopher Hitchens, being told how to teach by a non-teacher with a PhD in education is a bit like being told by a virgin how to get laid. His good intentions and intuitions can't replace the real experience of teaching children. Well-meant aphorisms about arming children to engage with the new learning society are easy to find inspirational, but they're empty. It's far harder to inspire someone with concrete and practical ideas. And abstracts, though they sound beautiful, are harder to both prove and disprove.

Thinking outside the box

Thinking outside the box is the by-now clichéd way of expressing an ability or tendency to think in new, unusual or creative ways, bringing surprising solutions to old problems. It assumes that existing paradigms (i.e. conventional conceptual schemes or ways of perceiving something) are inadequate for dealing with unusual or new challenges. And that is correctly perceived as a good thing. Like Alexander, mythically cutting through the fabled knot at Gordus, lateral thinking has become the new orthodoxy for intelligence.

But it assumes that existing paradigms are inadequate and that the original box wasn't fit for purpose. And it fails to take into account the wisdom of tradition; it assumes that the new paradigm will be a superior solution, when it is not. Or it may be a partially superior solution for one aspect of the paradigm's problems, but not for others.

Calling contemporary education 'unfit for purpose' is simply a statement of opinion, and an ill-informed one at that. There is a reason why a bowl of custard makes a poor key ring – that's unfit for purpose. But a small circle of metal with overlapping ends that require you to lose a thumbnail to access? Well, that works quite well, actually. Children and adults already think creatively – that's something axiomatic about human nature. I imagine that for every card-carrying, genius-level designer, artist and innovator – the Dysons, the Fosters, the Sinclairs, the Einsteins that we so admire had an education that was in many ways traditional – the box was a perfectly suitable start for them. It provided a framework, a structure, a skeleton of the best of previous generations' thinking, creating a springboard from which they could . . . well, spring.

Isaac Newton's famous quote 'If I have seen farther than others, it is because I have stood on the shoulders of giants' is a perfect expression of this art. No thinker exists in a state of solipsism; we all lean on the achievements of our predecessors, and the most inventive of us will adapt and improve that work, often in surprising ways, but rarely in a manner that is, literally, entirely new.

The internet is the product of prior discoveries in telecommunications, which can be traced back to the tinkering of Marconi and the embryonic machinations of Edison, Faraday and a million other explorers. Rap, grunge and garage can all be traced back to common ancestors of thought and ingenuity. We are a culture in a stream of cultures, and the biggest mistake we can make is to fail to discern that this is so. Creativity is a quality in the human spirit; it can, and should, be encouraged by bold experiments and grand failures, both in schools and in the greater world. Of course it should. But innovation isn't all, and paradigms that have existed for thousands of years might not benefit from constant and foundational innovation. Sometimes, like the shark, they have remained in a stationary state of evolution because they are exactly fit for purpose. Old ideas are not always bad ideas, and the endless advancement of novelty and the shock of the new is a poor reason to overturn everything. Revolutions must serve a purpose.

Take the chair I'm sitting on; as we speak it has four sturdy legs supporting its valuable cargo, tapping away. But hold! There's nowhere to put my Irn Bru. Thinking creatively, I give one of the chair legs a stiff tug, and attach it to the back rest with some Sellotape I have handy, in case the creative muse grips me. Oh dear, I now appear to be on my ass.

The chair, you see, was a pretty good shape for the purpose it was designed to fulfil. Now it's an unusual paperweight in the middle of my floor, and I'm wearing a soft drink.

Every time I hear about someone saying that kids learn in different ways these days, and that we teachers have to get on board or get off the bus, I despair. No they don't. People are the same as they've always been. And they learn in the same ways. And no amount of expensive software or digital popcorn will alter that fact. This isn't being reactionary – this is me trying to fight off the vultures that want to commodify education, and turn it into something they can sell us. Education takes place in a space where the teacher and student exist in a relationship; where the learned instruct and guide the learners. It isn't a software package; these things are tools, strategies, but not replacements.

And every time I hear people calling for a revolution in the curriculum, or a brand, brave new world of education where pupils turn up and give the lessons in semi-circles using the medium of the Haka to describe their physics homework, I roll my eyes and wonder when the bad noises in my head will stop.

The 21st Century Skills movement reminds me of the Moonies: it's a cult; a collaboration of well-meaning individuals and possibly, less well-meaning multinationals that have a dream. But the dream isn't based on evidence; it's based on a belief. Well, that's great. But don't pretend for a second that what you're selling is anything more than, as Jay Matthews says, 'a lot of buzzwords and jargon describing principles of teaching and learning that have been with us for many decades.' For children still struggling with the so-called nineteenth-century skills of numeracy and literacy, getting them to adopt all of these lovely twenty-first-century skills instead seems a pipe dream. Worse, the movement, so heavily attached to the love of creativity, imagination, problem solving and team work, is so in love with these principles that it has been deservedly scorned (by me) for its inability to teach knowledge and content. For people who claim that we know live in a knowledge economy, that is a very strange claim indeed.

View from the classroom

21st Century Skills: nice rhetoric, but empty of any evidence to back up its terrifying, prescient claims. Every time I hear a claim made by the movement about the absolute, vital and overreaching necessity that everyone, everywhere suddenly adopt these practices, I check out where they get their opinions from and find that, yes, they really are opinions. Opinions, based on opinions, based on opinions and we're back to the turtles all the way down again. It seems a tremendously shaky platform, by which to base a transformation of the entire education sector. It seems a bad grounding by which schools are turned upside down, classrooms flipped and content stripped from the classroom. But there it is; it's how it's been justified, and it's still happening. I kind of feel it's my duty to point this out as often as possible because so much is happening so fast and on such little evidence; in fact, no evidence. It is, in the clearest possible way, a scandal.

By all means encourage your children to be creative, work together (although steady on Captain – see Chapter 7 on group work), but don't think that these things can be taught dislocated from content. Nobody, prior to the 21st Century Skills movement, was taught in a way that focused on these matters, and people appear to have been educated regardless. We learn through content; any skills of manipulating that content can only come about through familiarity with the content. I don't learn ball control skills without kicking a ball; I cannot become a philosopher unless I learn some philosophy; I need numbers to calculate; I need words to write; I need facts from history to understand history.

Oh, and incidentally, seeing as how we're in the second decade of that century, I'd say they were a bit slow off the mark. Surely they should be future-proofing us with 22nd Century Skills? Now that really would be magic.

Chapter 10

Techno, techno, techno, TECHNO

Digital natives in flipped classrooms

I spoke at an educational conference where I had the pleasure of talking to Professor Alan Mycroft, one of the Brainiacs behind the Raspberry Pi. As I'm sure you hipsters know, that's the company that created a credit-card sized computer that costs less than a McDonald's family meal; the ultimate in stripped-down tech. It's cheap and easy enough that students at school can really start playing with programming, coding and computer design. He wasn't a corporate shark circling education; he was just worried about the decreasing skills he saw as a member of the University of Cambridge's computing department. Whereas kids in the 80s (like me) grew up with Ford Model T computers that were simple enough for us to start getting to grips with, by the third millennium, computers were black boxes that defied scrutiny by the casual user. Also, school IT had taken a disastrous turn, focusing on end-user applications. Kids were getting a lot of training about how to use Excel and PowerPoint, and not a lot about coding.

I mention this, because I think what Professor Mycroft was trying to do was brilliant: giving kids the ability to get their hands dirty with chips and solder, figuratively speaking, and prevent them becoming passive users of IT. IT is unquestionably one of the dominant technologies in most countries today. Like so many other inventions that changed the world, it's ubiquitous. This chapter follows on from the last chapter: it's the *Temple of Doom* to 21st Century Skills' *Lost Ark*.

There's a strange trend I've noticed on social network sites that I lurk around, especially Twitter. Many teachers put in their biographies that they are 'passionate about integrating technology into the classroom'. Given that you get about half-a-breath to say something in your bio, that seems quite a signifier of commitment to a cause. Not 'husband and father' but 'passionate about the digital classroom' or something.

Now, in part, I think that this is connected to the 21st Century Skills cult; one of the most prominent tentacles of that octopus is the commitment to skills in IT, and other emergent digital arenas. It's closely connected to the claim that children need to become digitally literate, that is, more conversant with the ways that computers and their related organs and instruments operate. Essentially, classrooms and schools need to adopt and integrate more and more IT and computer equipment into classrooms for two reasons.

First, children these days are digital natives; it's how they live – they eat and breathe computers in every aspect of their lives. They're comfortable with it, they like it, it engages them, and it's how they interact with the world. Wouldn't it be sensible for schools to get hip and start speaking the language that children do in order to motivate, engage and educate them?

Second, digital platforms offer enormous possibilities to actually improve learning and raise attainment.

Now, I love a bit of IT; I use it quite a bit in the classroom. I'm an interactive motorboat at home: I blog; I tweet; I built a website; as a kid I did a bit of coding (yes, BASIC, then machine code, in black and white, such as the ancients possessed). I am not Steve Jobs, but I'm not Arthur Askey either. I'm not anti-IT.

But the contemporary obsession with technology in the classroom is ridiculous. The claims being made for its efficacy are simply enormous; the insistence that it be one of the pillars of your lesson is now ubiquitous. Oh yes, and it's expensive.

Who makes these claims? Again, just stick a pin into Google and you'll hit someone claiming that IT is an essential part of learning, which must come as a surprise to Thomas Aquinas and Einstein.

> Independent studies in the United States and Israel show students who use a digital teaching platform achieve higher gains in language arts and mathematics than students in comparable schools using traditional teaching methods and curriculum. The digital teaching platform classrooms also show improved teaching quality, an improved learning environment with fewer disruptions, and an increase in student confidence, motivation and enjoyment of math and reading/language arts.[1]

1   Cohen, Aryeh Dean, Fixing Our Broken Classrooms. Israel21c, 2010. Nagel, David, Texas District Expanding Use of Online Teaching Platform, THE Journal, 2010. This paragraph is lifted from the Wikipedia page for Digital Literacy, not because I'm lazy (although I am) but because it's interesting to

Whoah! That is quite the claim. Let's follow the string a bit deeper into the labyrinth. The source given is an online article (on a website called 'Israel 21stC', no less, so maybe we can see where this is all going) writing about some amazing gains made by a start-up called Time To Know,[2] which rolled out in a few Israeli schools, before being an enormous success and impressing the then New York Chancellor of Education so much that he adopted the programme for use in NY schools. That's the same Joel Klein, incidentally, who now acts as the Head of Educational Marketing for News International, owned by Rupert Murdoch. So he's got legs in the business.

> Pupil and class performance and motivation soared in the US pilot of the program in Dallas last year, making a believer of New York City Chancellor of Education Joel I. Klein. South Korea and other countries have also expressed interest in the learning system company that the company's chief pedagogical officer Dovi Weiss believes can fix 'the classroom machine that's broken'.
>
> Current users are hoping for Dallas-like results: Dramatic improvement in writing, reading and math scores. A control group not using the system had 73 percent of the pupils in the class below, or at standard writing skills level, while the Time To Know group had 98 per cent at standard or recommended levels.[3]

Impressive claims, but are they magic beans? Of course, there are no references I could see for those claims, but I'm *sure they are true*. The rest of the website describes how the TTK detected 'bugs' in the way classes were taught: an emphasis on chalk and talk: 'But using this only one way of teaching suits no one' says Weiss.

---

see the popular ideas about topics, and then unpick the stitches a little. Incidentally, even Wikipedia had put, at the time of writing, a quality warning on this page, indicating that 'It appears to be written like an advertisement,' and, 'No other articles link to this page.' Probably from shame.

2   Journal of Research on Technology in Education for the TTK publication www.timetoknow.com/Data/Uploads/jrte-44-3-225.pdf. Accessed on 26 March 2013.

3   http://israel21c.org/social-action-2/fixing-our-broken-classrooms/. Accessed on 26 March 2013.

'Drill and kill' was next, with too much emphasis on over-preparing for tests. Then there was 'little feedback from pupils', and finally little extra help in the classroom, although it's not clear for whom.

Well, I can see that these might be seen as problems, although all of these problems can be viewed as non-problems too; chalk and talk can be funny, intense, engaging . . . however it is presented. Plus, learning is often just hard bloody work. Drilling is an essential part of memorisation in some aspects of education; feedback from pupils really isn't particularly high on my list of essentials, and I have no idea what the extra help thing is, but I'm sure it's a big problem (or bug, as they say).

The answer? Lots of lovely tech. 'It was time for a classroom make-over,' says Weiss. Gorgeous. This involved lots of training, lots of tech, lots of software, and presumably, lots of maintenance contracts and upgrade requirements every year. But what about those gains? They really are something. Luckily, even though the web article doesn't help us much, there's a link to the company TTK itself. Maybe they'll have some data? *clicks link*

There are some hopeful links: it says 'Proven results – click here.' So I did. It led me to an overview page, which sadly contained only more vague claims about 'improved results'. Apparently, though, it was based on the 'latest research'. So I browsed further and found the research, which you'd kind of hoped would be on the front page as it's so good.

Aha! I found a list of papers from 2011 and 2010. Not many, but a good start. Most of them seemed to have the same two men in common: H. Braun of Boston College and Y. Rosen. I couldn't find many of them online or even referenced, but I have no doubt this was just my clumsy internet skills and no doubt they're fine things bristling with factual evidence. But I did manage to come across 'Intertwining Digital Content and a One-To-One Laptop Environment in Teaching and Learning: Lessons from the Time To Know Program,' by Yigal Rosen, 2011.

Oh boy. Now we're talking: 476 4th and 5th graders from four schools in Dallas, Texas. It's not a huge study, but let's not be sniffy about it. Actually, let's be sniffy. Unless every one of those kids jumps from Fs to As, in the absence of any other influences, I'm going to be hard convinced that this is a large enough sample size. But that's just me. They were looking to find the link between the TTK programme of 'one-to-one computing program in terms of student

math and reading achievement, differentiation in teaching and learning, higher student attendance, and decreased disciplinary actions.'
OK, that sounds like things we can probably measure.

First paragraph: 'One of the main challenges for education systems
is to leverage the learning sciences and modern technologies to
develop engaging, authentic, and personalised learning experiences.'[4]

That sounds dispiritingly like a moral claim to me, and no matter
how many papers you cite, that's hardly a good way to start a
scientific analysis. I'm already worried that this project is setting out
to look for evidence to prove a point, rather than attempt to disprove
it and see how robust the claim is, but that could just be my own
inference.

There were 283 kids on the programme overall; the rest were a
control, carefully matched for demographics. It's still different people
though. So they tested 283 kids with 177 different kids in different
schools. Let's see where this goes. Well, when it comes to reading
and maths abilities, the kids on the TTK programme seemed to do
better after a year. Was this because of the TTK programme or was
there some other factor? Would it have happened anyway? Answers
are there none in this paper. More interestingly and oddly, the paper
seems to claim that discipline and absences went down in the same
period for the TTKers (which may very well be true) but then
attributes it directly to the programme:

> As a result of the program, the percent of unexcused absences
> reported in school records was reduced by 29.2 per cent from
> the beginning to the end of the school year (240 compared with
> 170 unexcused absences), whereas in the control classes, the
> unexcused absences increased by 56.6 per cent. In addition, it
> was found that the program reduced students' discipline issues,
> while the control students' discipline issues did not change . . .

I consider that a very large claim to make. You can't just say, 'Oh
these two things happened, they must be connected.' You have to
prove it; you have to test it. You can't just turn up and say, 'I bet
X caused Y.' Feynman is rolling and rolling in his grave.

4   Rosen, Yigal, 'Intertwining Digital Content and a One-To-One Laptop
     Environment in Teaching and Learning: Lessons from the Time To Know
     Program', 2012.

No mechanism suggested. No discussion if the TTK programme caused this, or could have been something else. No discussion of the Hawthorne effect, or confirmation bias, or anxious teachers keen to make sure they didn't screw up putting their backs into teaching that bit more; or kids enthused about the cool new computers and technology. Or the fact that the control kids presumably weren't being taught with computers and individual laptops, so they really were in a different environment. The experiment was testing for many things: the TTK programs; the teacher's competencies; the tech itself; the hardware . . . it's a lot to tease apart.

But I'll leave the best for last: the author, we find, is: 'Yigal Rosen is an assessment and evaluation team leader at Time To Know and a faculty member at the University of Haifa Faculty of Education.'

So the research was commissioned and paid for by Time To Know? Undoubtedly, there is no conflict of interest in conducting research into your own programme in order to assess its efficacy. This isn't to impute the authors in any way of course. Merely to suggest that many would view this, from the outside, as a difficult and delicate minefield of ethics through which to tiptoe.

I leave it to you to decide.

Incidentally, pulling up another paper by the same author, also investigating the effects of the TTK programme (this time on children of Low Socio Economic Status – 'SES'), pulls up the following belter, also in the first paragraph.

> The study described in the article is based on the assumption that one of the possible solutions for bridging the social gap between low-SES students and others can be based on narrowing the 'digital divide,' particularly by bringing a 1:1 computing social-constructivist learning environment to the low-SES students.[5]

It also contains this.

> Educational technology can play a significant role in enhancement of educational systems to address knowledge and skills

5   Yigal Rosen and Iris Wolf, 'Bridging the Social Gap Through Educational Technology: Using the Time To Know Digital Teaching Platform', 2011. www.timetoknow.co.il/Data/Uploads/Bridging%20the%20Social%20Gap%20 Through%20Educational%20Technology.pdf. Accessed on 26 March 2013.

needed for the 21st century. However, despite high efforts and significant investments of resources, educational technology programs have revealed relatively low effects.[6]

For a start, there's that assumption again, right in the introduction: this stuff can really work, and 'there are new skills required for the 21st century'. That's the starting point of the paper, and one suspects that everything after that will be an attempt to confirm it. But hold! What's this admission that there are relatively low effects? Have we given up before we've begun? Not a bit of it. The next paragraph reassures us that.

> Lessons-learned from past research show that mainly student-centred, appropriately implemented, technology-rich learning environments can more effectively promote educational goals, such as learning motivation, teamwork, and higher-order thinking skills, in comparison with traditional teaching and learning.[7]

You'll notice one of the co-authors of that paper. See all those people who said IT didn't seem to have much of an effect? You can ignore them. I wrote a paper. And I feel like I'm taking crazy pills again.

Actually, looking at those critical papers is interesting. Cuban, 2001, refers to Larry Cuban, an excellent researcher who has been working in this field for years, and who presents us with something quite novel in my experience as a teacher: a researcher in technology integration in schools who isn't funded by a tech firm and who publishes papers and research that doesn't religiously support the proposed findings. In other words, he comes to exactly the opposite conclusions from most tech-sponsored research: IT integration doesn't yield significant gains in the classroom.

Here's what Larry Cuban has to say:

> . . . many researchers see electronic devices in schools as hardware and software devices that are efficient, speedy, reliable, and effective in producing desirable student outcomes such as higher

---

6   Rosen, Y. and Wolf, I., 'Bridging the Social Gap Through Educational Technology: Using the time to know digital teaching platform', 2011.
7   Rosen and Manny-Ikan, 2011.

test scores. These researchers have designed studies that have compared films, instructional television, and now computers to traditional instruction in order to determine to what degree the technology has shown that teachers are more efficient and effective in their teaching and students learn more, faster, and better. Such studies have been dominant in IT research in the U.S. for over a half-century 'with the most frequent result being "no significant difference".'[8]

Larry Cuban writes extensively and well about this, and if you want to see the research – or more importantly, the lack of it to be found in support – then I advise you to read more of him.

In *Teachers and Machines: The classroom use of technology since 1920* he describes in loving detail how every new innovation in technology has followed the same pattern in the classroom: adaption to the school environment, claims by enthusiasts that education would be revolutionised by its adoption, frustration that problems in education weren't solved in any significant way (although perhaps exchanged), and then a new technology emerges. It happened with calculators, TVs, recording devices, and now it's happening again with IT equipment. And in this game, enthusiasm trumps evidence.

When we look at the type of research carried out by others, we find similar problems. After checking that they weren't working for some dastardly conglomerate of Luddite interests and manufacturers of pencils and scrap paper, I read it. What's interesting is that they make the very reverse claims to papers such as TTK:

> New communication, media, and computing technologies have long tantalised educators, policy-makers, and educational technologists as to their prospects for enhancing educational outcomes. (Saettler, 1990) Numerous tools ranging from Edison's film projector through Berners-Lee's World Wide Web were originally invented for purposes other than education, but they were quickly promoted by educational technologists and others as having enormous promise for enhancing the impact of teaching and learning. Devices now considered to be simple and omnipresent in educational settings were once considered revolutionary and capable of mending social inequity and

8   http://larrycuban.wordpress.com/2012/03/14/dilemmas-in-researching-technology-in-schools-part-2/. Accessed on 26 March 2013.

changing the face of education. For example, in the 1970s, access to handheld calculators was considered to be crucial to raising test scores for underachieving math students, and accordingly math educators and educational technologists led efforts to get calculators into the hands of children learning mathematics. However, once the access gap was closed, the results were found to be much lower than promised.[9]

The debate about IT in education has been hijacked by the zealots, the optimists and commercially interested parties; by the desire for a simple solution to the problems of education; by the rhetoric of improving social inclusion, of ironing out inequality and improving social mobility. These are all fine claims, and greatly to be desired as values. But promise is not the same thing as delivery. The difference between this and the optimism of the Raspberry Pi pioneers is that they offer a clear mechanism for kids to explore and improve in a designated, clear area – computer design. The claims of the IT zealots are enormous, and they are blinded by their own values and optimism. The evidence just isn't there to support their assertions.

By all means, use IT in your lessons where you feel it is appropriate: I love using clips; I love bringing up text and imagery; research projects are fun and far more broad. But it has its place. The mindless adoption of IT on a compulsory, wide-scale basis is an enormous mistake; there are many problems with IT adoption that zealots frequently fail to admit.

Take those who advocate smartphones in the classroom. This is an enormous distraction for many children. If you don't think that many of them will be tempted to text, tweet, chat and MSN instead of focusing on the lesson, then you have an odd view of children's need to socialise rampantly, like little animals.

Research on computers offers an enormous number of avenues for distraction that simply don't exist in an encyclopaedia:

- plagiarism;
- misdirection – working slowly on font design instead of working;
- bugs, viruses, crashed, reboots;
- equipment failure;
- light shining on whiteboards;
- unfamiliarity with equipment.

9   Amiel and Reeves, 2008.

And so on. Supporters of IT will argue that all of these problems can be countered or ameliorated by good training and repetition, but they conveniently ignore that these are issues that occur on a daily basis in the classroom. The more complex the system, the more frequently it fails, and the more effort it requires to maintain it. This is not a problem I have with marker pens and wipeable boards, it just isn't.

I don't scorn or salivate over tech; I use it where I see fit. If it looks like it slows me down, I don't use it; if it gives me a clear advantage than otherwise, I use it. If I want to discuss Martin Luther King's speech, it's a powerful ploy to be able to show them the thing. But it isn't the only way. It can be read with passion, it can be read silently, it can be discussed; there are a million ways to learn.

Remember it can slow you down; it can ruin a lesson rather than support it. It can make your life hell; it can also be brilliant. I could say the same about chalk and blackboard. Like the twenty-first-century learning cultists, they fail to appreciate that, given that these changes are still fresh to the tune of a generation, we must consider that everyone in the history of everywhere was *not* instructed using twenty-first-century techniques, hard-wired into the matrix and working on Virtual Learning Platforms. However did they cope? And at least we have significant evidence of how they did, which I'm going to call 'all history ever'.

The evidence that learning is better on a VLP?

So far, it's next to nothing. Use IT if it suits your style. Use it if it helps you. But don't use it because you must, and certainly (if you have a budget for such things) don't buy it because you don't know what else to do. Good teaching relies on things that have been around for millennia: good subject knowledge; good classroom control; good communication skills; heart and guts. You don't need anything else. Maybe a pen, if you're feeling profligate. Everything else is chaff. Everything else obscures the teacher. I don't need a damn thing other than my voice and a room full of kids. The rest is bull, dressed up as Buck Rogers.

So: from an industry-commissioned research paper with some significant questions to be answered, to an uncritical website promoting technology, to Wikipedia, the crowd-sourced encyclopaedia where, even by its standards, it isn't too sure about it . . . to my computer, on the very first hit I get when I type in Digital Classroom Wiki as search terms. That's not very far to go; that's the two degrees of separation. Everywhere I look for evidence backing up hard data to show that classrooms benefit from the introduction of hard tech and integration of digital learning platforms, I find the following:

1   small sample sizes;
2   industry-sponsored research;
3   research unpublished in academic journals;
4   research available only online;
5   research that references other research by the same authors;
6   research that references websites, or the web pages of other industry providers.

I mean, is it just me? *I feel like John the Baptist here, raving in the desert.* Many in the tech industry (with the undoubted exception of TTK) are in this up to their boots. Nutt was right; the claims are based on the kind of science that would make Aristotle weep, which is odd, given that it's designed to justify the adoption of some of the end processes of the most complex science we have. And if your references are from 'the internet', then I hope you have trouble sleeping.

I weep, and the civilised world weeps. Until someone shows me real proof, I choose to remain unconvinced of the benefits of VLP, personal laptops, lessons on PCs and tablets and so on. In fact, the more I look into it, the more I see it as an enormous con, designed to sell stuff to schools, to gullible educators and holders of purse strings who don't know any better, who don't have the time to read the research that claims to back up the claims, who believe it when they are told by their own line managers that this stuff works, because they themselves have fallen for it, or work closely with the companies that provide it.

Joe Nutt, who used to be a principal consultant with the CfBT, makes many of the same points in *Professional educators and the role of IT in schools.* (Nutt, 2010). Nutt's got form: English teacher for nineteen years, state and private; then consultancy work with a number of bodies; Teach First; helped implement the national intranet for Scotland, etc. He is, in many ways, righteous in matters IT and teaching, which makes him a rare beast.

His report says, among other things, that:

•   The implementation of IT has been driven by suppliers, techno-zealots and the surprisingly digitally illiterate.

- The push for digital literacy is simply a push for conventional literacies using new delivery mechanisms, and don't rely on anything ground shaking. In essence digital literacy is simply regular, ready-salted literacy with a funny hat.
- IT professionals are often the driving force for the adoption and implementation of resources in the classroom.
- The government works hand-in-hand with educational suppliers in partnerships designed, from the outset, to promote the adoption of greater IT in classrooms.
- Teachers can be marginalised from this process.
- There is a staggering paucity of data that supports the purported gains promised by the IT evangelists; that the gains they suggest in grades are spurious and unproven.

The great thing this report does is point to the paucity of information supporting the claims of those who seek greater integration between classrooms and IT. Again, the reasons that this idea gains so much traction is because:

- IT is novel; novelty is superficially attractive and interesting.
- Nobody wants to be old-fashioned. IT is almost the definition of cutting edge. It is very groovy, and gets groovier with every update and reboot.
- IT is concrete. It is something you can buy. It is something that you can say 'I have done THIS in order to improve problem X.' It is a substitute for actually doing something.

If that doesn't sound like a scandal, I don't know what does.

We need to reboot.

Chapter 11

The Holy Trinity of the three-part lesson

This is an easy one. I only include it because it's a good example of how dogma emerges without any credible authenticity or justification.

I'm talking about the noble three-part lesson. It's been around since I started teaching. I don't know many state school teachers who haven't used it, and most teachers I know have been told at some point to use it as a way to structure their lessons. I've heard Ofsted inspectors criticise lessons for not having three parts, and I've seen lessons being graded unsatisfactory because plenaries were too short, and starters too long, or starters blending seamlessly into main activities.

The wind has changed; now your face will be stuck like that (possibly: research isn't in yet). At the time of writing (the fabulously retro summer of 2012. Hello twenty-third century), the incumbent Head of Ofsted, Sir Michael Wilshaw, is clearly speaking out against the three-part lesson, or the 'any number'-part lesson:

> Inspectors will not adopt a formulaic, tick-box approach to the inspection of teaching, but will recognise that the most important features of a good lesson are that children are interested in what they are doing, engaged, learning and making progress.
>
> Inspectors will not – let me emphasise, not – determine what is a 'right' or 'wrong' style of teaching.
>
> Sir Michael Wilshaw, HMCI[1]

---

1   A speech at the annual Brighton College education conference, 10 May 2012 by Sir Michael Wilshaw, Her Majesty's Chief Inspector, Ofsted. www. ofsted.gov.uk/resources/brighton-college-education-conference-speech. Accessed on 26 March 2013.

So that's clear: the main inspectorate for state school education in the UK doesn't care about how many parts there are to your lessons. So why the attachment that many teachers and school leaders have? The odd thing is that there doesn't appear to be, as far as I can find, any research that supports the claim that 'learning is better in a three-part lesson'. Which is odd for something so dogmatic. Where did it come from?

One explanation is the Literacy and Numeracy strategies, introduced in the late 1990s in England and Wales, which recommended around ten minutes for a starter, fifteen minutes for a plenary and the rest for main body activities. Interestingly enough, by 2006, people had begun to criticise this, as this 2006 article in the *Times Educational Supplement* (TES) demonstrates:

> The three-part lesson, used in primaries since the late 1990s to teach literacy and numeracy, can damage learning, influential advisers have warned. Teachers should feel free to decide what works best and tailor their teaching to pupils' needs, rather than be restricted by government guidelines, according to the Advisory Committee on Mathematics Education (ACME).
>
> The committee, part of the Royal Society, also said the 'top-down' pressure on schools to improve test results has left some pupils feeling anxious about the subject.[2]

ACME went on to explain:

> Indeed, the impact of this structure on learning can be less than positive, even where schools believe they are doing an adequate job, e.g. where good key stage test scores are achieved . . .
>
> Margaret Brown, professor of mathematics education at King's college, London and an ACME member, said: 'It's not that the three-part lesson in itself is wrong. It's that more variety would be useful.'
>
> Some tasks, for example, investigative work or revision, worked better spread out over a series of lessons, she said. In these cases, it was not helpful to have starters and plenaries. Yet teachers often feared to depart from the standard format. In 2012, Ofsted was forced to warn inspectors not to insist on the three-part

2   www.tes.co.uk/article.aspx?storycode=2247419. Accessed on 26 March 2013.

structure, following complaints that some had marked teachers down when their starter was 'five minutes too long'.

How different it all was in 2001 when HMI inspectors were slapping it on the three-part back, saying: 'The National Strategy, through the daily three-part lesson, is having a profound effect on the way mathematics is taught in primary schools.' (HMI 2001:1). And they meant that in a good way.

> Effective teachers make good use of starters and plenaries in the context of interactive whole-class teaching to engage all pupils in constructive deep learning ... Starters exploit the prime learning time at the beginning of lessons when pupils are often at their most receptive and concentration levels are high ... Plenaries need to be planned as part of the planned learning episodes (spontaneous plenaries tend to be less effective). They should link carefully to the objectives, outcomes and success criteria of the lesson as a whole.[3,4]

So the guidance documents from the then DoE supported the structure. But what supported it? I'm already worried about turtles again. Luckily it points to some research. *At last.*

'Research studies frequently refer to the vital importance of structuring learning. Mortimore *et al.* (1988) concluded that the key classroom factors contributing to effective outcomes were structured sessions ...'[5]

A brief look at this material reveals that the authors in general support the idea that starters and plenaries can be used to good effect, which is a very different notion to the idea that the three part (or any part) lesson is to be favoured over any other way.

An odd but likely source for the temporary dominance of the three-part lesson is its intuitive correctness, absorbed from the old adage that, in order to get someone to understand, you first have to tell them what you're going to say, then say it, then tell them what you

3   Pedagogy and Practice: Teaching and Learning in Secondary Schools Unit 5: Starters and plenaries, DfEE 2004.

4   www.teachfind.com/national-strategies/pedagogy-and-practice-teaching-and-learning-secondary-schools-%E2%80%93-unit-5-starters-. Accessed on 26 March 2013.

5   Pedagogy and Practice: Teaching and Learning in Secondary Schools Unit 5: Starters and plenaries. 2004, DfE http://dera.ioe.ac.uk/5668/2/bd4ba685563fcd91f0f1f97eb1afa5e7.pdf. Accessed on 26 March 2013.

said. This was from Dale Carnegie, the early twentieth-century writer and lecturer on salesmanship and persuasion skills.[6]

It kind of makes sense; it's also the favoured narrative structure of most stories: a beginning, a middle and an end, and there's nothing wrong with that. But just as with stories, there's sometimes no need to have a formal beginning; the more you play with the art form, the more confident you get dispensing with such things. Many films and books launch straight into the drama (see: *Mission: Impossible III*); some stories are told in flashback, with the ending first (see: *Memento*). Some have no obvious structure (see: *Skyscraper*). The point here is that structure is a tool, not a trap.

Another way to look at it is that no matter what you do a lesson will have a beginning, middle and an end. You walk in, something happens, everyone walks out again. In that sense, a three-part lesson is inevitable. I would suggest that starters, plenaries and middle activities all have some extremely good functions, and you would do well to pay attention to its efficacy as a basic structure. But, as Dr W.H. Cockroft said:

> We are aware that there are some teachers who would wish us to indicate a definitive style for the teaching of mathematics, but we do not believe that this is either desirable or possible. Approaches to the teaching of a particular piece of mathematics need to be related to the topic itself and to the abilities and experience of both teachers and pupils. Because of differences of personality and circumstance, methods which may be extremely successful with one teacher and one group of pupils will not necessarily be suitable for use by another teacher or with a different group of pupils. Nevertheless, we believe that there are certain elements which need to be present in successful mathematics teaching to pupils of all ages.[7]

Ofsted reported in 2011 that one of the factors that characterised poor teaching in English was:

> An inflexible approach to planning lessons. School policies sometimes insist that all lesson plans should always follow the

---

6 Carnegie, Dale, *How to Win Friends and Influence People*, 1936.
7 The Cockcroft Report (1982). www.educationengland.org.uk/documents/cockcroft/cockcroft05.html. Accessed on 26 March 2013.

same structure, no matter what is being taught. In addition, evidence from the survey suggests that teachers often feel that they should not alter their plans during the lesson. The notion of a three- or four-part structure to lessons with certain key elements, such as a lively starter activity and an opportunity to review learning at the end, is helpful to teachers. However, teachers need to have the confidence to depart from their plans if early indications are, for example, that the pupils know more or less than the teacher had anticipated. The key consideration should be the development of pupils' learning rather than sticking rigidly to a plan.[8]

The final report of the Numeracy Task Force said that a three-part lesson was a typical lesson, but 'not a rigid structure to be followed.'[9]

A report by Dr Ros Fisher (2007) 'Plus ça change: change and continuity in literacy teaching' reviewed the outcomes of the literacy strategy. In its conclusion there were some very apposite comments about the difficulty in translating laboratory science into national strategies; they could apply to any educational reform propelled more by enthusiasm than evidence:

> Changing teaching is difficult. Leithwood *et al.* (1999) review evidence for what works in successfully implementing and sustaining reform. They recognise the difficulties of achieving and sustaining 'a reasonably uniform, widespread understanding of a single reform initiative.' (p15) Whereas the government's intention was to 'change for the better teaching approaches across the entire education service' (DfEE 1997 paras 26, 27) it is clear that at the individual level change in teaching covers more than programs and procedures. As Reynolds (1998) argues, 'It may be that the problem with literacy teaching . . . may not necessarily only be to do with the validity of the methods being utilised in schools, but more the reliability of their implementation. (p. 169)
>
> This analysis of . . . a period of large scale reform shows that further work needs to be done to investigate how teaching

8   www.educationengland.org.uk/documents/pdfs/2012-ofsted-english.pdf. Accessed on 26 March 2013.
9   www.leeds.ac.uk/educol/documents/chapter1.htm. Accessed on 26 March 2013.

reform becomes imbedded. It is important for reformers to realise the complex interactional context of the classroom and to acknowledge the importance of the individual teacher's pedagogical stance in how any reform will be implemented. Successful teaching of literacy (and no doubt any subject) relies as much on the individual teacher's capacity as any program of content or technique.[10]

In other words, what works for one, may not work for another; the chemistry between the teacher and the strategy is of vital importance, and this is something borne out by many experiences. Three parts, plenaries and starters may work for you; I would even argue that they are a powerful tool for achieving a large variety of ends: settling; stimulating; showing recall; evidencing learning; linking to the next or previous lesson; and so on. But to claim that they are the basic structure of the (and I mean every) good lesson is demonstrably nonsense. Perhaps no one ever explicitly even said this, but this is how guidance has/had been interpreted.

The problem isn't finding research that supports the use of structure in lessons – there's loads of evidence that teachers need to have a structure to their lessons. What there isn't, is any appreciable evidence that having three parts to a lesson leads to any kind of measurable improvement.

The view from the classroom

It might sound like teaching you to suck eggs, but my advice is to have some kind of structure to your lesson. That structure might look like a tripod, or it might look like a bicycle, or a centipede or any damn thing. The important thing is that your lesson structure suits the intention of your lesson: that it suits you, that it suits them. If I'm doing project work then I don't really care if I don't have a plenary at the end, because it isn't appropriate. If I want my kids to crack on immediately into preparing a speech, or if my lesson has been truncated for any reason then I might skip the starter. I might not – whisper it – I might not even put my aim on the board because sometimes I want kids to work out what we're trying to do for them.

10 https://eric.exeter.ac.uk/repository/bitstream/handle/10036/41914/plus %20%C3%83%C2%A7a%20change.pdf?sequence=1. Accessed on 26 March 2013.

It depends, it depends. If you're a new teacher, and you're still struggling to come to terms with how you deliver a lesson, then by all means use the three-part structure, so you at least get a feel for how you teach, what suits you and what suits them. And if I were observing a lesson and things just came one thing after another, with no progression or connection, I'd probably want to know why the structure was so loose. If there was a reason that could be understood, I might not think it wrong. Again, the key thing is to have a structure that is deliberate rather than one that is imposed from without.

Also, don't let structure be a straightjacket; if you've ever had to change a lesson mid-way due to unforeseen circumstances, then you'll know that lessons, like life don't always pan out as you plan. A wasp flies in. The kids don't get it, or some do but some don't. There's a fight. Someone farts. You forgot your IWB pen. The usual. A good teacher adapts the structure to fit the circumstances, like a host working a room. What you don't do is plod on through the list on your lesson plan in case the sky falls in. It will not.

It's worse when being observed; if you've ever been watched by Ofsted, you'll know the peculiar prickly fear in your saddle as you deviate from the liturgy in their hands. But to hell with that. You do what needs to be done, for the benefit of the children's education, and nothing else.

Structure is a tool; a climbing frame. All aspects of teaching are climbing frames. Use them when you need, dispense with them as you must. Putting the teacher back in charge of the classroom is my main aim as I search for research that, in this case, doesn't exist. Trust your feelings, Luke. Switch off your targeting computer. Use The Force.

Even Ofsted is now recommending we come down for the three-part climbing frame, I repeat, come *down* from the climbing frame.

Chapter 12

There are no such things as learning styles

Up until fairly recently, there was a column on every lesson plan and scheme of work I was asked to produce. Alongside columns indicating, not unreasonably, how tasks would be assessed, how I would differentiate and timings of each activity, was another column, headed 'learning style'. In this column, I was expected to describe how each activity related to a different style in which students learned, either Visual (V), Audio (A) or Kinaesthetic (K). The aim being was, of course, to show that I had planned and catered for different learning styles in each lesson, in order to ensure that students with different categories of approach had their needs met, and no one was left out of the lesson because they preferred to see information in a film (V) rather than, say, absorb it in the form of Japanese Noh theatre (K).

Here are some of the things that the VAK crowd say:

> There are three basic types of learning styles. The three most common are visual, auditory, and kinaesthetic. To learn, we depend on our senses to process the information around us. Most people tend to use one of their senses more than the others. Today's lesson will help you determine which of these learning styles you rely on the most.[1]

> Do you learn better by seeing, hearing, or acting out the information you receive? In other words, are you a mostly visual, auditory, or kinaesthetic learner? Actually, everybody learns by mixture of methods, but one method or type is usually dominant

---

1 'What's YOUR learning style?' http://people.usd.edu/~bwjames/tut/learning-style/. Accessed on 26 March 2013.

in each person. By determining your dominant learning style you can improve your memory and your grades.[2]

I suspect many of the teachers reading this will still have to do something like this. I was instructed to pay heed to it throughout my training, and for many years it was the very last word in good practice. Children learn in different ways to each other; the old model of one-size-fits-all learning had been smashed. If we paid closer attention to the different ways in which they learned rather than simply treat them as a mass of identical learners, then we would be able to encourage learning, engage them, motivate them and, like every educational innovation, transform the way children learned.

It's closely connected to other fashions in education, of course: personalised learning and independent learning. It also echoes the whole project of differentiation, by tailoring teaching to individual learning capacities and preferences. As indicated by the ubiquity of it in my teaching experience, learning styles was one of those strategies that essentially won the argument; it was, for a while, broadly accepted as a pillar of education.

And yet, there is no evidence for it whatsoever. None. Every major study done to see if using learning styles strategies actually work has come back with totally negative results. Worse, the whole theory of learning styles, while sounding plausible (that grain of truth again, leavening its acceptance), is itself without foundation. So how did this crock of – let's face it – moonshine get into the classroom?

It started, like disco, in the 70s, with writers such as Rita and Kenneth Dunn[3] who started the ball rolling. They went into schools and studied how students seemed to prefer to learn; they found that some preferred group work, some alone, some preferred different teachers, and so on. They identified several common factors in learning preference:

- Environmental considerations (How hot is the room? What's the lighting like?)
- Emotional support (Do they like lots of support or structure, for example?)

2   http://homeworktips.about.com/library/quizzes/bl_lstylequiz1.htm. Accessed on 26 March 2013.
3   Dunn, R. and Dunn, K. (1978). *Teaching Students through their Individual Learning Styles*. Reston, VA: Reston.

- Sociological composition (Alone or in groups? With whom?)
- Physiological issues (Are they visual, audio or kinaesthetic learners?)
- Psychological elements (Do they like to get stuck in, or reflect first?)

I've simplified, but that's what they found. Let's focus on the physiological issue: learning styles, or sometimes, learning modalities. What are VAK learning styles?

Visual learners

learn through seeing . . .

These learners need to see the teacher's body language and facial expression to fully understand the content of a lesson. They tend to prefer sitting at the front of the classroom to avoid visual obstructions (e.g. people's heads). They may think in pictures.

Auditory learners

learn through listening . . .

They learn best through verbal lectures, discussions, talking things through and listening to what others have to say. Auditory learners interpret the underlying meanings of speech through listening to tone of voice, pitch, speed and other nuances. Written information may have little meaning until it is heard.

Tactile/kinesthetic learners

learn through, moving, doing and touching . . .

Tactile/Kinesthetic persons learn best through a hands-on approach, actively exploring the physical world around them. They may find it hard to sit still for long periods and may become distracted by their need for activity and exploration.[4]

There's even a little picture of a hand in that last one to help you understand.

4   www.ldpride.net/learningstyles.MI.htm#Learning%20Styles%20Explained.
    Accessed on 26 March 2013.

David A. Kolb had a similar approach.[5] He argued that students had preferred learning strategies, although they could develop others with practice. He believed that the four learning styles were:

- Converger – good at solving problems, like to make the abstract concrete;
- Diverger – Imaginative, like to come up with new ideas;
- Assimilator – Abstract conceptualisers;
- Accommodator – Doers; like concrete examples.

Other researchers, such as Honey and Mumford, developed Kolb's theory, redrawing the categories as Activist, Reflector, Theorist and Pragmatists. They developed the Learning Styles Questionnaire (LSQ)[6] which is one of the most widely used tools in UK schools for identifying learning styles.[7]

There are others, but I'm getting tired just typing all the categories and wondering why they're all so different, and why the researchers can't agree. The most common learning style system, the VARK system (Fleming 2001) builds on Neuro-Linguistic Programming. Fleming defines learning style as:

> . . . an individual's characteristics and preferred ways of gathering, organizing, and thinking about information. VARK is in the category of instructional preference because it deals with perceptual modes. It is focused on the different ways that we take in and give out information.[8]

Incidentally, the moment someone mentions NLP in any educational discussion, put your coat on and leave because you just won the argument.

VARK (the R stands for Reading and Writing, incidentally) refers to every sense except taste and smell, and one wonders why that isn't a modality as well, although I suppose we don't teach many pythons or bloodhounds. Can you imagine VAK in a school of vipers? ('I prefer to be inssssssstructed using the modality of sssssmell,

5   Kolb, David (1984). *Experiential Learning.*
6   Honey, P and Mumford, A (2006). *The Learning Styles Questionnaire, 80-item version.*
7   www.campaign-for-learning.org.uk. Accessed on 26 March 2013.
8   Fleming, N.D. (2001). *Teaching and Learning Styles.*

ssssir . . .') The questionnaires for such things are self-assessed of course, and involve lots of questions about how you prefer to interpret the world. Apparently 41 per cent of the population have a preference for one modality, 27 per cent two modalities, 9 per cent three, and 21 per cent for four. Perhaps you sat one of these tests? They're a bit like questionnaires in *Cosmopolitan* about 'How sexy are you?' or something.

'Fleming (2001) discusses the validity of the instrument, presenting research that supports the use of the instrument in identifying learn-ing preferences of students. Beyond his reports, there is no other research on validity or reliability.'[9] Which is nice of Fleming to back up his research with . . . his research, isn't it? Sounds completely above board.

This research was all scooped up with gusto by the educational community, and children were assessed, categorised, their individual needs catered for by anxious teachers, terrified that they were denying the student's right to modal preference.

It is, of course, complete rubbish as far as I can see.[10] There is very little to the theory underpinning the idea of learning styles, and damn all evidence I can see to suggest that identifying and then delivering modality-specific lessons has any effect whatsoever on children's learning. It really is that stark. You could say that learning styles has as much scientific basis as the magic crystals you can buy in the King Arthur shop in Glastonbury, I'm afraid.

The empirical science fights back

Although the literature on learning styles is enormous, very few studies have even used an experimental methodology capable of testing the validity of learning styles applied to education. Moreover, of those that did use an appropriate method, several found results that flatly contradict the popular meshing hypothesis.

We conclude therefore, that at present, there is no adequate evidence base to justify incorporating learning-styles assessments into general educational practice.[11]

9 Thomas F. Hawk and Amit J. Shah, 'Using learning style instruments to enhance student learning', 2007
10 IN MY OPINION.
11 Pashler, H. *et al.* (2008). 'Learning styles: Concepts and evidence'.

And that's just some of the nicer things the recent research has shown. See, I've done a fair job appearing to trash social science in this book, but that's not what I'm about at all; and it isn't just a case of accepting social science that agrees with me and disputing that which doesn't. The article I've quoted above does what science – any science – does best, in fact what some would say it was designed to do: test hypotheses to the point of failure; to scrutinise, to be sceptical, to assess, to shake the papers as hard as they can to see if it holds together. And when it comes to learning styles, the evidence just isn't there.

Baroness Greenfield, the Director of the Royal Institute, said in the *Daily Telegraph*:

> Humans have evolved to build a picture of the world through our senses working in unison, exploiting the immense interconnectivity that exists in the brain. It is when the senses are activated together – the sound of a voice is synchronisation with the movement of a person's lips – that brain cells fire more strongly than when stimuli are received apart.
>
> The rationale for employing VAK learning styles appears to be weak. After more than 30 years of educational research into learning styles there is no independent evidence that VAK, or indeed any other learning style inventory, has any direct educational benefits.[12]

Stahl (1999)[13] says:

> The reason researchers roll their eyes at learning styles is the utter failure to find that assessing children's learning styles and matching to instructional methods has any effect on their learning ... over the past thirty years the names of these styles have changed ... but the research results have not changed. In 1978 Tarver and Dawson reviewed 15 studies ... thirteen of the studies failed to find an effect and the [other two] used unusual methodologies. One year later Arter and Jenkins reviewed 14

12 www.telegraph.co.uk/news/uknews/1558822/Professor-pans-learning-style-teaching-method.html#. Accessed on 26 March 2013.
13 Stahl, S.A. (2002). Different strokes for different folks? In L. Abbeduto (Ed.), *Taking Sides: Clashing on controversial issues in educational psychology* (pp. 98–107).

studies . . . all of which failed to find that matching children to reading methods by preferred modalities did any good.

And so on. In 2004[14] a team from the University of Newcastle concluded that: 'Despite a large and evolving research programme, forceful claims made for impact are questionable because of limitations in many of the supporting studies and the lack of independent research on the mode.'

A 2005 Demos report[15] said that the evidence for learning styles was 'highly variable', and that practitioners were 'not by any means frank about the evidence for their work'. Ouch. It goes on and on. Make no mistake, citizens, learning styles has taken a battering. Note that one of the critics I quoted above is writing in 1999 and talking about how rubbish evidence has been for the last thirty years. Even then the jig was up. Doesn't that say something dark and terrible about the way in which bad ideas can lurch on ('zombie facts') for decades after their satanic birth, despite enormous evidence to suggest that there isn't any evidence available?

Why did learning styles become so popular? Stahl, above, thought that there was an analogy with fortune telling: they managed to say just enough about you to keep you interested in what they were selling. I'd say that most people were fairly narcissistic: one of our favourite topics is always us; and just like those hideous, repellent questionnaires in magazines written by unpaid interns (and no, they aren't the pinnacle of science either) they appeal to our vanity. If you've ever been on Facebook then you'll be familiar with the million and one surveys you can do, all in exchange for your personal details, for a test written by a sixteen-year-old. Bargain.

They also appeal, I think, to the belief that we are all unique, that we are special in some way. It also appeals, of course, to the idea that there is a magic bullet in education. The reality is, of course, that education is an enormous, complicated hydra of a creature, whose reformation or improvement involves many hundreds of small and large changes administered over a long period of time and using many people and much time. Like dieting, it's reassuring to think that there might be a pill we can pop. Learning styles fits the bill.

---

14 Coffield, F. *et al.* (2004). *Learning Styles and Pedagogy in Post-16 Learning. A systematic and critical review.*
15 Hargreaves, D. (2005). *About Learning: Report of the learning working group.* Demos.

It also ties into one of the normal 'modes' of most teachers: kindness. Most teachers I know believe that they can help every single kid if they just figure out the right way to teach them, and learning styles offers the promise that there is, at last, a way into the inner workings of the student mind. There probably aren't many simple ways. Certainly not modalities, or learning preferences.

Teacher's eye view

Another reason this appeals is because, as ever, there is a germ of sense that appeals to us: everyone does, of course, prefer to do things in a certain way. You might call it personality, or prejudice, or whatever. I like to watch films more than I like to go to concerts. Maybe that . . . maybe that means I'm a V more than an A! Also, I hate sport. So cross off my K! But that doesn't mean I learn in a particularly different way than anyone else. Oh, I might have a preference, in the same sense that I prefer a bedroom a little cold than a little hot, or my coffee with extra milk and my books made of paper.

But that doesn't mean I have one way to learn that works better than another. The problem with the Dunn research is that they mistook expressed *preferences* for learning, for real modalities. Just because someone claims they learn better one way, means very little. If you asked half my students how they prefer to learn, they'll probably tell you 'On a couch, eating Pringles, listening to my iPod, yeah?' or something. So flicking what? If I told you I preferred to be carried into work on a golden sedan by the cast members of *Chicago*, while the Pussycat Dolls trumpeted my arrival, scattering blue petals before, would that refer to anything beyond my own peculiarities? Would it suggest that London Transport really had to raise their game a bit? Or would it just mean that I, like every other human being, have dreams?

There's another trap for teachers here, beyond the obvious ones of falling for yet another faddish piece of educational moronism: the trap of exhaustion, self-blame and guilt. We work hard enough as it is to try to make the lesson accessible to everyone, brainiac or blunt instrument. The added requirement that we tailor things for every individual learning style really is too much. You can hear teachers cracking from the effort. This affects new teachers more than old, who will look at it with the justified suspicion of the old lag; but new recruits genuinely worry themselves into a spot over this.

As Stahl mentions, after a year, most people who attend courses on VARK usually end up, within a year, not using it.

On Twitter recently, I mentioned that learning styles was a pile of demonstrable guano. The response I got from many, many people suggested to me that, although Dracula has had a stake thrust into his gizzards, he still needs to have his head cut off and stuffed with garlic by Dr Van Helsing. It isn't quiet dead yet. Even though it died decades ago. Doesn't this say terrible things about the way in which bad ideas won't quit? The longevity of guff is one of the reasons I wanted to write this book. I lived through learning styles; let me be a lighthouse to you all.

Here be dragons. VAK ones that prefer learning through mime.

Chapter 13

Game over

The gamification of education

This is so hot, it's scorching, although that usually means it'll be out of date by yesterday and this chapter will resemble your dad wearing a cardigan with patches, dancing to the Spice Girls. Right now, it's lava. Here's a quote from Allan Gershenfeld, founder and president of E-Line Media, a publisher of digital games to help kids and parents learn. His bio helpfully informs us that 'He's an advocate for games used in the classroom as a learning tool.' That will become apparent:

> Video games, if effectively harnessed, are an ideal platform for learning. And there are a number of reasons why. Unlike film or television or other linear media – even books – games are interactive. They're participatory. You lean forward, not back. Games let people step into other shoes, make decisions, explore the consequences. In games, the player has *agency*, which is very, very powerful. Games are participatory. You're interacting, which is very, very powerful. Games are adaptive. They're personalised. You can go at your own pace, advance at your own pace. They're scaffolded for folks who go slower. So in many ways, the platform itself is perfectly set up for effective learning.[1]

The claims

An increasing number of people are getting in on this: we witness the infancy of a movement. Gamification has barely reached the shores of School Island, but already the claims are being made of its

---

1   http://earthsky.org/human-world/alan-gershenfeld-on-video-games-for-learning-science. Accessed on 26 March 2013.

efficacy. In 'Gamification in education: What, how, why bother?' by Hammer and Lee (2011) we read that introducing gaming aspects into the classroom can have many benefits. What might they be?

> Games provide complex systems of rules for players to explore through active experimentation and discovery. For example, the apparently simple mobile game Angry Birds asks players to knock down towers by launching birds out of a slingshot . . . In short, players' desire to beat each level makes them small-scale experimental physicists. These techniques, applied to schools, can transform student perspectives on learning. . . . Gamification can help students ask, 'If I want to master school, what do I do next?' . . . Crucially, they also help players persist through negative emotional experiences and even transform them into positive ones . . . Developing a strong school-based identity helps engage students with learning in the long run (Nasir and Saxe, 2003). However, many students do not feel like they can 'do school' (Pope, 2003). For these students, gamified environments can provide an opportunity to try on the unfamiliar identity of a scholar.[2]

You are kidding me on, surely? No that's churlish. Where's the evidence? The authors are careful to remind us that gamification 'is not a universal panacea', which, of course, shows us how reasonable they are. But the whole tone is speculative: this *might* work; that *might* improve their esteem, etc.

Now as I'm careful to point out, I have no problem with rewards-based systems in school as such, although I'll point out some snags in a minute. And I have no problem with someone who is interested in education, and gaming, looking into ways that this could go well together. I'm certainly delighted for teachers to try anything that works for them.

What I'm very prickly about are spurious claims about the efficacy of a project without any evidence to back it up. This article seems to me to be a piece of advocacy and speculation, and that's absolutely fine. What I don't think it is, is proof of any kind, and I'm sure the authors didn't intend it to be either (I actually enjoyed it as a teacher; it gave me some ideas). But I've already seen it cited in a number

---

2   Lee and Hammer (2011). 'Gamification in education: What, how, why bother?'.

of articles and features (mostly online) in support of the idea that gamification is somehow supported as a classroom technique by the academic community. There is no such thing.

On the contrary, there is a lot of evidence looking into the ability of rewards and punishments to incentivise people in the workplace and schools. There's a lot about incentive schemes, mainly because industry and marketers are very interested in how to encourage people to buy all their stuff. Governments are also interested in getting people to act one way or another; economics deals with this kind of question all the time.

The papers cited by the article above are no assistance to anyone seeking to prove the claims of the gamifiers, most of which, unsurprisingly, seem to be involved heavily with tech, IT or software suppliers, who all want to sell us stuff. Isn't that *weird*? What a coincidence.

If you've read the last few chapters, you might see a common thread emerging between people who want to sell schools stuff and research that shows that schools need to buy stuff in order to teach kids *real good*.

Which mostly they don't.

> To be fair, you can do some really brilliant things with this gear as a teacher: take this article about a teacher from Indiana University who teaches online game design; he decided to make part of the course . . . an online game. That is, without question, very cool.
>
> Class time is spent completing quests (such as presentations of games or research), fighting monsters (taking tests or quizzes), and 'crafting' (writing game-analysis papers and a video-game concept document). The 40-person class is divided into six 'zones,' named after influential game designers, in which students complete group tasks.
>
> Mr. Sheldon says last semester's students performed a full letter grade better in the course than students had under the traditional approach — the class average was a B instead of a C.
>
> 'They are more engaged,' Mr. Sheldon said. They are 'the gamer generation, they are the social-networking generation, so this class is couched in the terms that they understand.'[3]

3   http://chronicle.com/blogs/wiredcampus/at-indiana-u-a-class-on-game-design-has-students-playing-to-win/21981. Accessed on 26 March 2013.

Isn't that great? He sounds like a top teacher. I'd worry about the speculation regarding the grade rises; but he's not projecting this as a national rollout, so there's no quarrel there.

The Institute of Play and Quest to Learn

A pioneering public school in New York City that offers a promising new model for student engagement. Designed from the ground up by a team of teachers and game designers, and firmly grounded in over thirty years of learning research, Quest to Learn re-imagines school as one node in an ecology of learning that extends beyond the four walls of an institution and engages kids in ways that are exciting, empowering and culturally relevant.

Quest to Learn's unique standards-based integrated curriculum mimics the action and design principles of games by generating a compelling 'need to know' in the classroom . . . Quest to Learn opened to its first class of sixth graders in 2009. In 2010 a seventh grade was added. By 2015 the school will offer a complete middle and high school education.

Research is under way to generate comparative data on student proficiency in twenty-first-century skills like systems thinking, creative problem solving, collaboration, time management and identity formation. Preliminary results are promising. In addition, students are performing at or above New York City public school averages on standardised tests. And in 2010 the school ranked in the ninety-seventh percentile in student engagement across city schools.[4]

Well that's all very promising isn't it? No data yet, but all very hopeful. I'm sorry, it's easy to be negative (especially in educational research) and I wish these people all the best. But there's no data yet. We don't know what kind of background these children have; we don't know how useful the techniques would be . . . in short there isn't any data. I hope these kids all come out like gangbusters, but there just isn't the evidence to persuade me that schools would benefit from gamification.

---

4   www.instituteofplay.org/about/context/additional-resources/. Accessed on 26 March 2013.

Reading the Institute of Play website is interesting. One of its sponsors is the Bill and Melinda Gates Foundation, but actually that scores points with me because they're fabulous philanthropists. Some of the research quoted in the evidence section of their website isn't available any more, but some is.

None of it, that I could see, is evidential. What every paper cited seems to do is to draw useful links between the way they believe people learn, and the features of video games, or games in general that could either correlate or support them. Which is very interesting – genuinely. But none of this points to anything other than speculation. I consider it so far from evidence that it can scarcely be used as such.

But schools have adopted these programs; some teachers wonder if they should adopt them. Schools expand their rewards structures, and salesmen peek their heads in and wonder if they can just have five minutes of our time. Once again, as soon as something becomes possible, someone does it. Five minutes later, someone tells you it can cure cancer and tries to charge you for it.

I am reminded, in some way, of superhero comics (I confess that this happens a lot). When I was a lad, I used to devour old *Marvel* comics. The secret origins of these leotard Olympians often revolved around radiation: Spiderman was bitten by a 'radioactive spider'; Bruce Banner's exposure to gamma rays turned him into the Hulk; the Fantastic Four were pummelled by cosmic rays ('Who knows *what* they'll do?') and turned into the world's premier super family until the Incredibles, and so on. It seems quaint to us that they didn't simply get cancer and die, but that was the era; radioactivity seemed strange and mysterious, a doorway into the Twilight Zone. A century ago, speculative authors were doing the same with electricity: Doctor Frankenstein animated his mortified creation Adam with the magic powers of this novel new source of wonder. When something is new, it is both frightening and, in its incomprehension, suffers from endless speculation of its protean form.

I think this is what's occurring with emergent technologies. They are so new that we have had no chance to understand the impact they will have on us; only perspective grants us this boon. Until then, they seem to occupy a million possibilities all dancing in front of us. We simply have no credible data to suggest in what ways gamification could help us in the classroom.

The moral/abstract problem

There is also another dimension: the problem of motivating children using external rewards itself. When we are very young, and socially acceptable value systems are unknown to us, just as most empirical knowledge is absent from the blank slates of our mind, we need to be taught right and wrong (or, if you're a moral non-realist, accepted from non-accepted values). This process is considerably accelerated by the use of incentives: positive ones (like carrots, if you're a donkey) or negative ones (the goad, the reprimand, the sanction). Children come to associate discouraged behaviour with punitive experiences, and more agreeable behaviour with comfort and acceptance. It's not exactly nuclear physics; every animal with a decent cognitive ability can master it.

The problem lies in that we use these reward systems as a means to an end: that the child should become habituated into seeing certain courses of actions as desirable, and others undesirable. The purpose of the activity is not to emphasise the desirability of the reward, but the desirability of the behaviour associated with the reward. In other words, if I give a kid a Smartie for tidying his room, I'm hoping that he'll eventually learn to do it because it's the right thing to do, not because he's a Smartie addict. In other words, the reward for the action itself, which initially is extrinsic to the action, becomes intrinsic. And this, according to the Categorical Imperative, is what we might call duty.

Duty is considered by some deontologists to be the only perfectly moral motive. Why? Because it is the only motive that excludes self-interest and consequential gain. If I teach a child that every time he hands in his homework he'll get a lollipop, the question I must ask myself is, is he doing it because he's conscientious and dedicated, or because lollipops float his boat? The only way to find out is to take the lollipops away and find out. You might not like the answer.

Self-interest has always been one of the world's most ancient and powerful motivators. Adam Smith took it as one of his central assumptions in the *Wealth of Nations*: that competition was the engine of human psychology. Darwin, too, took it to be a foundational truth: when resources are scarce we compete. Shaw called it the Life Force, and Kant claimed that we all instinctively had the love of our own lives uppermost in our basic desires. What's in it for me? Is it such a universally acknowledged motivator that it scarcely needs to be expressed in the creation of any contract, tacit or formal. But the answer we should be seeking, if we are to consider ourselves in any way enlightened beings, is sometimes 'Nothing: there's nothing in it for me.'

If you help an old lady across the road for a fiver, you might be doing a good thing for a bad reason, because it suggests you wouldn't do it without the reward. If however you do it because you believe it's the right thing to do, regardless of your benefit, then you'll be reliably inspired to do so in the absence of reward. Altruism, while not the exclusive litmus of goodness, is probably more reliable a barometer than naked self-interest. Egoism, even of the enlightened variety, will only support moral conduct as long as the participants visibly, perceptibly benefit. Which means the system collapses when our interests are perceived to be at risk. Even societies based entirely on this structure (the 'social contract' beloved of Hobbes, Locke and other legislative forefathers) contain this weakness: that morality can never be based entirely on self-interest, no matter how cleverly constructed it is to be mutual. In other words, kindness can never be conceived as entirely a rational enterprise, because it's a value, and not reducible to articles of fact or quantity. It can only be conveyed by parenting and education.

And because moral action is a value rather than a fact, we have to be careful how we reward students. If we make the link between good conduct and palpable benefits too direct, we risk encouraging good conduct only when rewards are available. The reverse of this is a frightening acceptance of bad conduct in the absence of reward. So any system of treats, stars, codes or gamified assets has to be treated carefully, otherwise we might just find that we're teaching our students laziness, selfishness and egocentricity.

If you're a good teacher, you don't bust your backside trying to help your students because there's a bonus, or a power-up, you do it because it's the right thing to do. Any benefit to you should be incidental – although recognition and a warm rosy glow are nice of course. Alasdair MacIntyre would draw a distinction between external and internal goods: in his book *Beyond Virtue*, he discussed how the value of an activity should reside in the activity itself; Aristotle thought that the Good Life was, among other things, people pursuing actions that were ends in themselves rather than means to an end.

I agree. Rewards, if overdone, lead to vice, not virtue; when they are achieved, they should be for actions that merit them, not actions that are merely expected, not at the post-adolescent stage. To do otherwise is to devalue the currency of reward, and to imply that all normal conduct should be accompanied by reward. Well, life isn't like that. I don't want to teach children to be complacent; I want them to appreciate self-sacrifice and restraint as well as hedonism: the former are vital to understanding the latter, and no reward system should teach children that life is an enormous chocolate box of increasing levels of diversity and sensuality, without also informing them that somewhere inside every box there, too, lurks the horrors of the ginger or the macaroon.

Jesse Schell, a video game designer, uses the term 'Gamespocalypse' to describe the way the world might be if gamification is used to exploit and corrupt people, perhaps in an effort to make them more obedient consumers, or by attaching exploitative values coded into the reward algorithms of the gaming process. We can see this effect on a much more subtle level in the way we reward our pupils.

Less is more. There are no Level Bosses to bash in life. I suspect it's a good deal more complex than that.

Continue? (Y/N)

Chapter 14

Learning to learn to learn to learn . . .

Currently enjoying its 1000th week in the pop charts of fashionable educational orthodoxy, is Learning to Learn (L2L), which, as its name suggests, is about teaching children to learn about the process by which they become more intelligent, and understand. It's meta-learning, and I promise you I will never use that phrase again. Just try and think what learning to learn about learning might look like, and if your eyes aren't crossing then I salute you. The problem with L2L is, at the least, it doesn't seem to mean anything specific; it means many things to many people: 'It is a well-used phrase in contemporary educational debates around the world, but the idea lacks conceptual clarity.'[1]

Brother, you said it. Learning to learn. It isn't even a thing. We've been hoaxed. Again. *Punked*!

> Since we cannot know what knowledge will be most needed in the future, it is senseless to try to teach it in advance. Instead, we should try to turn out people who love learning so much and learn so well that they will be able to learn whatever needs to be learned.
>
> John Holt[2]

That quote is from John Holt, the American educator, who is closely connected with the twenty-first-century movement. He believed that the primary reason that children failed to do well at school was fear – fear of wrong answers, of ridicule, and also of studying things that they weren't interested in, which doesn't seem

---

1   Steven Higgins, 2009, www.beyondcurrenthorizons.org.uk/learning-to-learn/. Accessed on 26 March 2013.
2   www.learning3pointzero.com/2011/12/09/life-is-too-short-not-be-a-lifelong-learner/. Accessed on 26 March 2013.

like a fear at all, but I'll gloss over that. In his 1964 book, *How Children Fail*, he described how children failed school not despite the efforts of school, but because of school; he was perhaps unsurprisingly a champion of home-schooling. Here's another belter: '. . . the human animal is a learning animal; we like to learn; we are good at it; we don't need to be shown how or made to do it. What kills the processes are the people interfering with it or trying to regulate it or control it.'[3]

This philosophy is also echoed in such projects as the Montessori movement and Steiner schools, and can be seen threaded through many sectors of the state sector, as such progressive ideas gained momentum in the early quarter of the twentieth century following from the ideas of reformers such as Dewey. It is interesting that the notion of progressive education, which contains in its own name the connotations of innovation and modernity, is rooted firmly in ideas that were current at the same time as Henry Ford was wondering what colour to paint his automobiles, and the Kaiser was looking at a map of Europe and touching himself. It suggests change, improvement and the nouveau. In reality, it is one ideology among many, and not a new one. But I digress.

L2L suggests at its core that learning is not something that merely occurs through exposure to content; that learning is a process that some can be better at than others, and that this process can be improved by instruction. The organisation Campaign for Learning has this to say:

> The Campaign defines 'learning to learn' as a process of discovery about learning. It involves a set of principles and skills which, if understood and used, help learners learn more effectively and so become learners for life. At its heart is the belief that learning is learnable.[4]
>
> In brief, 'learning to learn' offers pupils an awareness of:

- how they prefer to learn and their learning strengths
- how they can motivate themselves and have the self-confidence to succeed
- things they should consider such as the importance of water, nutrition, sleep and a positive environment for learning

3   A Conversation with John Holt, Interviewer: Marlene Bumgarner, *Mothering Magazine*, 1980. http://naturalchild.org/guest/marlene_bumgarner.html. Accessed on 26 March 2013.
4   www.campaign-for-learning.org.uk/cfl/learninginschools/l2l/index.asp. Accessed on 26 March 2013.

- some of the specific strategies they can use, for example, to improve their memory or make sense of complex information
- some of the habits they should develop, such as reflecting on their learning so as to improve next time.

The Campaign for Learning seems as good a place to start as any other. They're a lobbying group for L2L, and other topics that seem to revolve around 21st Century Skills, lifelong learners, and enabling children to be citizens in a turbulent world of lightning innovation and upset. There is mention of world citizens. Happily, they provide links to research, so I thought I would take a peek.

They produced a research document for the CfBT, reviewing the literature on L2L in FE, with a view to establishing best practice. Which already puts the research firmly in the camp that assumes L2L is a worthwhile project, and now what we need to do is establish what flavours are best. And of course, the research defines for itself what success would look like. So, that's two large assumptions before the first page is turned.[5]

Oh, and in case you were in any doubt that they were in some way neutral on the matter, we have this in their own words:

> The Campaign is working for a society that recognises active participation in learning as the key to improving life chances, fulfilling potential and promoting citizenship. We run national campaigns, provide support for practitioners, run projects, undertake research and evaluation and lobby to influence policy. We have been running our Learning to Learn action research project in schools since 2000 and in FE since 2008.

So they're a campaigning, lobbying group that works to promote a certain view of learning. Forgive me, but might that rather suggest any research they promote as being somewhat partisan, or is that just me? 'Hi, I work for the Society of Coca Cola, and I have some research for you about the health benefits of taking a bath in Coke every night.' I'll pass, brother.

This is important; this is a huge factor in the quality of the research. In this case, and I'm sure in all cases by the Campaign, their research

---

5   www.campaign-for-learning.org.uk/cfl/assets/documents/Research/ LearningToLearn_v5FINAL.pdf. Accessed on 26 March 2013.

is quite impeccable, but in order to be taken seriously by others, I'd say it isn't sufficient. But let's look at the research and see what it says. What evidence is there that there is a separate skill set called 'learning to learn', and what evidence suggests that, even if such a thing exists, it has any impact on the learning process? Now I find this surprising, because my intuitive default is that learning is a process that occurs anyway. Clearly not.

I remember as a child watching TV in the 70s with my parents when we learned that apparently people in England had succumbed to the vice of actually paying for water in a bottle instead of just getting it free from the tap. This was clearly the Beast spoken of in the Apocalypse. And yet, see how we eagerly pay for the translucent stuff now, and how we feel a shudder of guilt when asking the waiter for 'just tap water please'. There are even gourmands for different springs and natural reservoirs.

So too with L2L: we now have people to tell us how children learn, and how to teach them how to learn. I have some strong opinions about this: I suspect that children learn when they are told stuff, and forced in some way to remember it, and practise it.

Actually, the Campaign for Learning is interesting in itself. It began in 1995 as the RSA (the Royal Society for the encouragement of Arts, Manufacturers and Commerce – yes, Ken Robinson's video platform wallahs), and became an independent charity in 1997, with a remit to 'champion lifelong learning'. What is that? Well, it's the idea that schools don't equip children for the twenty-first century and that in order to combat this brave new world we have to become lifelong learners and, oh dear, is that the time? zzzzzzzzzz. This is another thing that always gets me in education; there is a lot of this stuff, particularly the twenty-first-century learner gas, that all rests, not in evidence, but on speculation; not in research into what has happened, but rather what they think might happen, and what they think the most appropriate response is. (I rather suspect they're de-skilling us all to hell, but that's just my groovy belief.)

Back to the research

The Campaign for Learning was formed in response to the Kennedy Report in 1999.[6] This report (Learning Works), chaired by Baroness

---

6   Based on the work of the Further Education Funding Council (FEFC) founded in 1994.

Kennedy, was an attempt to tackle the 'learning divide' in society, and suggests ways in which as many people as possible could participate in learning; it was one of the first sources to discuss the concept of 'life long learning', it encouraged widened participation, and stated, as one of its axioms, that 'Learning is the common foundation for prosperity and social cohesion. The report contains a persuasive statement of the case that learning is the key to economic prosperity and social cohesion.'[7]

This is a beautiful thing, although it would be easy to take issue with: learning is the common foundation of social cohesion? You may very well send everyone to university, but if what they learn is of variable value (e.g. a law degree versus a degree in hairdressing) then you still replicate disparities of opportunity. Perhaps issues of social cohesiveness aren't located in education, but in other sources, such as the tax bracket one finds oneself in. As ever, education and schools are seen as the principal vehicles of social change and improvement.

The Kennedy Report (Learning Works) was well received and endorsed by the then Secretary of State for education, David Blunkett, who produced a response called *The Learning Age: Further education for the new millennium*,[8] and we already see where this is going. The same broad assumptions: learning is all different now, eeeh, it's all X-boxes and that round here now.

In 2003, the Campaign published its findings of a two-year (2000–2002) project called Learning to Learn in Schools; the focus of the project was:

- The emergence and preference of learning styles and multiple intelligences in children;
- The impact of studying learning how to learn for year 7;
- Performance in specific curriculum subjects based on the effects of teaching metacognitive skills . . .[9]

You will be delighted to learn that the report concluded that multiple intelligences, learning styles, VAK, all that guff were just

7   http://archive.niace.org.uk/organisation/advocacy/Archive/Kennedybriefing. htm. Accessed on 26 March 2013.

8   DfEE, 1998.

9   www.learntolearn.org/documents/CfLReport4pp.pdf. Accessed on 26 March 2013.

splendid ways of helping children, and that 'teachers who were informed about and experienced in learning to learn approaches found extensive benefits in teacher effectiveness, professional development, motivation and confidence'.

Isn't that lovely? A piece of their report in 2010 defines L2L as:

> . . . a process of discovery about learning. It involves a set of principles and skills which, if understood and used, help learners to learn more effectively and so become learners for life. At its heart is the belief that learning is learnable.[10]

This research is, of course, a piece of research conducted by the Campaign itself, but no harm done. The report is very concerned that more learning to learn needs to happen:

> Successful teaching and learning, which are central to learning to learn practice, lie at the heart of colleges' effectiveness, are key to retention and achievement and a central focus of Ofsted teams during college inspections. The sector therefore has much to gain from an explicit focus on learning to learn.

No support offered for this assertion, but we'll take that as read. Government must:

> acknowledge the key importance of effective teaching and learning throughout all learning phases in order both to motivate learners to continue learning throughout their lives and to equip them with the skills to do so. The importance of flexible, transferable 'soft' skills as well as vocational skills cannot be overestimated in the current economic climate.

Anyone who still thinks this is a piece of science rather than advocacy can check themselves into the rubber room. *But these are the kinds of papers quoted as supporting the projects.*

The evidence that is often quoted throughout the website (it only stores fairly recently published papers) is based on the book *Teaching Pupils How to Learn: Research practice and inset resources.*[11]

---

10 Amalathas, E., 2010.
11 Lucas *et al.*, Campaign for Learning/Network Educational Press, 2002.

Fortunately some of their findings are available in summary form online.

In addition to the VAK claims and multiple intelligences, above, it also states that: 'Pupils perform better if they have free access to drinking water.' Yes, we don't want their brains drying out. 'Exercise in the form of Brain Gym® and sport has a positive effect on pupil enjoyment and motivation for learning.'

Referencing the largely discredited Brain Gym® is a cause for concern. Plus is it true to say that all kids enjoy gym and sport? 'Students are happier and perform better when they have teachers who are flexible, open minded, willing to experiment and embrace change.' That's a beautiful sentiment, but I worry that it is more of an aesthetic judgement than a factual one. Can we prove it in any way?

> Learning to Learn courses help primary and secondary students identify and apply a range of strategies that they think helps them learn at home and school. The techniques considered most useful include Brain Gym®, Mind Mapping, memory techniques, posters and diagrams, interactive whiteboards and working with peers.

Which just goes to show you what kids know about improving their own education if they think Brian Gym helps them. This is, of course, connected to another favourite piñata of mine, Student Voice; the idea that kids can't learn unless we're asking them how they like to learn. Of course, the possibility that they actually don't know, and that teachers might know what they need more than what they think they need as children, doesn't seem to conceptually occur to the architects of such ideas. It does to me.

So far we have precious little research to suggest that children actually can improve their learning by learning about learning, or even that conceptually, such a thing might exist. It really is quite curious, and I'm not entirely sure where it actually came from? By that I don't mean I don't know where and when it happened, and from whom – I simply mean, as Hume might put it, that I cannot trace it back to any observable evidence; I can't find a single statement of fact that supports its existence or its efficacy. That's a big problem for a movement that alleges that, not only do L2L skills exist, but that they are vital in helping kids face the future. They are not. As far as I can see as a teacher, they are pretty much a waste of time.

Every minute you spend teaching a kid about L2L skills is a minute you aren't teaching them . . . well, the subject you're supposed to be teaching them. Whole days off the curriculum, well-meaning teachers wasting millions of staff hours, millions of pounds and for what? No observable improvements. Just the feeling that you might be doing something good. Well, as far as the evidence goes, you aren't.

My advice? Go back to teaching them the subject on the door. That's how they learn. I am reminded of my favourite PowerPoint slide show called 'How to Study'. It goes like this:

1   Open your books.
2   Study the *hell* out of that thing.

Couldn't have put it better myself.

The idea that children are natural learners has its ecological roots back in Locke, and further into the romanticism of Rousseau. They believed that children were natural learners, and that society, the polis, corrupted and perverted their natures and prevented them from learning, and we're back to the quote from John Holt again at the start of this chapter. It is, of course, demonstrably untrue; children are certainly instinctively curious, and want to know more about their surroundings, but the idea that this then translates into a passion for learning in general is an odd one. They want to know what pleases them and assists their comfort. The idea that a child, left alone, would teach itself language, poetry, art and music is palpable guano. In Burroughs's excellent *Tarzan of the Apes*, the titular shipwrecked alpha male finds the cabin of his infancy, wherein he describes finding a series of children's alphabet primers. Rousseau would have been overjoyed to know that Tarzan teaches himself to read from just such a resource.

Alas, I suspect Tarzan might be an unreliable evidence base, on account of his fictional status.

L2L is one of those dogmas that many now revel in, feeling that it makes them cutting-edge innovators at the very edge of educational practice. Well they are in one sense; they're on the edge of something, but I fear it is more likely to be the edge of reason, because there isn't much science that backs the whole project up.

The University of Cambridge, in a four-year project (2001–2004) with Kings College and the Open University, published The Design of the ESRC TLRP 'Learning How to Learn' Project.

One of their assumptions, laid out cold in the first few pages, is:

> The project design was based on the following theoretical, methodological or practical assumptions:
>
> - The concepts and practices underpinning 'assessment for learning' cohere theoretically with concepts and practices associated with 'learning how to learn'; thus work to promote AfL is expected to enhance L2L although this hypothesis needs to be tested and the relationships properly examined.
> - The development of new AfL/L2L practices need to be stimulated through some form of intervention because previous research indicates that they are not widespread in teachers' current practice.[12]

In other words, this four-year project will assume that L2L is useful and more schools should be doing it. Which doesn't strike me as demonstrably proven. In fact I'd say it was downright hostile to the possibility that L2L doesn't cohere or exist in any meaningful way, and no one can even agree what it means or what it looks like. There's another peach of a problem, alluded to by the authors when they consider how to assess programs of L2L. Some of the proxy indicators will obviously be something like attainment, attendance, punctuality and so on. But the authors also consider that they might want to create some way of assessing L2L in itself. Which leads us to the very weird possibility that we might have classes on how to learn learning to learn. And then we could have classes on that. Infinite regress is a joy.

> However, our interest in learning how to learn as an outcome, as well as a process, led us to attempt to develop an L2L assessment task (SLL). This has proved to be problematic[13] and we have decided not to use it as a 'test' of learning how to learn 'ability', although it has value as an activity to prompt discussion of learning with teachers.

12 Mary James and David Pedder, University of Cambridge, Paul Black and Dylan Wiliam, King's College London, Robert McCormick, Open University. 2.1 Assumptions and principles.
13 See Swann, J., Wiliam, D. and Black, P. (2003) 'Assessing learning how to learn', paper presented in a symposium entitled 'Learning how to learn: More than just study skills?' at this conference.

This paragraph is essential:

> Even the earliest days 'in the field' convinced us that this was
> too simplistic. Schools, particularly at this time, are experiencing
> such a plethora of initiatives that isolating 'our' interventions
> would be extremely difficult.

In other words, we realised quickly that we couldn't just see if it
was our project that was having an effect, or other projects. Aren't
humans just frustratingly complicated? Although I'm in permanent
scoff mode, I don't want to disparage these researchers; Wiliam, for
example, produced one of the most sensible and influential pieces
of school research that led to action in the last quarter century with
his research into formative assessment, AFL and the best-selling (I
fuss you not) *Inside the Black Box.* These guys aren't stupid, nor do
I assume them to be so. But it still staggers me that the practical
difficulties of social science appears to be almost a distraction to many
people in the field rather than, as I perceive them, elephants in the
lab. It's almost as if people want their research to be successful, so
they ignore the practical problems with translating human observation
and data gathering into a meaningful scientific model predicated on
predictive and explanatory mechanisms.

The conclusions of the study also need a bit of scrutiny. You'd
think that, after such an enormous project, you'd get some kind of
indicators that L2L (or as it was referred to here, LHTL, Learning
How To Learn – presumably there were copyright issues) was the
bee's knees. Er ... not a bit of it. The researchers make these
findings:

> Pupils' measured academic performance varied between project
> schools. These results need to be treated with caution as possible
> outcomes of the project. All schools were responding to
> numerous initiatives at the time, each of which could be expected
> to have some impact.[14]

So out of forty schools, three showed significant improvement,
although a few more showed improvement in 'engagement with the
project' and other such mysterious unquantifiables. As they say at

14 Teaching and Learning Research Briefing, July 2006. www.tlrp.org/pub/
documents/no17_james.pdf. Accessed on 26 March 2013.

the end, it really *was* a 'striking success story'. If that's what success looks like, I'd love to see failure.

Is there no end to the ability of true believers to see success in the most meagre of evidence bases? Believe me, I contacted quite a few people right at the heart of this industry, and this was the best I could squeeze out of them in terms of an evidence base that L2L has any effect at all. The researchers admit that this has only ever been examined on a small scale, and that scaling it up has never been done. Clearly it hasn't even been proven on a small scale, so why would we do that? And why would we, as some schools have already done, started to teach discrete, compartmentalised 'learning skills' lessons, as if it was something that could be taught separately from the respective subjects? The researchers themselves say that's pointless, and probably conceptually impossible.

It just isn't good enough to go into a school loaded with the assumption that L2L works, and then look for evidence that it does. It just doesn't. I'd call that a fundamental flaw.

Sure, students can learn good habits and dispositions towards schools. The four-year project found that L2L wasn't a discrete skill, but 'a family of learning practices that enable learning to happen'. So it isn't a thing. It's a bundle of things. I could probably have told you that diligence, liking your subject, dedication, effort and focus were good ways to behave as a learner, but apparently we need millions of pounds to tell us the obvious.

The report doesn't enlighten us to what these practices are. Which I found a bit disappointing, to be honest.

I could go on, but the deeper I go into it, the more I find exactly the same. Opinions dressed as evidence. Data gathered and carved into the shape of the desired conclusion. Learning to learn? I'm not even sure there is such a competency, except at the broadest, most conceptual level. That it can be meaningfully taught in any other way than instilling in children a sense of dedication, self-discipline and an insistence that they focus and work hard, which is kind of what good teachers do already. The hipsters are selling snake oil on this one, whether they know it or not. Don't waste your time. Just teach them, instead.

Chapter 15

The hard smell

Smell/dance/box/sing yourself
smarter/happier/healthier

In every man's life there is a drawer, a very special one; it is the drawer where everything goes that does not go anywhere else. In my drawer is, among other things, pencils, old passports, fuses, contact lenses, travel shampoo, foreign coins with no value, and left-handed scissors.

This chapter is that drawer. There are so many claims about educational innovation every day that it is hard to keep up with the latest trend. Most of the things I've discussed so far have been real movements, global phenomena that have formed the topography of the landscape. But for every movement, there are a million smaller organisms, all vying like animals for Darwinian dominance. Most of them don't last; most of them simply rise and fall in the same week, although in some cases they latch on to some fertile habitat, some receptive department where they can survive and thrive, like lichen on the wet side of a coastal rock.

Most of them don't even stand up to a cursory examination, so this chapter will involve a degree of shooting fish in a barrel. Still, shooting fish in a barrel sounds like a lot of fun, so until someone affords me that opportunity, it might be worthwhile to quickly look at a few 'initiatives' and 'exciting new research' that has two main unifying themes: they all promise exciting possibilities for educational innovation; and they're all – I think – daft.

Come with me now.

Smell yourself smart: Can scents make you remember things?

I was hugging myself with glee to read an article in the *TES*[1] a few years ago: Sydenham High School, where parents drop £12K a year to have their girls turned out, has introduced scented oils with the 'pungent aromas of lavender, grapefruit and mint' into their classrooms. Which sounds very lovely, actually. Nothing wrong with making your class smell of something other than Lynx, desperation and paper mould.

At this point, the article bicycles off the cliff of 'fair enough' into the abyss of 'you're kidding me on, right?' The school claims it has adopted these oils in order to 'aid students' recall of key facts in exams'. Let me check that I'm on the right page: having a nice smell in the classroom will help students remember things? I'm not saying that a nicer, more pleasant classroom doesn't have a general beneficial influence on how people feel – and it's fairly uncontroversial to claim that people will enjoy lessons more if the room doesn't stink of tummy gas and KFC boxes.

But that's not the claim being made here, which is something delightfully specific: that performance can be measurably improved by the use of what appears to be Body Shop bath bombs. And what a wonderful world that would be, ladies and gentlemen; forget complicated strategies to raise attainment in students via well-trained professional teachers, improving social welfare and tackling other deeply unsexy civic fractures – we can massage their memory cortexes by teaching them through their noses.

Says who? Anthony Padgett, the owner of Memory Oils, who claims that a handkerchief soaked in grapefruit oil helped his dyslexic daughter through her exams. 'She was predicted Bs and Cs in her GCSEs,' he said. 'But she came out with A*, As and Bs. She puts it down to the oils.' A pupil who was predicted Bs and Cs ends up with, er . . . Bs, and better.

A pupil exceeding their predicted grades. Have you ever heard of such a thing? That would suggest that grade predictions aren't some kind of immutable engine of predestination that can only be thwarted in some nightmarish dream.

I wonder how Mr Padgett established beyond clinical refutation that his daughter carrying around a smelly handkerchief in class was

1   www.tes.co.uk/article.aspx?storycode=6060248. Accessed on 26 March 2013.

the significant factor in her impressive performance. That's the problem with anecdotal claims about specific outcomes; unless proper, controlled procedures have been put in place to test any hypothesis to exhaustion, any reliance on an unrepresentative sample is doomed to pointlessness. In other words, I might have worn my lucky pants to the interview, but it doesn't explain why I got the job.

Stories like these are adorable; and then they're just depressing, because it indicates at least two things:

- Professionals – teachers, SLT, LEA wallahs – waste their time on spurious, feel-good, medicine-man quick fixes, rather than focus on issues that we know create good schools; effective behaviour, well-trained subject experts, and supportive parents, to name a few.
- Lazy thinking: if the people responsible for educating our youth are satisfied with the non-thinking required to support these kinds of non-scientific claims to efficacy, then I worry for the students who follow, who need to be trained to discern between verifiable fact and fiction.

I repeat my earlier assertion: I'm all for classrooms that smell nice. Give me your petition and I'll sign it. But to claim that it has a measurable effect, and roll out a few dubious papers of dodgy provenance to support it, is inadequate. Education has enough on its plate, without people pimping out their pet theories on unsuspecting children. People who adopt large-scale programs of perfumed classes should admit they like it because it 'just smells nice'.

Steve Garnett, quoted in the article as the author of . . . well, some smelly learning, suggests the following:

> To Reduce stress – spiced apple, rose and chamomile.
> –   Reduce anxiety – vanilla, neroli and lavender.
> –   Relax – basil, cinnamon and citrus flowers.
> –   Energise – peppermint, thyme and rosemary.
> –   Relieve tiredness – woody scents, cedar and cypress.

What's the evidence base for this claim? You *must* look at the website for Memory Oils[2]. It's a joy. 'Effortlessly boost your recall,'

2   http://memoryoil.co.uk/. Accessed on 26 March 2013.

the website breathes. 'The oils that help you remember!' And who am I to argue? I'm sure the owners of this business have the best intentions and believe with sincerity that their oils really do help you remember things. So what's their evidence base?

Because they're all about the science, they have a research page. What does it tell us?

1　A link to a BBC iPlayer article about kids designing an experiment with smelly pencils. What? The link didn't work, so because I am nothing if not rigorous, I Googled it. It came up with a link to a BBC pop-science show called *Bang Goes the Theory*. The show was available on DVD, but already I was beginning to suspect that this wasn't exactly published research. I moved on. If this was the kind of evidence to back up their claims, I wasn't optimistic.

2　The second link didn't work either. Luckily the internet does; it was a paper by D.G. Laing and G.W. Francis, 'The capacity of humans to identify odours in mixtures.'[3] Oddly though, the paper discussed the fact that 'the capacity of humans to process information about odours perceived simultaneously may be limited'. Or in other words, we can't tell smells apart very well. I couldn't see what that had to do with memory oils aiding learning.

3　Another broken link to an article called Cortical contributions to olfaction: plasticity and perception by D.A. Wilson, M. Kadohisa and M.L. Fletcher.[4] It seems to be, from the Abstract, about how the cortex is involved in processing smells, and doesn't seem to offer any support to the claim that specific smells aid learning in a meaningful way. Still, at least it was about smell.

4　I started to give up the ghost by this point, so I stopped. So far, nothing seems relevant to me, other than that they are something to do with smelling.

There's even a button for 'More research' but I'm still looking for the first stuff. I persevered a little, and found one link that actually worked: a link to an online newspaper *The Harvard Gazette*, which isn't exactly an academic journal. The report claims that Harvard researchers have found out a little about how the brain remembers

3　www.ncbi.nlm.nih.gov/pubmed/2628992. Accessed on 26 March 2013.
4　www.ncbi.nlm.nih.gov/pubmed/16750923. Accessed on 26 March 2013.

smells. Which is great. But it doesn't help us with the claims we're looking for. It even seems to contradict the second piece of research quoted, about our ability to distinguish smells; this paper seems to suggest we can remember up to 10,000 notes of smell. Weird.[5] The author, Linda Buck, is a bona fide olfactory scientist. I don't know if she's authorised the use of her name with Memory Oils.

So the research quoted strangely enough doesn't seem conclusive. I've no doubt it's out there. Somewhere.

Anyone else backing up this theory? You bet. As the *TES* says:

> In the US, Dr Rachel Herz, an expert on the psychology of smell based at Brown University, Rhode Island, has performed experiments which showed that the ability of children to solve puzzles was improved with the use of certain aromas.

Dr Herz is a neuroscientist, although it must be said, one that is now 'consulting for many of the world's leading multinational fragrance and flavor companies'.[6] Also, the research I read from her suggested that, while there is undoubtedly a link between memory and smell, it is a broad one – we remember smells, and some smells are very potent and evocative of emotional situations and events in our lives. But so are sounds and pictures. Her research suggests that emotional 'salience' (i.e. importance) is what makes smell memories seem more evocative than other memories.[7] Which may well be true, but that still doesn't get us closer to the claim that 'Smell X' will help you remember 'Content Y'. Nothing to do with it at all. Thankfully there is a voice of balance:

> However, Roger Pope, head of Kingsbridge Community College in Devon, urged caution. 'Other than the fact that the exam hall will smell like a perfumery, I think it's nonsense,' he said. 'Memories can be triggered by sensory experiences but the whole idea is highly suspect. To say that you will remember your calculations by smelling grapefruit is contrived.'[8]

5   www.news.harvard.edu/gazette/1999/04.08/smell.html. Accessed on 26 March 2013.
6   http://en.wikipedia.org/wiki/Rachel_Sarah_Herz. Accessed on 26 March 2013.
7   http://rachelherz.com/uploads/Are_Odors_the_Best_Cues_to_Memory_1998.pdf. Accessed on 26 March 2013.
8   www.tes.co.uk/article.aspx?storycode=6060248. Accessed on 26 March 2013.

Thank you, Mr Pope. We'll leave it there, shall we? By all means dress your classroom in any scent you savour; anything has to be better than the heady aroma of flatulence and sweets that pervades most classrooms, no matter how groovy they are. Smells are a powerful trigger for memories, we all know that – the scent of marzipan whisks me back to my nursery like a time machine – but that's very different from saying a smelly oil can help you remember specific facts and sequences. That's one of those crazy claims with, I should say, no serious evidence.

I might close by saying that, at a school meeting I attended, one of my colleagues turned to me and said, 'Why don't we try smelly air fresheners to aid their memories?' to which I said, 'Well, there's no evidence to suggest that actually works.' He then said, 'Well, it can't hurt, can it? There might be something in it.' And I wept.

Busta Rhymes: can rhyming make you clever?

Fortunately many are now aware of the dubious premises upon which the science of Brain Gym® rests, especially after Ben Goldacre's famous assault on it in *Bad Science*. But not before thousands of schools had (in my opinion) wasted their time, and most importantly that of the students, on pointless, pointy-headed, miracle, crystal exercises that made extraordinary claims to efficacy but without concomitant extraordinary evidence. Any efforts accrued from Brain Gym® could be replicated from giving your pupils a break every now and then and getting them to stretch their legs a bit. Which, you know, people do anyway, unless you treat your students like laboratory beagles (and even they get very long fag breaks).

Some theories still endure, though. Fans of feeling sad and slightly intellectually superior weren't disappointed if they read the news in February 2011 on the BBC website that 'Moving to rhyme may boost pupil results.' What the research appears to be telling us here is that doing exercises set to nursery rhymes helps children to develop:

> The Primary Movement project involves getting nine-year-olds to do set exercises to nursery rhymes and will be tested in 40 schools in north-east England. The exercises mimic the earliest reflexes made by babies and foetuses. The theory is that children can be held back if such reflexes persist. Trisha Saul from the Primary Movement project said: 'Some of the songs and the nursery rhymes will be familiar, it's the movements that are

different.' These are designed to replicate movements the foetus makes in the womb and the baby makes in the first six months of their life.[9]

Again, these are specific and impressive claims. What supports these assertions? This appears to be based on a study by the Queen's University Belfast in 2000.

> The small-scale, little-known research project found that children who carried out systematic physical exercises for a year gained 15–20 months progress in reading compared to a control group which did not do the exercises.

'Small scale'. 'Little Known'. It doesn't inspire. They could have said 'obscure', but I think the Beeb draw a line somewhere. Trisha Saul, from the Primary Movement Project, said this: 'It's a bit like a caterpillar turning into a butterfly, but the butterfly still has bits of the caterpillar attached to it.'

That's *exactly* what it's like. What?

I had a look a Primary Movement's website (the body coordinating the project, which was taking place in *40 schools* in England and Wales). It's far from illuminating, although it links to a sole credit – a press release from Queen's University, Belfast (oddly enough from 2006, and the article published by the *Journal of Research in Special Educational Needs* – available online only – was in the November 2005 issue, so I don't know where 2000 comes from).

What it *does* offer is a number of courses that you can apply to take. There isn't a price list on it. I'm guessing it isn't free, for either the *Foundation* or *Advanced* Level certification. The website advises that as a parent, you should check if your local teacher is trained properly in the method, and to me it starts to sound a bit mystical and Alexander techniquey, and only the elect are chosen etc.

> The Primary Movement programme developed at Queen's University, Belfast has been shown to have a significant impact on reducing reflex persistence. It has been evaluated in a number of formal studies that have been published in peer-reviewed scientific journals.
>
> In a school-based study of children in their first year at primary school, it was found that the Primary Movement programme had

9   www.bbc.co.uk/news/education-1697141. Accessed on 26 March 2013.

a significant effect on the development of fine motor control. In another large, school-based study, involving more than one thousand children, it was found that the Primary Movement programme had a significant effect on ATNR persistence. This led to improved academic attainments in reading, spelling and mathematics.[10]

That last sentence interests me, because that's where programs like this intersect with my work as a teacher. The PMP is, I'm sure, beyond reproach, has impeccable academic credentials and works solely to promote the well-being of children. Its authors and board are undoubtedly motivated by nothing but the noblest of motives.

My concern is that it is far from clear that instigating a programme, however well endorsed, of physical exercises has anything like a substantial effect on a child's learning ability, and if it does, can be replicated on anything more than laboratory conditions, on all, or even merely most children. And that it is far from clear that such a programme has any significant difference from any other programme of simple physical exercises. That the suggested increases in learning can be accounted for solely by reference to the exercise programme, and can't be accounted for by other means, such as the children and the teachers feeling that there should be some kind of benefit. Maybe, maybe, maybe. That's my problem with this kind of research.

The problem remains with all forms of educational research: controls aren't real controls; exact conditions can't be replicated and tested against. High causal density in human interactions means that causal relationships can rarely, if ever, be inferred from any pool of data, and researcher bias can overwhelm in both the design, execution and interpretation of any such project.

My verdict: unproven.

10   www.primarymovement.org/background/index.html. Accessed on 26 March 2013.

Chapter 16

Thinking hats on!

I'll finish on one of my favourite/least favourite fairy tales. You've all heard about Edward de Bono: an inventor, a prodigious writer and allegedly the man who suggested that the Middle East conflict was in part due to the low-zinc diet of unleavened bread, and could be abated by simply sending them plane-loads of Marmite, which is resplendent in the stuff. I promise you I didn't make that up.[1]

So his pedigree is impeccable. He's also the man responsible for children all over the world wearing multi-coloured felt hats and being asked, 'But how do you feel about the number seven, Jimmy,' a lot. His famous *Six Thinking Hats*.

De Bono is a celebrated polymath and innovator; he doesn't just think outside the box, he thinks outside of the xob. Sometimes, he thinks inside the box just to mess with everyone's heads, before he jumps out and shouts, 'There is no box!'

In fairness, he's also a Rhodes Scholar at Christ's Church Oxford, a Nobel nominee, an appointee of Oxford, Cambridge and Harvard Universities and – less impressively – the Da Vinci Professor of Thinking Chair at University of Advancing Technology in Phoenix, USA, which is a bit of a let-down frankly after all that CV artillery. I wouldn't mention him – play the ball not the man and all that – but his name's in the theory, so I thought I would have a punt.[2,3]

Learning hats: the core idea is that, in order to release student's ability to think about familiar concepts in unfamiliar ways and utilise

---

1   www.independent.co.uk/news/world/middle-east/de-bonos-marmite-plan-for-peace-in-middle-yeast-740189.html. Accessed on 26 March 2013.
2   De Bono, Edward (1985). *Six Thinking Hats*.
3   De Bono, Edward (1990). *I am Right – You are Wrong. From this to the New Renaissance: From rock logic to water logic.*

the power of lateral thinking, they imagine that they are wearing a different hat every time they consider a concept. So 'the thinking hat tool provides a means for groups to think together more effectively, and a means to plan thinking processes in a detailed and cohesive way.'

The hats refer to the following ways of thinking about a problem:

Blue Hat Thinking	–	Thinking about thinking
White Hat Thinking	–	Facts, information and data
Green Hat Thinking	–	Creativity
Yellow Hat Thinking	–	Benefits, positives, plus points
Black Hat Thinking	–	Cautions, difficulties, weaknesses, dangers
Red Hat Thinking	–	Feelings, intuition, hunches, gut instinct

This stuff is going gangbusters in schools, by which I mean it is very, very popular. It was even trialled in the UK civil service as a way to teach lateral thinking. Can you imagine the committee meetings where miserable looking civil servants glumly passed round the little hats, although, as they do in many primary schools, perhaps they substitute it for a teddy or a mug or something. It comes up on every INSET I attend, and it's been a huge part of the L2L movement for as long as I can remember. That, VAK and Mind Maps, and you've got a full day with sugar paper and break-out groups right there.

Here are the goals of De Bono For Schools, a company that sells the programme to schools:

> Our main goal is to equip educators, administrators, and students with practical, good quality tools that support proactive thinking as a necessary life skill for productive participation in our global society.
>
> Our secondary goal is to start a *thinking revolution in our schools.* The debate is over. Our students have fallen behind in science, math, reading, you name it. We have a lot of catching up to do with many other countries throughout the world. Thinking is the most basic of all skills. We need to develop effective thinkers if we are to equip our youth to lead us well into the future.[4]

4   www.debonoforschools.com/asp/about_us.asp. Accessed on 26 March 2013.

And here are the claims that they make:

> We believe equipping students to be productive and independent thinkers will help:
>
> 1   Increase test scores.
> 2   Improve reading and writing skills.
> 3   Students make informed choices.
> 4   Sharpen problem-solving skills.
> 5   Nurture creative thinking skills.
> 6   Strengthen collaboration skills.[5]

Now you know how much I like a few specific claims. You will, of course, notice the modifying 'I believe', which enables it to be categorised with 'I believe that every time a baby cries, a candle glows' and no one can seriously take issue with the content of my claim. But schools must be doing this for a reason. And the reasons are usually those given above.

So, two things: what evidence do we have, other than de Bono's gut, that these hats are a way to process and think about things differently, and what evidence do we have that anything is improved by this? We might strap on a tertiary concern: should schools be doing it? Where's de beef, de B?

> Research evidence obtained by the De Bono Foundation suggests his tools can have a positive impact on academic achievement and behaviour. As part of the Government's New Deal job-finding programme, teaching youngsters the De Bono thinking systems for only six hours improved their employment rate by 500 per cent.[6]

Now that is a claim worthy of investigation.

If I could I would parachute in there and rescue every one of their sad twenty-first-century faces. Just scoop them up and say, 'There there, it's all gone, here's a felt brain, tell me where the bad man made you think.'

---

5   www.debonoforschools.com/asp/about_us.asp. Accessed on 26 March 2013.
6   www.independent.co.uk/news/education/schools/put-your-thinking-hat-on-how-edward-de-bonos-ideas-are-transforming-schools-1518507.html. Accessed on 26 March 2013.

The school in one of the most deprived boroughs in the country, is also always in the top 15 per cent of primaries in the country for academic results. Bullying is rare and there have been only 11 disciplinary incidents since February 2008. Before the introduction of the thinking tools that figure would have represented a half term.[7]

The article quoted above continues:

Traditional subject areas have been thrown out. Thinking books replace exercise books. The curriculum is taught entirely in seven themes such as problem solving and reasoning, creative development or knowledge and understanding of the world. But all subjects are taught with creative thinking tools at the fore. Images of the coloured hats crop up all over the school and lessons are peppered with references like 'let's apply some green hat (creative) thinking' or 'White hats on – what are the facts?'

I'd love to be the secondary school teacher that gets them after all that and asks them if anyone knows what the capital of England is, to be met with thirty pairs of confused eyes, who then huddle together and form a learning bubble about how they would find out the answer to that question, and how everyone felt about London. OK, so: White Hats on – what are the facts? 'Research evidence obtained by the De Bono Foundation suggests his tools can have a positive impact on academic achievement and behaviour.'

If you noticed the name that preceded the word foundation, then you might – if you're me – wonder about the possibility of bias inherent in such research. Although I'm sure it was conducted with stringency and impartiality. But it would be understandable to at least speculate about the neutrality of such a body towards the work of De Bono.

Debonoforbusiness.com provides us with numerous cases studies where clients are happy to testify that using de Bono helped them:

Using Hats, the team was able to bring more people back into the creative process. And meetings went much more quickly and were far more productive. 'In just three hours we were able to put together our plan – probably in two-thirds less time than it would have taken without Hats. And the quality and quantity of ideas we could take into production were incredible. Because

Hats made team members comfortable voicing their ideas, we maximised creative input,' says Hallas.[8]

The Memorandum of Understanding was a big breakthrough for the committee because changes in seniority rules were usually obtained through formal bargaining. This was a significant move away from a conventional method to a more compassionate approach. It occurred, in part, as a result of the synergy created by *Six Thinking Hats*. Participants had finally managed to set aside their personal agendas so everyone could work collaboratively toward a positive outcome.[9]

They're testimonials more than case studies; client feedback. But at least they're happy. So we have a number of happy customers, which is great, and I hope they knock themselves out with this stuff. But any evidence to support the claim that anything went on that couldn't have been achieved by people thinking, you know, really hard about stuff? I asked my network of teachers (OK, Twitter) and I got a lot of 'I like it' but no one could tell me what it actually did, or what difference it made to their classes that couldn't be achieved in other ways. I mean, the claims are pretty big on the websites – developing twenty-first-century learners for the twenty-second century and all that. Apparently if we don't use this stuff then we'll be destitute in a decade and we'll all be eating each other for fun. OK, I'm exaggerating, but the twenty-first-century wallahs seem pretty convinced that if we don't do all this thinking skills stuff then we're in trouble.

So I popped over to the de Bono Foundation. Because if anyone has the goods when it comes to research, it's going to be these people. If they don't have what I need, then no one has, surely? I found an action research programme, which sounded very dynamic. The website said:

> Two hundred and eighty three geography pupils at Key Stage 3 have been involved in an action research project on Six Thinking Hats. The research covered two thirds of the geography Key Stage 3 curriculum, and was conducted by a teacher at a large South Wales Valley school.

8 www.debonoforschools.com/pdfs/JWalter-Thompson-Ford-Focus-Six-Hats-Case-Study.pdf. Accessed on 26 March 2013.
9 www.debonoforschools.com/pdfs/Boeing-Union-Six-Hats-Case-Study.pdf. Accessed on 26 March 2013.

The teacher who undertook the research says, 'The driving force for the research was a feeling of improvement I had when using the Six Thinking Hats – both in pupil participation and their development of complex ideas. I wanted to do a real investigation to get a clear understanding of what the effects were.[10]

So the research is conducted by a teacher (which is a novelty in my experience), and was inspired because a teacher thought that her existing Thinking Hats work was great, and wanted to show why and how. Hmm, I'm not feeling the complete impartiality here. I'm sure I'm wrong.

Five different methods for gathering data about the effects of using the hats were used:

- Pupil questionnaires
- Pupil self-evaluation
- Lesson observation (conducted by the Head of Department looking at collaboration, engagement and idea development of the pupils)
- Structured and qualitative interviews with a sample of 44 pupils
- Assessment of pupil work before and after implementation of the strategy.

Oh good, self evaluation. That's a Blue Hat activity. And a lesson observation by the HOD, looking at utterly unquantifiable variables. Structured interviews. But was it science?

Dr. Adrian West, The Edward de Bono Foundation UK's Research Director commented 'I'm greatly impressed by the sheer amount of work put in to this, and the thoroughness of the approach. Whilst teaching full time too – it's quite an achievement'.

Dr West may be impressed, and I'm delighted for him. It certainly sounds thorough.

What were the results? They were, you may be surprised to learn, *in favour of the process*.

10 www.debonofoundation.co.uk/schoolresearch.html. Accessed on 26 March 2013.

The conclusions of the research were that 'Thinking is a learned activity and that the structured approach of Dr. de Bono has a positive impact on pupils' higher order thinking skills'. For one group project, year 9s who received some of their previous teaching using hats could be compared to those who had not. 'It was evident from the quality of work and the number of those achieving level 6 and above (63 per cent vs 87 per cent) that the strategy does impact on pupil creativity and higher order thinking'.

In other words, 'Well, *we* think it works.' That was the finding. It was also the evidence. Do you see where I'm going with this? Without some kind of way of knowing if they were more or less creative brainiacs than before this is just . . . well, I feel awful being so mean, because I'm a teacher and I like teachers doing new things, but this all just seems . . . well, so thin. I don't see this as evidence. It's barely data in any meaningful way. I see it as wishful thinking and self-congratulation. There was a pie chart in the research, but I would have been embarrassed to present it at a staff meeting let alone as a piece of evidential research.

The rest of the website was just testimonials from happy clients in the schools and business sectors, but I couldn't stomach any more 'Cheers, Edward, you're the best,' so I searched further and wider. I did find this paper: 'Using the "six thinking hats" model of learning in a surgical nursing class: sharing the experience and student opinions.' Erginer, Saritaş, Karadağ[11]. It was based on questionnaires and forty-one nursing students.

> Findings: The majority of the students stated that this method facilitated their empathising with the patient; sharing different ideas and opinions; considering the patient holistically; generating creative ideas; looking at an event from positive and negative aspects; and developing their system of thinking. They recommended that this class be taught using this method.[12]

Forty-one people. Well, it's a start. Not a great one. But at least they had a nice time, and I hope someone got a good grade for this

11 Karadağ, A., Saritaş, S., Erginer, E., 2009, 'Using the 'six thinking hats' model of learning in a surgical nursing class: Sharing the experience and student opinions.'
12 www.ajan.com.au/vol26/26-3_karadag.pdf. Accessed on 26 March 2013.

paper. A few dozen people saying they felt that they had developed their empathy seems an impossibly small study, and with impossibly nebulous outcomes. Has the thinking actually been perceptibly better in any way? And how would that even be assessed? Answers there are none, not here. The vast majority of literature that looking into de Bono unearths is based around papers that express the need for students to have high-level thinking skills, and creativity, and deep learning. But didn't they always? It's odd to suggest that somehow we don't value these things, and that what kids really need is to learn how to consider things from different angles.

This seems to be the summary of the argument proposed by De Bono advocates:

P1: We need to develop critical thinking skills

P2: De Bono's Thinking hats are a thinking skill tool

Conclusion: Thinking hats all round!

Obviously the first premise is the one I'd take issue with. There is a lot of research by earnest researchers to say that we need brand new thinking skills to replace the rubbish old ones that brought us to the edge of the twenty-first century. You know those rubbish skills, that gave us Mozart and Einstein and gene splicing and so on? Yes they're all *old* skills. We need *new* thinking skills.

There's no evidence for this; it is pure conjecture, pure advocacy; it is a set of values wrapped up in a survey; it is futurism at its most naked. The definitions of thinking are so vague, so unfeasibly subjective, that one can barely believe anyone took them seriously as scientific ontological evidence. This is no abstruse philosophical debate; this is a field that proposes something exists that needs to be developed. To say the findings are contentious would be to understate matters. It is so maddeningly vague and metaphysical that it would make you weep. That anyone would base a national school programme on it beggars belief. But such is the world of education: the Butterfly effect is everything, at times; the flap of an imaginary wing can cause a hurricane in England.[13]

I'm not against thinking about things in different ways. And I support any teacher who likes using this to get kids thinking in

---

13 Rizvi, A.A. *et al.* (2011), 'Application of six thinking hats in education', pp. 775–779.

different ways if they find it helps – and I mean really find it helps, not just like to think it helps. Whatever works, works. But I can't see this technique doing anything else that couldn't be achieved by simply asking them to think really hard about something. In other words, it's a nice way to achieve something that could be achieved in a hundred other ways.

Then there's the charge: is it useful beyond this? Does it really achieve the results that some of its exponents claim? Improve grades? Increase sociability? Improve self-esteem? All the evidence I could find was self-reported, based on testimonials and so on. There were no negative findings; no angry papers from depressed disappointed teachers or researchers who said this is useless. In fact, even research – and I mean published research[14] by people with letters after their names, in magazines that vaguely alluded to educational research – was hard to find. Most of what I could find was on websites, usually those selling *Thinking Hats* literature. It is very hard to find any kind of evidence that it has any demonstrable effect whatsoever. There are all kind of converts and dilettantes telling us how wonderful it is, but unless you accept the argument presented before, then all we have to go on is testimony of happy customers:

> We have moved from the Information Age to the Concept Age. There is simply too much information out there, far too much for our children to be mere regurgitators of facts. Schools cannot hope to give a child even a fraction of the knowledge that he will come across in his lifetime – for example the US Department of Labor estimates that current secondary school students will have between 10 and14 different jobs . . . by the age of 38! It has been claimed that the top 10 jobs that will be in demand in 2010 did not even exist in 2004 – we are preparing students for jobs that don't yet exist, and to solve problems that don't yet exist. What schools must do, of course, is give their students the tools to cope with what life will throw at them, and in particular the ability to deal with new concepts and situations.[15]

14 Kenny, L.J. (2003) Using Edward de Bono's six hats game to aid critical thinking and reflection in palliative care.
15 Wells, Kim, Gifted and Talented Update, Issue 62, March 2009, from website 'Blue Sky Thinking'. Accessed on 26 March 2013.

That was by Kim Wells, who according to the website 'Blue Sky thinking' is one of three De Bono Master Education Trainers in the UK. There are *three*? We are indeed blessed in these isles.

To be honest, it doesn't look good for Thinking Hats. By all means use it; but if it works, it's because you're a good teacher who could help them think in any number of ways. Also I counsel caution: make sure you ask yourself, 'Do I really need to ask this child how they feel about the number seven?'

My Black Hat suggestion is that this is unproven.

Chapter 17

School uniform Armageddon

Here's a thing that gets dragged out more often than Paul McCartney: should schools have a uniform or not? Few things polarise the edu-debate more lazily than a good old toe-to-toe on the uniform issue. It animates schools councils, Radio 2 phone-ins, reformers, reductionists, rebels and reactionaries alike. It is the debate that dares to speak its name constantly. Most schools in the UK require students to wear a uniform: 82 per cent of all schools, 98 per cent of secondary, 79 per cent of primary.[1] English schools have a largely free hand in the implementation and guidance on uniforms; Scottish schools are encouraged to have them, but are given no guidance about what constitutes uniform. So, uniforms in schools – do they help with anything? What impact do they have? Educational research, give me a beat I can follow.

One paper I looked at doesn't think much of uniforms.

> Our findings indicate that student uniforms have no direct effect on substance use, behavioural problems or attendance. A negative effect of uniforms on student academic achievement was found. These findings are contrary to current discourse on student uniforms. We conclude that uniform policies may indirectly affect school environment and student outcomes by providing a visible and public symbol of commitment to school improvement and reform.[2]

1   www.oft.gov.uk/shared_oft/reports/consumer_protection/schooluniforms summary.pdf. Accessed on 26 March 2013.
2   Brunsma, D.L. and Rockquemore, K.A., 'The Effects of Student Uniforms on Attendance, Behavior Problems, Substance Use, and Academic Achievement', 1998. www.members.tripod.com/rockqu/uniform.htm. Accessed on 26 March 2013.

OK, so uniforms have no effect. But hold! Here's the 2001 report from the Scottish Executive[3] Better Behaviour – Better Learning Report of the Discipline Task Group:

School dress code

3.42 A common feature of schools with a positive ethos of achievement is that they have high expectations of their pupils in terms of their behaviour, commitment, participation, academic progress and completion of homework. In many schools with a high ethos of achievement, there has also been a sustained effort to either maintain or introduce a dress code to the school. The benefits of a dress code can be summarised as follows:

- differences between pupils are reduced, which in turn reduces some of the causes of isolation and bullying
- the self-esteem of particular groups of pupils can be improved
- security (particularly in large schools) can be improved – it is easy to spot who does and who does not belong to the school community
- pupils can feel a stronger sense of belonging and commitment to the school
- it can improve the image of the school in the local community
- it can create a sense of purpose within the school environment.

3.43 The DTG take the view that the benefits outlined here, coupled with the experience of schools and authorities which have pursued this, lead us to believe that there is merit in schools giving serious consideration to the continuation or formation of a dress code policy. It is also our view that the nature of the school dress code is for the school community to decide.

So broadly in favour; of course, this is research based on a few case studies, but at least it has the benefit of being a tentative suggestion rather than an imperial statement of final arbitration. However, such documents do persuade and influence schools heavily; schools with poor behaviour who have not implemented 'guidelines' often find themselves having to justify why. Any more evidence?

3   www.scotland.gov.uk/Resource/Doc/158381/0042908.pdf. Accessed on 26 March 2013.

I found the Brunsma report (above) quoted quite a few times, often on blogs or parent websites who basically took the line that uniforms weren't useful, despite what people said. Reference was made to the Halo effect,[4] where our judgement of someone is influenced by our overall opinion of someone – so for example we might not believe someone is lying because we find them attractive, or we believe school uniform helps students with behaviour because we remember seeing well-behaved students in uniform. That could well be true. The Brunsma report was big, too; based on around 26,000 students, over 800 schools; quite a piece of work. Any more evidence in favour of uniform?

Plenty: studies show they are involved in lowering student victimization (Scherer 1991), decreasing gang activity and fights (Kennedy, 1995; Loesch, 1995), increasing student learning and attitudes towards school through: enhancing the learning environment (Stover, 1990), raising school pride (Jarchow, 1992), increasing student achievement (Thomas, 1994), raising levels of preparedness (Thomas, 1994), and promoting conformity to organizational goals (LaPointe *et al.* 1992; Workman and Johnson, 1994), increasing attendance rates, lowering suspension rates, and decreasing substance use among the student body (Gursky, 1996), increasing self-esteem (Thomas, 1994), increasing spirit (Jarchow, 1992), and increasing feelings of 'oneness' among students (LaPointe *et al.* 1992).

It's a blur; the data seems to point in both ways, or more accurately every way. Looking at most of this, we see a lot of data gathered and causal relationships made with some abandon, perhaps even in cases when the causality of the relationship is somewhat suspect. There's also a lot of self-reporting, a lot of questionnaires based around questions such as 'Do you think uniform has helped with attendance?' and so on. There was a lot of this:

> Although proving causality is difficult, almost all individuals interviewed for this report indicated that the implementation of a school uniform policy had improved school safety . . . Although scientifically based research is limited, previous qualitative research and the case studies conducted for this report indicate that parents, teachers, and administrators in schools and districts that have successfully implemented school uniform or dress code policies believe that uniforms can play an important role in

4   Thorndike, E.L. (1920) 'A constant error in psychological ratings.'

improving school culture; making schools safer, more positive learning environments; and improving student outcomes, including attendance, grades, and test scores.[5]

That last one is from a report by Dr Scott Joftus. Although it didn't offer any evidence to suggest that uniforms were a good thing, it included in its recommendations that schools should have one, yup. And it was subsequently cited and reported as evidence by other exponents of uniform that uniforms were good things. You see how this all works? Turtles all the way down again.

Oh yes, I nearly forgot: 'The study was funded by French Toast, the country's leading manufacturer of children's apparel and school uniforms.'[6] How about that? If you've read this far, then perhaps you're starting to see some patterns forming in how education research works.

What's the answer?

As a teacher, I think the answer is surprisingly easy. The key to understanding this is in the kinds of questions asked, and the kinds of answers sought. If you're looking for a clear correlation between schools with uniforms and attendance, punctuality, behaviour or grade levels, then you won't find any, because there isn't one. As a teacher, I can say that I've seen schools that were falling apart but had uniforms; I've also seen schools with no uniforms that turned out angels. It's fairly obvious that there is no single dimensional relationship.

That's because human behaviour is a bit more devious than that. We interpret, we weigh up multiple factors in our behaviours and motivations, subconsciously or not. Uniforms by themselves do nothing more than clothe a body; it's what a school then does with the uniform that matters. Members of the armed forces will know the attention to detail insisted upon regarding uniforms; this is not because your CO thinks that well pressed fatigues make you invulnerable to sniper fire, but because of the part it plays in the

5   Joftus, Scott (2004) 'School Uniforms: New Study Finds Positive Impact on School Environment and Student Achievement.'

6   www.educationnews.org/articles/school-uniforms-new-study-finds-positive-impact-on-school-environment-and-student-achievement.html. Accessed on 26 March 2013.

whole life of the soldier's attitude towards detail, discipline and inflexibility of commitment. If your shoes are polished madly, then it rolls over into other aspects of your attitude. When I worked for a theme diner, they insisted we had fourteen sweeteners in the sugar condiment, all facing the same way, and seven full fat sugars on the other side. This was madness; it took ages; but it ramped up our commitment to detail that was expressed across the board. Besides, if you let one standard slip, it meant that nothing important fell by the wayside (unless you are very picky about your sugars).

That's the power – or lack – of a school uniform; a school can introduce uniform, or crack down on standards if it has them already, and use them as an indicator of how strict they are about appearance, details and discipline. In conjunction with other efforts this can assist the students (and staff) understand that school is a special place, they're part of a community and that they should pay attention to details.

But this is only one way to promote this strategy; a school doesn't have to use uniform to do this. It could forget about uniform entirely and focus on other aspects of communal life, such as behaviour, courtesy or punctuality, as the lever for the programme. This is what is sometimes called the Steel Pole theory in management; it almost doesn't matter what you pick to hold up the tent, as long as it does the job. If a school has a uniform (which is an easy decision to take, and easy to maintain as long as you don't care how it's worn) and then doesn't do much with its pupils, no amount of cardigans, polo shirts and badged blazers will have any effect on children's behaviour and attainment. On the other hand, if a school is tight on behaviour, punctuality and cares about the well-being of staff and students, then no uniform is required. It's a tool, a lever, not a magic wand.

That's why the debate about school uniforms displays a huge misunderstanding about how change is made and maintained in large institutions. It would be like asking everyone to wear Superman T-shirts and then asking, 'Why haven't these T-shirts changed everyone for the better? Why is no one rescuing cats from trees?' Uniforms aren't magic. Asking 'are they a good thing' is like asking if a pencil is a good thing. It is if you need to make a soft confirmation of an appointment; it isn't if you've lost your glasses and you can't find the sharpener and the cat's asleep next to you.

Part III

What do we do now?

Chapter 18

What everyone in education should do next

In *Pinnochio*, the wooden hero dreams of being a real boy; Frankenstein hopes to be loved and accepted by his creator as a son; Data in *Star Trek* wonders what it must be like to be human; in Robert Howard's *Conan the Barbarian*, the ape pretends to be a king, and smashes every mirror to avoid being reminded that it isn't.

So too with the social sciences. In its quest to emulate the success of science, it has copied its every quirk, mannerism and accessory, like a child pretending to be its mother by walking around in heels and pearls, or an eager junior sibling clinging to its elder brethren. Or perhaps it is more akin to an adolescent exploring its emergent desires by swearing, smoking and affecting worldliness.

They adopt the form of the research paper, but many of them go their own way from there, assuming ridiculous axioms, basing their conduct and methodology on whim, affectation and fancy, prejudice and yearning. Imagination plays a part in any science, to be sure, but only in the social sciences do we see this creative aspect often placed on a pedestal, replacing empirical evidence as a guiding principle.

Because the truth is that a lot of social science belongs in the arts, not the humanities; that it discusses matters aesthetic, not empirical. The sadness of it all is that I'm not sure that some of the writers even realise this; they assume that, because they have flow diagrams, and learning bicycles, and abstracts, and data, and in some cases clipboards and white jackets, they have reached the mountain top. They actually believe that what they do has predictive, explanatory efficacy, when all they actually have is an opinion, a hunch, demonstrated in a piece of art, which I deliberately link to artifice. It is creation, not discovery; it is invention, not explanation.

I have heard social scientists scoff at this; they say that my claims about what works in the classroom are not evidence based. Well, as long as men and women who have barely stepped in a classroom believe they have a right to tell me how to do my job, I'll feel free to tell them how to do theirs.

The crime is that there are an enormous number of social scientists earning their bread honestly: making careful observations; testing their own hypotheses as carefully as the form permits; making clear the limitations of their methodologies, their theories, their conclusions; not twisting data into ludicrous shapes it cannot sustain, but making cautious, tentative conclusions that invite discussion rather than closing it down, that don't seek to justify their own theories, that retain a scepticism for themselves, that stick as much as possible to data that can be quantified and analysed by others; conclusions that are not merely self-reported, or if they are, they are discussed as subjective except in those parts that can be measured. There are social scientists out there who don't whore themselves out to PR companies seeking to make outlandish, eye-catching claims to promote this soap brand or that; who don't work for big businesses, desperate to create the illusion of efficacy; who publish negative statistics as well as positive findings; who do their best to survey the literature already; who attempt to replicate effects from previous experiments. I correspond with, admire and respect many people in the humanities who work in this way.

But, for whatever reasons, they aren't heard enough. Everyone still wants a magic bullet; everyone still wants to hear the guy with the big idea, wrapped up in modernity and novelty. No one wants to hear the possibility that what works in classrooms is often very simple indeed, very cheap, very boring and quite time-consuming. No one wants to go on a diet; everyone wants a gastric band.

So what makes a school successful, and what is successful teaching?

Oddly enough, there is research, and plenty of it, that seems to back up what every good teacher already knows. I'll quote Jan Scheerens and say roughly this:

- strong educational leadership
- emphasis on the acquiring of basic skills
- an orderly and secure environment

- high expectations of pupil attainment
- frequent assessment of pupil progress.[1]

This is the same Jan Scheerens whose ideas about lesson structure were incorporated, among others, into the numeracy and literacy strategy. I think there's an intrinsic flaw in the bureaucratic model: as soon as someone says something eminently sensible, it gets seized, hijacked and dragged across the country. When he said structure was evident in most good teaching, as exemplified by the three-part lesson, it was received by a nervous, over-inspected profession as orthodoxy, as received wisdom. I've lost count the number of times a well-meaning colleague in authority has dropped another policy shibboleth on my desk and said, 'Yes, this is backed up by real evidence this time,' tapping their nose. Pretending it isn't absurd.

Also, one of the best places a teacher can go to find out about meaningful research data for the classroom is Hattie's *Visible Learning*. Go and buy it now. It's not exactly a laugh a minute, but it's thorough, and it chimes with the experience of most teachers I know.

What can teachers do?

By now you've seen some of the wily tricks that the educational research sector gets up to in an attempt to convince you that you're holding your chalk, sorry, tablet, upside down, and that the best way for children to learn is in individual thought bubbles in break-out zones while independently performing group work in sessions designed to enhance their brain activity. Meanwhile, you're weeping into your cognitive-enhancement soup and wondering when the children will allow you to have a pay rise. The school sector has become the educational market, and you are now a customer. The only reason you might not think you are is because you don't actually put your hand in your pocket and buy anything. In fact, you're often not even a customer, you're a consumer. Educational research isn't the cause of the problem, but it sure forms part of the problem. Wishy-washy pseudoscience has infected the everyday idiom of educational discourse, so that even the language we use is based on the Orwellian absurdities and inanities of the quacks and hucksters trying to hustle the latest fad and fashion. Ministers buy it because

1   http://unesdoc.unesco.org/images/0014/001466/146695e.pdf. Accessed on 26 March 2013.

they don't know any better; school authorities buy it because it sounds good; companies hawk it because it secures them dollah. And schools buy not because they have to, or because they're assessed on their use of the latest ideologies in education. You, my friend, are crushed underneath all this. How can you possibly escape? There's only you, against all of them.

Well, I would consider that good odds. Here are my suggestions about what we can do, and now I'm not just speaking to teachers, but everyone in education, because no one is an island. We all exist in the same universe. What you do affects me, and what I do . . . well, affects maybe no one. I'll trust Newton that each force produces an equal and opposite force.

What you can do as a researcher

If you're involved in research in any way, then ask yourself: am I conducting this research in an ethical way? Am I simply attempting to prove something I already believe? Is my research being skewed by my employer? Why do they want the research? In ancient Greece, rhetoricians were scorned by Socrates because they were simply philosophers for hire, trained to train others to win arguments, not to be right. Is this you? Why are you doing it? Wouldn't you rather tell the truth, or at least the best form of it you can?

Try and achieve something as close to a scientific model as possible, and when this is not possible, don't just write it off as irrelevant, or ignore it. Report your sample sizes. How did you obtain the data? Whom did you ask? How did you ensure that bias was minimised? When you come to write your conclusions, are your summaries more wish-fulfilment than what the data is actually saying? Are you really building on previous research, or have you just selected research that agrees with you? How might you actively try to disprove your own hypothesis?

Do you publish negative findings, or only results that confirm what you want to demonstrate? Do you publish? Where do you publish? Are you peer reviewed? Do you publish in magazines and journals that attract critical discussion, or do you simply publish on websites? Are your primary supportive references also from websites? From blogs? From journalism? From popular non-fiction books? How convincing is your data really?

That's a lot of questions to ask. I'm sure there are more. But I think they'll do to begin with. As I have been at pains to mention, this is not an all-out assault on all educational research. This is an assault on bad research, because it is not carbon neutral; it does not exist in a vacuum. Make no mistake: *it hurts us.* It makes my job more difficult, and it makes children's lives harder. And the children whose lives it makes harder are disproportionately from poorer backgrounds, harder lives. These are children who already often face a mountain of shit in their lives. We owe it to them to provide the best education we can, not some hideous laboratory experiment of the first quarter of their lives where years get pissed away in the name of novelty, innovation and pseudoscience. Think of them, because I have to, every single day I spend in my job.

What can media outlets do?

Some of that applies to you. Popular perception is heavily affected by popular media, especially in areas where people aren't expert. Fortunately, many people still have a gut instinct about what they want from an education, but please never forget that many parents choose to believe what you write, which is sort of what you were hoping for. When you write a piece about how water improves grades by 5 per cent don't be surprised (because I am not) when parents phone up and ask why Jimmy isn't allowed 2 litres of Evian in the RS class, or why I'm not doing yoga with them. Because that's what happens, I kid you not.

Report honestly; don't simply report what the summary of research says – criticise it. Don't be afraid to consider if it's really true or not, just as you would consider reporting anything anyone else said as true. Researchers make mistakes; they make outrageous claims sometimes. Sometimes it's the media outlets that make the mistakes, who take careful, nuanced research and blow it to enormous levels of misrepresentation by punishing the most lurid form of the conclusion imaginable. I've read many headlines like 'PE causes blindness' or something, to find that in actual fact the research is about attitudes towards citizenship or something, and the words blindness and PE were stitched together like Frankenstein's monster.

Try to have balance; if a press release told you to vote Labour, you'd try to run it with Tory fluff that said the opposite. To the outlets, I would ask that you employ journalists with either a science background or an understanding of the scientific method. I'm just a philosophy teacher, although I'm a geeky one. I've probably made hundreds of basic scientific errors while writing this book, but I've tried my best to understand what separates good science from bad. My interest in this area was triggered because so much of what I was being told seemed at odds with my classroom experience. And there was a lot of money, it seemed, behind many of the initiatives; these were not free magic beans. That's the scandal. That's the story, if you want one. Why are so many people getting rich from educational magic beans?

What can teachers do?

If there's one thing I've found from my job, it is that teaching is a load of hard work, but it isn't expensive, in the main. It doesn't require a box of Buck Rogers tech, it really doesn't. It doesn't need IWBs or special pens that, once lost, render your board inaccessible. It doesn't need software packages; it shouldn't require more expensive training than that already offered by teacher training and time; it doesn't need many books (apart from this one obviously), or special learning to learn from dreadful one-day conferences. All of that tat has only existed in common form for a few decades; it barely existed when I was a child. Maybe some of it could un-exist?

I'm not encouraging mindless Luddism here; as I say, I'm not anti-innovation; I'm anti-pointless innovation. I'm not anti-groovyness. I am very groovy; I am Huggy Bear. I train a lot of teachers, and here's my completely free guide to what it takes to get kids learning. You can photocopy and email this to anyone you like and I won't chase you for royalties because I want children to learn and teachers to be able to teach.

OK, deep breath, here goes:

1   Children need to attend school as a default. Truancy means less school, means less syllabus covered. Kids that skip classes don't do as well. If I wanted them to teach themselves at home, I'd be working for the Home Schooling Network. I believe in school; I believe in its transformative powers. I believe that education is one of the greatest social inventions. That is my value; I have no research. But I'll happily show you countries where children don't have to go to school, and you can tell me if you'd like the same results it produces. If a child isn't in your lesson, enquire why. The school should have someone in place to monitor this, and other mechanisms to insist upon it. Incidentally, there is a lot of good research to show a link

between attendance and outcomes, but I regard it as being so intuitively obvious that I won't insult you.

2   Punctuality; this follows from (1). They need to be at your lesson on time to maximise the benefits of the lesson.

3   Behaviour. This is probably number one for me. The single biggest barrier to children learning in the UK, or any other country, is the behaviour of the children. If they're mucking about, shouting at each other, then they're not focused on the lessons. I also offer this to you as demonstrably obvious. If they're swinging from the loft, then they aren't learning maths or geography. Anyone who cares to dispute this is, frankly, a bit simple and I think they're a danger to children. The idea that kids can learn while mucking about is quite mad. I have seen some really bright kids behave like monkeys throughout school and still do quite well, but they are such outliers that building a mainstream system around them is also madness, and one has to consider how well they could have done if they focused and worked hard. Also, their behaviour makes learning for the majority absolutely impossible.

I sometimes wonder why this isn't headline news, and the top of every agenda in every school ever. It's behaviour, stupid. Schools fretting about L2L programs while kids are swarming in the corridors, cussing each other, playing with their phones and putting on make-up is idiocy of the highest order. It quite offends me, because I can see that what these kids need are boundaries so they can learn, but instead we get the magic bullets of group work and other inanities. You want social mobility? You want kids from poor backgrounds doing well? You want everyone doing well? Give them what they need, and stop being such cowards about it. Schools – some schools – need to buck up on this. They mean well, but they've lost their way. Teachers, step up to your classes; confront the poor behaviour. Apply sanctions; call home; expect the school to help you. If the school doesn't, it doesn't deserve to have you. Leave.

4   Hard work. Every kid should be working at the edge of their ability. Every kid should have something meaningful to do for the entirety of every lesson. Schools aren't playgrounds. Of course they can have fun while they're working, but this is incidental, not primary. Sometimes learning can be a lot of fun; I bloody loved it. But sometimes it's a pain in the ass, and you just have to accept that nothing worthwhile was ever created

without sweat and grief. This is life, and any attempt to confuse school with the Disney channel or Habbo House is sadly mistaken, and bound for rocks.

5   Regular feedback to the kids about how well they're doing, and how they can improve. AFL (at least parts of it) is one of the free programs in the last few decades that has any use whatsoever. I'm tempted to mention that this is because it contains the nuggets of what good teachers were already doing, but at least research that confirms what expert practitioners already know does more help than harm. Don't let kids flounder; if you look at their work, you understand what they understand, and you can do something about it. I don't mean some crucifying programme of individual personalised learning, just making sure that, broadly, all needs are catered for. In streamed classes this is easier. In mixed ability, it become more difficult. We do our best.

6   High expectations. I tell every single kid I can teach that they can get an A or a top grade, or whatever you consider success in the classroom. I tell every kid that hard work can make up for most inequalities of existent ability (although between you and me, I mean most kids – 1 or 2 per cent of kids have difficulties so significant they need genuinely individuated attention; at the other end, there are the rare outliers who possess an incredible X factor that indicates genuinely exceptional aptitude). I expect them all to do extremely well. Some will not, but many will. Tell them they're failures and watch them fail. If a kid isn't trying hard, call them out on it.

7   Solid subject knowledge. If I am to teach a class, I should expect to know exactly what they need to learn. The practice of allowing non-specialists to teach specialist subjects is crazy; only someone who believes that teachers are extraneous to the learning process would do such a thing, or who believed that kids could essentially teach themselves. They can't. They never have. Oh, they can learn, but it might not be the kinds of things you want them to learn. That's not to say that great non-specialists can't rise to the challenge, but we should dilute the need for expertise at our own peril.

8   Teaching ability. This is a huge subject in itself, so I'll summarise it as knowing how to communicate knowledge in a way that achieves some kind of genuine transference. There are a million strategies to achieve this. The reason why I rebel against the metrification of this process is because what works for one class

might not work for others, for one teacher as opposed to another, on one day rather than another. While I believe that there is a core of universal principles that apply to all schools and classes (for example, that behaviour underpins good learning) because we are all humans with a common genetic and societal heritage, even on the broadest of terms, there is also enormous scope for nuance and subtlety of expression within that core set of axioms. I love telling stories; other teachers do well with quizzes; others use odd taxonomies invented on the back of a matchbook. Fine; if it works, it works.

Just don't try to make everyone do it like you, if what you're doing is specific to you. I read a lot of advice books for teachers, and enjoy around 10 per cent of them. One of the things that repels me at times is that the author is telling the reader to do things their way, when doing things their way is only achievable for . . . well, them. That's why I don't try to flog anyone the Tom Bennett Teaching Tool Kit; I only ever advise people to do things that I think the vast majority of people could do. I once got a kid to stop playing with a mobile phone by implying he was playing with himself. *Job tightrope klaxon.* But I got away with it because of the extremely good relationship I had with my class. I would never recommend it as a course of action for someone else.

And that's pretty much it, in summary. That's what I would do as a teacher if I were you. But what do you do to defend yourself against all the poor research that often dominates the discussion?

Have integrity

Up to a point, you have autonomy. You don't always have to use the latest technique or fad, even if the school recommends it. In fact, I would wait until the school demands you do something specifically before you follow the fashion. Even then, you can reasonably claim that you don't believe it works for you. Schools can make reasonable requests from you, such as setting homework, even if you don't agree with it, as some don't. But can they expect you to really use VAK, for example, in your lessons? Of course not.

Feed the beast

I call this feeding the beast. Give the beast what it needs to leave you alone, and then do what you would do normally. So when you are being observed, make sure you record the VAK properties of the lesson, show that you've planned for it, and if necessary, demonstrate it in an observation lesson . . . and then completely ignore it for the other 99.5 per cent of your career. Ofsted and inspections, that's the only time to get the monkey dance and the jazz hands out. The rest of the time I teach the way I believe suits the best interests of the children's education, and I have no problem admitting that. I also recommend everyone else does the same. As long as your class is well served, well educated and does well, what right does anyone have to interfere? Of course, you're in trouble if your grades are rubbish, so make sure they're not. In fact, if they really are, and there's no simple reason why, that's when a conscientious teacher examines their own practice and asks, 'Do I need to do things differently?' Because this isn't a charter for arrogance; I'm not saying, 'Teach as you please and damn their eyes!' There is some very terrible teaching out there, and it's only proper that the educational system wants to monitor and regulate the process. It costs the UK taxpayer billions every year; you don't get that kind of dollar for nothing.

But don't let the fashions crush you. And so many of them are so, so very bad. The thrill of innovation, the desire for simple answers, and the mistaken belief that educational research will shine a guiding light to a smarter, more efficient system, has proven the undoing of us, and will undermine us further if we let it. So we mustn't let it.

Stand up for what you believe in as a teacher; raise it at staff meetings; if you are in a leadership/management position, promote the things you believe actually help, rather than the things you think will please your line manager. I was once asked, after an examination series where my cohort had performed exceptionally well, what I was doing to improve things next year. 'Continue to teach them to the best of my ability, every lesson,' was my simple answer. It didn't please. 'But what about the learning to learn courses? Have you integrated it into your lessons?' I was asked. I said no. And I didn't. It wasn't the droid I was looking for. The middle leader had mistaken innovation for improvement. The Golden Goose was at risk of ending up in a hot, buttered pot.

Be vocal. Resist the introduction of simple answers for complex problems. Read research papers for yourself if you have time. It's easier than you think now that the internet has brought the world into a phone box. Make your own judgements as to whether or not the research has been done properly. If it hasn't then consider your response to it. Write blogs about it. Write books about it. Share your views with other people. Aim for public office and fix the whole damn world with your bare hands if you can.

Sometimes it can feel like you against the world. But if you care about the children, then it's a fight that is endlessly worth fighting; more, it's endlessly worth starting, or picking. Next time you read some crappy report that informs you that you need to get the kids beat-boxing their geography in order to achieve deep learning (whatever the hell that is – does anyone really know? Answer: No), then fling it in the bin, or pin it to the staff-room wall with the word *flatulence* written across it.

Teaching is, as I endlessly advocate, one of the best careers in the world. It really is a vocation; I have never been happier since I encountered my educational Damascus. It saved me. I love teaching; I love to see kids learning; I love their little faces when they realise that I won't permit them to do anything less than their best. I suspect, if you're reading this, that you do too. It is practically a holy mission that we give them the best education we can, for our own self-esteem, their life chances, for our communal dignity's sake. Good research can help us with this. Bad research makes it harder.

Learn to separate the good from the bad. Make yourself teacher proof.

Good luck, and spread the love.

Tom Bennett, London, 2012

Further reading

Anyone interested in raiding further and deeper into the Mordor of comedy educational research could do a lot worse than read *Bad Science*, by Ben Goldacre, which broke the seal on the coffee jar of Cargo Cult science for me. Then, just about anything by Richard Feynman for an example of what real empirical proofs look like. Daniel T. Willingham's *Why Don't Students Like School?* is a must read for teachers and educators who want to survey what science really tells us about how we learn rather than what people wish it was like. *When Can You Trust the Experts?* by the same author is also seminal. *Visible Learning* by John Hattie should also be your go-to reference manual for the best research into what does and doesn't have an impact in the classroom. Larry Cuban's blog is an excellent source of ammunition against the neuromantics, as is OldAndrew's perpetually incisive blog *Scenes From the Battleground*.

Don't forget to wear your Thinking Hat while you read them. I'll be rubbing my brain buttons.

Bibliography

Aaronovitch, D., *Voodoo Histories – The Role of the Conspiracy Theory in Shaping Modern History*. Jonathan Cape, London, 2009.

Abass, F., Cooperative Learning and Motivation. (8 December 2009) Available online www.leo.aichi-u.ac.jp/~goken/bulletin/pdfs/NO18/02 FolakeAbass.pdf. Accessed on 26 March 2013.

Adey, P. and Dillon, J., *Bad Education: Debunking Myths in Education*. Open University Press, Berkshire, 2012.

Allix, N.M., 'The theory of multiple intelligences: A case of missing cognitive matter', *Australian Journal of Education*, 2000, 44: 272–88.

Amalathas, E., Learning to Learn in Further Education: A literature review of effective practice in England and abroad. CfBT, 2010.

Amiel, T. and Reeves, T.C., 'Design-based research and educational technology: Rethinking technology and the research agenda', *Educational Technology & Society*, 2008, 11(4): 29–40.

Aristotle, *The Politics*. Penguin, Essex (London), 1962.

Baines, E., Rubie-Davies, C. and Blatchford, P., 'Improving pupil group work interaction and dialogue in primary classrooms: Results from a year-long intervention study', *Cambridge Journal of Education*, 2009, 39(1): 95–117.

Bandler, R. and Grinder, J., *The Structure of Magic: 1*. UK: Science and Behaviour, Oxford, 1975.

Bandler, R. and Grinder, J., *Frogs into Princes: Neuro Linguistic Programming*. Real People Press, Colorado, 1981.

Bennett, N. and Dunne, E., *Managing Classroom Groups*. Simon & Schuster Education, London, 1992.

Blum, P., *Surviving and Succeeding in Difficult Classrooms*. Routledge Falmer, London, 1998.

Brody, N., 'What cognitive intelligence is and what emotional intelligence is not', *Psychological Inquiry*, 2004, 15: 234–8.

Bruner, J., Vygotsky: A historical and conceptual perspective. In J. Wertsch (ed.) *Culture, Communication, and Cognition: Vygotskian perspectives*. Cambridge University Press, Cambridge, 1985, pp. 21–34.

Brunsma, D.L. and Rockquemore, K.A., 'The effects of student uniforms on attendance, behavior problems, substance use, and academic achievement', *The Journal of Educational Research*, 92(1): 53–62, September–October 1998.

Burke, E., *On Government Politics and Society*. Fontana, New York, 1975.

Butterworth, J. and Thwaites, G., *Thinking Skills*. Cambridge University Press, Cambridge, 2005.

Capel, S., Leask, M. and Turner, T., *Learning to Teach in the Secondary School – a companion to school experience*. Routledge, London, 2001.

Carnegie, D., *How to Win Friends and Influence People*. Simon & Schuster, Inc., New York, 1936.

Carrithers, M., *Why Humans Have Cultures*. Oxford University Press, Oxford, 1992.

The Cockcroft Report (1982). *Mathematics Counts*. Report of the Committee of Inquiry into the Teaching of Mathematics in Schools under the Chairmanship of Dr W.H. Cockcroft. www.educationengland.org.uk/documents/cockcroft/cockcroft05.html. Accessed on 26 March 2013.

Coffield, F., Moseley, D., Hall, E. and Ecclestone, K., *Learning Styles and Pedagogy in Post-16 Learning. A systematic and critical review*. Learning and Skills Research Centre, London, 2004.

Cohen, Aryeh Dean (28 September 2010). Fixing Our Broken Classrooms. Israel21c. http://israel21c.org/social-action-2/fixing-our-broken-classrooms/. Accessed on 20 February 2013.

Cohen, Elizabeth G., *Designing Groupwork: Strategies for the heterogeneous classroom*, 2nd edition. Teachers College Press, New York, 1994.

Cuban, L., *Teachers and Machines: The classroom use of technology since 1920*. Teachers College Press, New York, 1986.

De Bono, E., *Six Thinking Hats*. Little, Brown and Company, Boston, 1985.

De Bono, E., *I am Right – You are Wrong. From this to the New Renaissance: From rock logic to water logic*. Penguin Books, London, 1990.

Devilly, G.J., 'Power therapies and possible threats to the science of psychology and psychiatry', *Australian and New Zealand Journal of Psychiatry*, 2005, 39: 437–45.

DfE, 'Pedagogy and Practice: Teaching and Learning in Secondary Schools Unit 5: Starters and plenaries', 2004.

DfE, 'Your Child, Your Schools, Our Future: Building a 21st Century Schools System', 2009.

DfEE, 'Further Education for the New Millennium', 1998.

Dunn, R. and Dunn, K., *Teaching Students through their Individual Learning Styles*. Reston, Reston, VA, 1978.

Eysenck, H.J., *Intelligence: A new look*. Transaction Publishers, New Brunswick, NJ, 2000.

Feynman, R.P., *Surely You're Joking Mr Feynman!* Vintage, London, 1992.

Feynman, R.P., *The Pleasure of Finding Things Out*. Penguin, London, 1999.

Fleming, N.D.,*Teaching and Learning Styles: VARK strategies*. N.D. Fleming, Christchurch, New Zealand, 2001.

Galbraith, J.K., *The World Economy Since The Wars*. Sinclair-Stevenson, London, 1994.

Gardner, H., *Frames of Mind: The theory of multiple intelligences*, Basic Books, New York, 1983, 1993.

Gardner, H., *Multiple Intelligences*. Basic Books, New York, 1993.

Gardner, H., 'A Reply to Perry D. Klein's "Multiplying the problems of intelligence by eight"', *Canadian Journal of Education*, 1998, 23(1): 96–102.

Gilbert, I., *Why Do I Need a Teacher When I've got Google? The essential guide to the big issues for every 21st century teacher*. Routledge, London, 2010.

Gladwell, M., *Blink*. Penguin Books, London, 2005.

Gokhale, Anuradha A., 'Collaborative Learning Enhances Critical Thinking', *Journal of Technology Education*, Fall 1995. http://webcache.google usercontent.com/search?q=cache:cfg9eMI647gJ:scholar.lib.vt.edu/ ejournals/JTE/v7n1/gokhale.jte-v7n1.html+&cd=1&hl=en&ct=clnk&gl =uk&client=firefox-a. Accessed on 26 March 2013.

Goldacre, B., *Bad Science*. Fourth Estate, New York, 2008.

Goldstein, N.J., *Yes – 50 Secrets From the Science of Persuasion*. Profile Books, London, 2007.

Goleman, D., *Emotional Intelligence: Why it can matter more than IQ*. Bloomsbury, London, 1996.

Gottfredson, L.S., Social consequences of group differences in cognitive ability (Consequencias sociais das diferencas de grupo em habilidade cognitiva). In C. E. Flores-Mendoza and R. Colom (eds) *Introducau a psicologia das diferencas individuais* (pp. 433–56). ArtMed Publishers, Porto Allegre, Brazil, 2006.

Gursky, D., '"Uniform" Improvement?' *The Education Digest*, March 1996, 46–8.

Hargreaves, D., *About Learning: Report of the learning working group*. Demos, 2005. http://demos.co.uk/files/About_learning.pdf?1240939 425. Accessed on 20 February 2013.

Hattie, J., *Visible Learning – A synthesis of over 800 meta analyses relating to achievement*. Routledge, London, 2009.

Hawk, T.F. and Shah, A.J., 'Using learning style instruments to enhance student learning', *Decision Sciences Journal of Innovative Education*, January 2007, 5(1).

Heap. M., Neurolinguistic programming: An interim verdict. In M. Heap (ed.) *Hypnosis: Current Clinical, Experimental and Forensic Practices*. London: Croom Helm, 1988, pp. 268–80.

Higgins, S., 2009, www.beyondcurrenthorizons.org.uk/learning-to-learn/. Accessed on 26 March 2013.

Hitchens, C., 'Mommie Dearest', *Slate*, 20 October 2003, www.slate.com/ articles/news_and_politics/fighting_words/2003/10/mommie_dearest. html. Accessed on 26 March 2013.

HMI, *The National Numeracy Strategy. The second year*. London, OfSTED, 2001. www.ofsted.gov.uk/resources/national-numeracy-strategy-second-year. Accessed on 26 March 2013.

Hobbes, T., *The Leviathan*. Penguin Classics, London, 1982.

Honey, P. and Mumford, A., *The Learning Styles Questionnaire, 80-item version*. Maidenhead, UK, Peter Honey Publications, 2006.

Hume, D., *Enquiries Concerning Human Understanding*. Oxford University Press, Oxford, 1989.

Humphrey, N., Lendrum, A. and Wigelsworth, M., 'Social and emotional aspects of learning (SEAL) programme in secondary schools: national evaluation.' Research Report 049, DfE, 2010.

James, M., Pedder, D., Black, P., Wiliam, D. and McCormick, R., 'Deepening capacity through innovative research design: Researching learning how to learn in classrooms, schools and networks', paper presented at the 2003 Annual Meeting of the American Educational Research Association, Chicago, in the BERA-1 Symposium. www.leeds.ac.uk/educol/ documents/00003913.htm. Accessed on 26 March 2013.

Jarchow, E., 'Ten Ideas Worth Stealing from New Zealand', *Phi Delta Kappan*, 1992, 73: 394–5.

Joftus, Scott, 'School Uniforms: New Study Finds Positive Impact on School Environment and Student Achievement', *Education News*, 2004. www. educationnews.org/articles/school-uniforms-new-study-finds-positive-impact-on-school-environment-and-student-achievement.html.

Johnson, R.T. and Johnson, D.W., 'Action Research: Cooperative learning in the science classroom', *Science and Children*, 1986, 24(2): 31–2.

Johnson, S.J., 'Enhancing Human Performance: Issues, theories, and techniques'. In Daniel Druckman and John A. Swets (eds). National Academy Press, Washington, DC, 1988.

Jones, K., *Education in Britain – 1944 to the present*. Polity Press, Cambridge, 2003.

Karadağ, A., Saritaş, S. and Erginer, E., 'Using the 'six thinking hats' model of learning in a surgical nursing class: Sharing the experience and student opinions', *Australian Journal of Advanced Nursing*, 2009, 26(3).

Kennedy, Michael, 'Common Denominator: Schools See Less Violence When Kids Wear Uniforms.' *Los Angeles Times*, 21 August 1995.

Kenny, L.J., 'Using Edward de Bono's six hats game to aid critical thinking and reflection in palliative care', *International Journal of Palliative Nursing*, March 2003, 9(3): 105–12.

Kolb, D., *Experiential Learning: Experience as the source of learning and development*. Prentice-Hall, Englewood Cliffs, NJ, 1984.

Landy, F.J., 'Some historical and scientific issues related to research on emotional intelligence', *Journal of Organizational Behavior*, 2005, 26, 411–24.

LaPoint, V., Holloman, L. and Alleyne, S., 'The Role of Dress Codes, Uniforms in Urban Schools', *NASSP Bulletin*, October 1992, 20–6.

Leaman, L., *Managing Very Challenging Behaviour*. Continuum Books, London, 2005.

Lee, J.J. and Hammer, J., 'Gamification in education: What, how, why bother?' *Academic Exchange Quarterly*, 2011, 15(2).

Levitt, S.D. and Dubner, S.J., *Freakonomics*. Penguin Books, London, 2006.

Levy, F. and Murnane, R.J., *The New Division of Labor: How computers are creating the next job market*. Princeton University Press, Princeton, NJ, 2004.

Lewis, J. and Cowie, H., 'Cooperative group work: Promises and limitations: a study of teachers' values', *Education Section Review*, 1993, 17(2): 77–84.

Locke, E.A., 'Why emotional intelligence is an invalid concept', *Journal of Organizational Behavior*, 2005, 26(4): 425–431.

Lucas, B., Greavy, T., Rodd, J. and Wicks, R., *Teaching Pupils How to Learn: Research, practice and INSET resources* (Campaign for Learning). Educational Press Ltd , Stafford, 2002.

MacIntyre, A., *After Virtue*. University of Notre Dame Press, Indiana, 1981.

Mill, J. S., *On Liberty*. Penguin Books, London, 1985.

Morris, D., *The Naked Ape*. Corgi Books, London, 1969.

Nagel, D., 'Texas District expanding use of online teaching platform', *T.H.E. Journal* (September 27, 2010). http://thejournal.com/articles/2010/09/27/texas-district-expanding-use-of-online-teaching-platform.aspx. Accessed on 20 February 2013.

Nutt, J., Professional educators and the evolving role of ICT in schools. Perspective report, 2010, CfBT. www.cfbt.com/evidenceforeducation/pdf/ICTinSchools-web.pdf. Accessed on 26 March 2013.

OECD, '21st Century Learning: Research, Innovation and Policy Directions from recent OECD analyses', CERI, 2003.

Ofsted, 'Moving English forward – Action to raise standards in English', 2012.

Pashler, H., McDaniel, M., Rohrer, D. and Bjork, R., 'Learning styles: Concepts and evidence', *Psychological Science in the Public Interest*, 2008, 9: 105–19.

Phillips, R., 'Making history curious: Using initial stimulus material (ISM) to promote enquiry, thinking and literacy', *Teaching History*, 2001, 105 (December).

Plato, *The Republic*. Penguin, London, 1955.

Rizvi, A.A., Bilal, M., Ghaffar, A. and Asdaque, M., 'Application of Six Thinking Hats in Education', *International Journal of Academic Research*, 2011, 3(3): 775–9.

Roberts, R.D., Zeidner, M. and Matthews, G., 'Does emotional intelligence meet traditional standards for an intelligence? Some new data and conclusions', *Emotion*, 2001, 1: 196–231.

Robinson, K., *Creating Tomorrow's Schools Today: Education – Our Children – Their Futures*. Continuum, London, 2010.

Roderique-Davies, G., 'Neuro-linguistic programming: Cargo cult psychology?' *Journal of Applied Research in Higher Education*, 2009, 1(2): 58–111.

Roger, T. and Johnson, D.W., An Overview of Cooperative Learning. In J. Thousand, A. Villa and A. Nevin (eds) *Creativity and Collaborative Learning*. Brookes Press, Baltimore, 1994.

Rosen, Y., 'Intertwining digital content and a one-to-one laptop environment in teaching and learning: Lessons from the time to know program', *Journal of Research on Technology in Education*, Spring 2012, 44(3): 225–41.

Rosen, Y. and Manny-Ikan, E., 'The social promise of the time to know program', *Journal of Interactive Online Learning*, Winter 2011, 10(3).

Rosen, Y. and Wolf, I., 'Bridging the Social Gap Through Educational Technology: Using the time to know digital teaching platform', *Educational Technology*, September–October 2011.

Rousseau, J.J., *The Social Contract and Discourses*. Everyman, New York, 1988.

Saettler, P., *The Evolution of American Educational Technology*. Englewood, IL, Libraries Unlimited Inc., 1990.

Scherer, M., 'School snapshot: Focus on African-American culture', *Educational Leadership*, 1991, 49: 17–19.

Sharpley, C.F., 'Predicate matching in NLP: A review of research on the preferred representational system', *Journal of Counseling Psychology*, 1984, 31(2): 238–48.

Sharpley, C.F., 'Research findings on Neuro Linguistic Programming: Non supportive data or an untestable theory?' *Journal of Counseling Psychology*, 1987, 34: 103–7.

Stahl, S.A., 'Different strokes for different folks? A critique of learning styles', *American Educator*, 1999, 23(3): 27–31.

Stahl, S.A., Different strokes for different folks? In L. Abbeduto (ed.) *Taking Sides: Clashing on controversial issues in educational psychology*. McGraw-Hill, Guilford, CT, 2002, pp. 98–107.

Sternberg, R.J., 'Death, taxes, and bad intelligence tests', *Intelligence*, 1991, 15(3), 257–70.

Stover, D., 'The dress mess', *American School Board Journal*, 1990, 177: 26–9.

Swann, J., Wiliam, D. and Black, P., Assessing Learning How to Learn. Paper presented in a symposium entitled 'Learning how to Learn: more than just study skills?' at this conference, 2003.

Taleb, N.N., *Fooled by Randomness – The Hidden Role of Chance in Life and in the Markets*. Penguin, London, 2007.

Thomas, Susan, 'Uniforms in the schools: Proponents say it cuts competition; others are not so sure', *Black Issues In Higher Education*, October, 1994, 20: 44–7.

Thorndike, E.L., 'A constant error in psychological ratings', *Journal of Applied Psychology*, 1920, 4(1): 25–9.

Thousand, J., Villa, A. and Nevin, A. (eds) *Creativity and Collaborative Learning*. Brookes Press, Baltimore, 1994.

Trilling, B. and Fadel, C., *21st Century Skills: Learning for life in our times*. Jossey-Bass, San Francisco, CA, 2009.

Vygotsky, L.S., *Thought and Language*. MIT Press, Cambridge, MA, 1962.

Vygotsky, L.S., *Mind in Society*. Harvard University Press, 1978.

Waterhouse, L., 'Inadequate Evidence for Multiple Intelligences, Mozart Effect, and Emotional Intelligence Theories', *Educational Psychologist*, Fall 2006, 41(4), pp. 247–55.

Weare, K. and Gray, G., 'What Works in Developing Children's Emotional and Social Competence and Wellbeing?' Report 456, The Health Education Unit, Research and Graduate School of Education, University of Southampton, 2002.

Wells, K., 'Thinking hats on', *G&T Update*, March 2009, 62.

Willingham, D.T., *Why Don't Students Like School? A Cognitive Scientist Answers Questions About How the Mind Works and What It Means for the Classroom*. Jossey-Bass, San Francisco, CA, 2010.

Willingham, D.T., *When Can You Trust the Experts? How to Tell Good Science from Bad in Education*. Jossey-Bass, San Francisco, CA, 2012.

Witkowski, T., 'Thirty-five years of research on Neuro-linguistic Programming. NLP research data base. State of the art or pseudoscientific decoration?' *Polish Psychological Bulletin*, 2010, 41(2): 58–150.

Workman, J. and Johnson, K., 'Effects of conformity and nonconformity to gender-role expectations for dress: Teachers versus students', *Adolescence*, 1994, 29: 207–23.

Zins, J.E., Weissberg, R.P., Wang, M.C. and Walberg, H.J. (eds) *Building Academic Success on Social and Emotional Learning: What does the research say?* New York: Teachers College Press, 2004.

Index